DESEGREGATION AND THE LAW

DESEGREGATION AND THE LAW

THE MEANING AND EFFECT OF THE SCHOOL SEGREGATION CASES

ALBERT P. BLAUSTEIN

and

CLARENCE CLYDE FERGUSON, JR.

RUTGERS UNIVERSITY PRESS
New Brunswick   *New Jersey*
1957

To
PHYLLIS and DOLORES

CONTENTS

Preface		ix
Acknowledgments		xiii
1	The Supreme Court Speaks	3
2	Nine Men	15
3	Oliver Brown Goes to Court	39
4	Interpreting the Constitution	54
5	Interpretation and Amendment	68
6	Turning Back the Clock	76
7	Separate but Equal	95
8	Classification and Equal Protection	114
9	The New Equality	126
10	The Color-Blind Constitution	138
11	Impact of Decision	158
12	Brown Becomes a Precedent	180
13	Trend of Decision	198
14	Patterns of Compliance	210
15	Avoidance, Evasion and Delay	240
The School Segregation Cases		273
Table of Authorities		289
Table of Cases		321
Index		329

PREFACE

Here is the story of a case which was decided by the Supreme Court of the United States. And the purpose of this book is to explain the background, significance and future of that case.

The story of the Supreme Court decision in *Brown* v. *Board of Education,* more popularly known as the *School Segregation Cases,* has been told before; it will be told again and again; it will remain a constant source of comment and discussion as long as there is law and as long as there are lawyers. For this was the most important legal decision of the twentieth century, and it may well have been the most important legal decision ever rendered by an American court.

Ten per cent of the American people are Negroes. And, solely because they are Negroes, they were subjected to the special laws of twenty-one states and the District of Columbia requiring them to be "segregated." These laws provided, among other things, that Negroes could live only in specified areas, that Negroes could sit only in the backs of buses, that Negroes were forbidden to share with whites the same public parks, playgrounds and beaches—and that Negroes had to be educated in separate, all-Negro schools. These laws, many of them nearly a century old, represented a way of life to the forty million Americans below the Mason-Dixon Line.

Then came *Brown* v. *Board of Education*—and immediate conflict.

"Not in recent times," wrote *Life* magazine, "has any issue so divided the U.S. people as has the Supreme Court's historic decision on segregation. Galvanized by the court's edict, the nation has clashed in explosive debate. At the extremes of the forum are the zealots and bigots who fill the air with harangue and hate. And in the middle ground are the thinking Americans of North and South. The court, in now interpreting the law, has reversed centuries of tradition. But most citizens wonder how and how soon the conflict between conscience and custom will be resolved." [1] *

This is not a book about either that "conscience" or that "custom." Nor is it a study of either the philosophy or sociology of segregation in America. This is a book about the law, devoted to an explanation of how the courts have resolved, in legal terms, the issues of segregation. And this is an examination of America's court-oriented constitutional system and the way it translates human problems into legal issues which can be and are decided by judges.

"There are hundreds of leading citizens, many of them jurists and practicing attorneys, who sincerely believe that the court decision was an *unconstitutional encroachment* on state prerogatives." [2] There are thousands of leading citizens, many of them jurists and practicing attorneys, who question the wisdom of an exercise of judicial power which appears contrary to accepted law and precedent. There are tens of thousands more—still including jurists and practicing attorneys—who have mixed feelings on the legal rights and wrongs of what the Supreme Court did in *Brown* v. *Board of Education*. And, finally, there are millions of other Americans who have strong personal reactions to the human issues involved, many of whom earnestly desire to know just how the Supreme Court reached its decision and what other courts can do to hasten or delay the course of desegregation.

* Notes to references in text will be found in a separate section starting on page 289.

All these persons—regardless of their varying attitudes—
need to know more about "desegregation and the law."

Brown v. *Board of Education* was admittedly a radical decision. And because it was a radical decision, it well warrants
special analysis to determine whether the case was correctly
decided. Even more important than such analysis, however,
is the fact that the decision exists—and that all informed
judgments on the human and social aspects of desegregation
must be preceded by legal understanding.

Understanding *Brown* v. *Board of Education* is no simple
task. And it cannot be achieved through the all-too-brief
commentaries in the newspapers and magazines which, of
necessity, can treat only the highlights of the desegregation
issue. What the Supreme Court said and what the Supreme
Court did can only be understood as part of a pattern of decisions long predating the Civil War—and far from ended in
the year 1957. Just as the decisions of prior courts constitute
an indispensable guide to the meaning of *Brown* v. *Board of
Education,* so do the decisions of later judges shed additional
and necessary light on the significance of the Supreme Court
action. Understanding the *School Segregation Cases* requires
information about the legal system in which such a decision
could be made and came to be made. It requires knowledge
of the judicial process and knowledge of what a judicial decision can and cannot do. And it necessitates a special study
of that extraordinary document known as the Constitution of
the United States which encompasses a vast number of meanings, all but hidden behind the words of the framers.

This book makes its appearance at a particular stage in the
developing pattern of decisions. Three years have gone by
since the Supreme Court declared the rights of Negroes to
attend nonsegregated schools, and the authors have enjoyed
the advantages of three years of hindsight. Enough time has
gone by to assess and understand. Yet, it is impossible for
anyone to tell the whole story in any single book—unless the

book be bound in loose-leaf form to allow for supplemental pages.

While the basic legal principles have already been settled, understanding *Brown* v. *Board of Education* requires an understanding of the fact that additional law is being made on this subject virtually every day. Tomorrow's cases may well reveal aspects of existing law which go beyond present perspectives. Thus it is essential to recognize the likelihood of growth and change, and to arrive at an understanding flexible enough to allow for new insights.

The final chapters on racial segregation are a long way from being written. Laws alone cannot bring about the social adjustments necessary to accomplish complete desegregation for either the North or the South. But whatever action is taken to hasten or delay the end of racial discrimination in days ahead must be accomplished within the legal framework created by *Brown* v. *Board of Education*. And to understand the nature of these social adjustments, one must first understand what the Supreme Court can do and has done.

ALBERT P. BLAUSTEIN
CLARENCE CLYDE FERGUSON, JR.

Camden and Newark, New Jersey
May, 1957

ACKNOWLEDGMENTS

To the many people who played such important roles in the preparation of this book, the authors wish to express thanks. Our colleagues on the Rutgers Law School faculty contributed in substantial measure to the scope and content of the volume. Professor Robert E. Knowlton was at our side during the important outlining phase; Professors Alfred W. Blumrosen, Saul H. Mendlovitz, Gerard R. Moran and Malcolm D. Talbott read large segments of the manuscript and made many helpful suggestions; and Professor Vincent E. Fiordalisi performed yeoman service in guiding the authors to unexplored areas of legal research. And an additional expression of appreciation goes to Dean Lehan K. Tunks and Assistant Deans Charles W. Heckel and Donald Kepner whose constant understanding and encouragement made this book possible.

Miss Beatrice B. MacCarter, Librarian at Rutgers College of South Jersey, was an infallible guide to nonlegal materials, and Gibson B. Witherspoon, Esq., of Meridian, Mississippi, graciously supplied us with data on the Southern viewpoint which could not be obtained through library sources.

Two second-year students at Rutgers Law School's South Jersey Division also made substantial contributions to the volume. Andrew H. Field served as an invaluable research assistant, and Eugene P. Chell prepared the table of cases. Both, joined by Mrs. Field and Mrs. Florence Wotherspoon, also performed a large share of the vital, though unrewarding, tasks connected with manuscript preparation and proofreading. But the real credit for transforming the authors' penmanship into corrected typed pages goes to Miss Zimme Cherkinian, assistant to the law librarian at the South Jersey Division.

The authors also wish to express their sincere appreciation to Miss Helen A. Stewart, executive editor of the Rutgers University Press, for her untiring efforts in helping the authors translate complicated legal concepts into language which, it is hoped, will be understood by nonlawyers as well as lawyers.

DESEGREGATION AND THE LAW

Chapter 1

THE SUPREME COURT SPEAKS . . .

Monday is decision day in the Supreme Court of the United States. It is the day when the eyes and ears of the legal world are turned toward Washington and the marbled temple of justice which houses the most powerful judicial body in the world today. It was on a Monday that the Supreme Court delivered the pronouncement which ended the era of the National Recovery Administration.[1] And it was on a Monday a generation later that the Court denied the power of the Chief Executive to seize the nation's steel mills.[2] Monday is a day of history. Vacation and recess periods excepted, no Monday can draw to a close without some judicial dictate that affects the life, liberty or property of tens of thousands— or tens of millions—of people in the United States.

One Monday in the year 1954 was destined to be more important, more historic, more dramatic than any of the others. Before the high tribunal on December 7, 1953, had come some of the foremost talent at the American bar. For three days they spoke—and for three days the Supreme Court listened. Oratory—blended with rare eloquence—was the order of the day. John W. Davis, Democratic nominee for President of the United States in 1924, veteran of more Supreme Court battles than any other lawyer in American history, was the principal spokesman for the South. Thurgood Marshall, chief counsel of the National Association for the Advancement of Colored People (NAACP), key figure in a quarter century of hard-fought legal combat on behalf of the Negro, pleaded

3

the cause of desegregation. Another able lawyer, Assistant Attorney General J. Lee Rankin, spoke for the United States. Other outstanding advocates, such as Virginia's Attorney General J. Lindsay Almond, Jr., Delaware's Attorney General H. Albert Young and Paul E. Wilson, First Assistant to the Attorney General of Kansas, argued in favor of the segregation laws of their respective states. T. Justin Moore of Richmond supported the contentions of the South. Spottswood Robinson, III, also of Richmond, Louis L. Redding, of Wilmington, and Jack Greenberg and Robert L. Carter, both of New York City, stated and restated the desegregation position.

And then there was silence.

As days grew into weeks and weeks added up to months, the tension heightened. Five months of Mondays passed. June would mark the beginning of summer recess; the question "When?" became more and more insistent. The answer was May 17, 1954—a day which was soon to enter the lexicons below the Mason-Dixon Line as "Black Monday."

A full cast looked down from the raised platform. Associate Justice Robert H. Jackson, recovering from a heart attack, had left his hospital bed only that morning, so that all nine justices could be together when the decision was read. His presence was a clue to the great event to follow. But no one in the audience could be sure. Departing from custom, the Court had not even given newsmen advance printed copies of the opinion.

At 12:52 P.M., May 17, 1954, 335 years after the first Negro slaves arrived in America in chains and 91 years after the Emancipation Proclamation, Earl Warren, Chief Justice of the United States, began reading the Supreme Court opinion in *Brown* v. *Board of Education*.[3] As he spoke, reporters began to stuff hastily written messages into the pneumatic tubes which lead to the telegraph room on the floor below. Early in the reading they reported that Warren was attacking school segregation, but the 1:12 bulletin of the Associated Press cautioned that "the Chief Justice had not read far enough in the court's opinion for newsmen to say that segregation was being struck down as unconstitutional." [4] The reading of the unanimous decision ended precisely at 1:20 P.M. Laws requiring racial segregation in the public schools were held to be in violation of the Constitution.

"We conclude," said the Court, "that in the field of public education the doctrine of 'separate but equal' has no place. Separate educational facilities are inherently unequal. Therefore, we hold that the plaintiffs and others similarly situated for whom the actions have been brought are, by reason of the segregation complained of, deprived of the equal protection of the laws guaranteed by the Fourteenth Amendment."

The Supreme Court had spoken.

PASSION AND PREJUDICE

What the Supreme Court said and what the Supreme Court did on that fateful May 17, 1954, have caused a deeper schism between North and South than any since Reconstruction days. There is agreement that this is the "most controversial and far-reaching decision of the Twentieth Century." [5] Agreement stops at this point. Beyond it, invective has supplanted reason. "Both sides have been shouting at each other so loudly that it is difficult any longer to hear facts through the din of name-calling." [6]

And there are facts to be heard. The complexities and ramifications of the school segregation problem are many and diverse. There are legal arguments both for and against segregation. Sound legal doctrine has been marshaled both for and against the conclusion reached by the Supreme Court. The issues must be explored in an atmosphere devoid of passion and prejudice.

It is meaningless to echo the New York *Times* and cheer

the decision as a "monumental constructive stride in constitutional law and fundamental justice." [7] It is useless to join
the Washington *Evening Star* in condemning the decision as
"a blow to fundamental American institutions." [8] It is foolish
to cloud the vital legal, sociological and psychological issues
of the decision by creating an atmosphere where everybody
calls everybody else a communist.

If the South is somewhat more vehement than the North
in its analysis of *Brown* v. *Board of Education,* the proponents of desegregation must meet that vehemence with understanding. "Right or wrong" represents but one facet of the
legal problems of desegregation. Northern lawyers may phi-
losophize on the jurisprudential phases of the decision;
Southern lawyers face the day-to-day problems which followed their "Black Monday."

In 1951, when the first of the recent public school segregation cases began its tortuous climb up the judicial ladder
toward Supreme Court decision, twenty-one states and the
District of Columbia had laws either compelling or permitting the separation of white and colored in educational institutions. Here was the breakdown: Constitutional provisions,
state statutes and local ordinances made segregated schools a
requirement in seventeen Southern and border states and the
District of Columbia.[9] In four other states—Arizona, Kansas,
New Mexico and Wyoming—legislation did not require but
permitted the maintenance of segregated schools on an optional basis.[10] It is possible to discount the assertion of Mississippi Congressman John Bell Williams that "the Supreme
Court drove a knife into the heart of the U.S. Constitution,"
but impossible to deny that the Supreme Court has *in effect*
rewritten state constitutions and regional laws against the
wishes of the citizens who promulgated such constitutions
and laws.

"Black Monday" occurred at a time when 40 per cent of
the nation's public elementary and secondary school enroll-

ment was in segregated schools. In September, 1953, three
months before Supreme Court argument and eight months
before decision, the Board of Education of Topeka, one of
the defendants in the case, voted to abolish elementary
school segregation under Kansas's local option clause. In
Delaware, decisions had already been rendered in the state
courts enjoining local officials from refusing Negro children
admittance to schools for whites.[11] And, immediately after the
Supreme Court decision,[12] education officials in the District
of Columbia were ordered to commence integration of students by the next registration date, September 2, 1954.[13]
Elsewhere, among the 8,200,000 white and 2,530,000 Negro
children [14] in the pro-segregation states, there has not been
so easy a solution.

Mississippi's Congressman Williams coined the term "Black
Monday" in a 1954 speech before the House of Representatives. Congressman Williams is a lawyer. Mississippi's Circuit
Judge Tom P. Brady, who adopted "Black Monday" as the
title of his widely circulated pro-segregation tract, is, of
course, another lawyer. United States Senator James O. Eastland, also of Mississippi, is likewise a member of the bar. So
is Sam J. Ervin, Jr., United States Senator from North Carolina. And there is no more distinguished lawyer in the South
than South Carolina's James F. Byrnes. They have all advanced tenable legal arguments against desegregation; they
have all, in varying degrees, obscured these same arguments
by permitting passion and prejudice to cloud their contentions. Others of the legal profession below the Mason-Dixon
Line have followed suit.

Judge Brady's pointed comments on the principle of *stare
decisis*—the legal doctrine that courts should follow prior decisions—are lost in the midst of his "Black Monday" attack
on the NAACP and others "drugged with the lotus of Social-
ism." He raises questions as to the sociological and psychological aspects of the decision, and continues:

"You and I know that the NAACP has been sponsored and fostered by these left-wing Liberals (I will call them that), these Marxian Christians in our churches, and these Neo-Socialists, teachers and preachers in the schools. . . . [The Southerner] has the God-given right to keep his blood white and pure. . . . If God in His infinite wisdom had wanted a Mongrelized, mixed man, that man would have been on this earth." [15]

From the pen of Senator Eastland have come many searching observations on the competence of the Supreme Court, as a court of law, to pass upon the questions of sociology and psychology argued in the case. But lawyer Eastland soon loses his lawyer audience. It is just not true that "the country has entered an era of judicial tyranny" and that "the Court has responded to a radical, pro-Communist political movement." [16] And the validity of the authorities cited by the Supreme Court cannot be impeached by calling them communists.

The Senator is correct in saying that the Supreme Court was influenced by the economic and psychological writings of Dr. Gunnar Myrdal. Footnote 11 of the decision of May 17, 1954, does indeed conclude with the words: "And see generally Myrdal, An American Dilemma (1944)." And conceivably, the Senator may be correct in his criticism that Dr. Myrdal's book "has no scientific validity, either from the standpoint of biology, sociology, or psychology." [17] The Senator is wrong, however, in challenging Dr. Myrdal's competency on the basis that he wrote his book under a Carnegie grant, and on the theory that "on this project Myrdal naturally found himself in the company of those recommended by the Carnegie Foundation, *of Alger Hiss fame.*" [18]

More urbane and scholarly than their legal brethren in Mississippi are the gentlemen from the Carolinas. Senator Ervin, a Southern moderate, has made penetrating commentary on the process by which the Supreme Court interprets the Constitution. Ex-Justice Byrnes (who has also served as Governor of South Carolina and Secretary of State) has written learnedly and well on the legal implications of the decision. Their arguments, and the meanings and ramifications of their arguments, comprise a significant portion of this volume. Yet even Senator Ervin speaks of desegregation advocates as "interfering outsiders," "political opportunists" and "zealot[s] blinded by fanaticism." [19] Even Jurist Byrnes looks upon the present trend of Supreme Court decisions as bringing "joy to Communists," and colors his legal arguments by invoking again the passion and prejudice which surround the question of miscegenation. "Southerners fear that the purpose of those who lead the fight for integration in schools is to break down social barriers in childhood and the period of adolescence, and ultimately bring about intermarriage of the races," [20] writes the former Justice.

On June 23, 1955, the members of the Mississippi State Bar Association heard an address by Hugh V. Wall entitled "A Lawyer Challenges the U.S. Supreme Court." [21] Thunderous applause followed the address. The speech was voted on and unanimously endorsed by the approximately five hundred lawyers present. Its tone may be judged from a few excerpts:

"On May 17, 1954, the form of our government was changed. . . . [The Supreme Court] usurped the most sacred right that is guaranteed our people, the right to educate our own children in our own way in our own schools. . . . [I]t is a strange coincidence indeed that following the political doctrine of the Communists, we find the Supreme Court of the United States outlawing segregation. . . . [I]f the blood of our white race should become corrupted and mingled with the blood of Africa, then the present greatness of the United States of America would be destroyed and all hope for the future would be forever gone."

Equally intemperate are some of the expressions of public opinion which have come from the "enlightened" North. *Life* magazine's "Letters to the Editors" page of February 27, 1956,[22] reflects some of this thinking: "If the South wishes to secede from the union, I will certainly vote that their petition be granted." And from another reader: "Our greatest Americans were not Washington and Lincoln. I now vote for Grant and Sherman." And even: "The South richly deserves the plaudits of Russia for their attempts at undermining our prestige abroad."

The Supreme Court has spoken. Its words and deeds require analysis and understanding. Whether the Supreme Court was right or wrong—and what made the Court right or wrong—can be determined only in an atmosphere cleared of personal predilections and prejudgment.

LAW, SCIENCE AND POLICY [23]

Whether the decision of May 17, 1954, was based upon law or upon science or upon policy will provide a source of debate among lawyers and social scientists for generations to come. Certainly what the Supreme Court held did touch upon sociological and psychological areas. This does not mean, however, that the decision necessarily went beyond the boundaries of the law. The important questions are whether these sociological and psychological issues were before the Court as a matter of proper legal procedure, and whether (and to what extent) sociological and psychological factors may *become* matters of law.

In the famous 1896 case of *Plessy* v. *Ferguson*,[24] the Supreme Court upheld the validity of a Louisiana statute providing for "separate but equal" accommodations for white and colored passengers on railroad trains. What the Supreme Court held in *Brown* v. *Board of Education* was that in the public schools "separate" facilities *could not* be "equal." All

nine judges agreed that "in approaching this problem, we
cannot turn the clock back to 1868 when the [Fourteenth]
Amendment was adopted, or even to 1896 when *Plessy* v.
Ferguson was written." What the Court meant was that conditions had changed; that "today, education is perhaps the
most important function of state and local governments";
that "whatever may have been the extent of psychological
knowledge at the time of *Plessy* v. *Ferguson,* this finding [of
inequality] is amply supported by modern authority." [25] But
does such a conclusion constitute "law" or "science" or
"policy"?

As Oliver Wendell Holmes, Jr., put it back in 1881, twenty-
one years before his appointment to the high tribunal, "the
felt necessities of the time, the prevalent moral and political
theories, institutions of public policy, avowed or uncon-
scious, even the prejudices which judges share with their
fellow-men, have had a good deal more to do than the syllo-
gism in determining the rules by which men should be governed." [26]

"It is not remarkable," writes Harvard Law Professor
Paul A. Freund, "that the process of constitutional decision
has become more self-conscious, more avowedly an expression of political philosophy, than ever before." [27] But what
is "political philosophy"? Is it politics, in the sense of the
ever-present struggle between Republicans and Democrats?
Does it extend to include the implications of foreign relations and the "cold war" between the countries on both
sides of the Iron Curtain? Or is it the resultant of long years
of legal research and analysis which sees different judges
come to different conclusions on the role of the judiciary in
the political order?

Foreign policy entered the briefs submitted by counsel to
the Court. The lawyers for the NAACP wrote: "Survival of
our country in the present international situation is inevitably tied to resolution of this domestic issue." [28] And in

the brief submitted on behalf of the United States, *amicus curiae, i.e.,* as friend and adviser to the Court: "It is in the context of the present world struggle between freedom and tyranny that the problem of racial discrimination must be viewed . . . [for] discrimination against minority groups in the United States has an adverse effect upon our relations with other countries. Racial discrimination furnishes grist for the Communist propaganda mills, and it raises doubts even among friendly nations as to the intensity of our devotion to the democratic faith." [29]

It is inconceivable that the international discord between East and West had no effect upon the nine men who were to determine a national discord between North and South. Unlike the mythical judge of a recent popular novel who scorned the press and radio in order to devote his nonjudicial efforts to translating the works of Faith Baldwin into ancient Greek, the men of the high tribunal know very well the problems of coexistence and the search for allies. True, the Supreme Court said nothing of foreign affairs in its decision. But others did, and the Supreme Court did not reject the references as immaterial.

After summing up the effect of the decision on the children in the segregation states, *Time,* in typical *Time* style, observed: "The international effect may be scarcely less important. In many countries, where U.S. prestige and leadership have been damaged by the fact of U.S. segregation, it will come as a timely reassertion of the basic American principle that 'all men are created equal.' " [30] *Time's* companion publication, *Life,* supported this position with the assertion that the Supreme Court "at one stroke immeasurably raised the respect of other nations for the U.S." [31] From *Newsweek* came these words: ". . . the psychological effect will be tremendous . . . segregation in the public schools has become a symbol of inequality, not only to Negroes in the United States but to colored peoples elsewhere in the world. It has

also been a weapon of world Communism. Now that symbol
lies shattered." [32] More pointed is the statement from *Citizen's
Guide to De-Segregation:* "The Voice of America carried the
news around the world. Hundreds of national and international leaders wired congratulations. Only radio Moscow was
silent." [33] More dramatic was the summary in the tenth anniversary issue of the Negro magazine, *Ebony:* "Negro America
fashioned a chain of political, social and economic victories
that were discussed in Europe, applauded in Asia and imi-
tated in Africa . . . the [legal] advances of the last decade
strengthened the cause of freedom everywhere." [34]

Other observers have analyzed the decision in terms of the
domestic political scene, and their comments have often included accusations of playing grass-roots politics. Supreme
Court critics are quick to quote the cryptic analysis by the
celebrated Mr. Dooley of more than half a century ago that
"no matter whether the constitution follows th' flag or not,
th' supreme coort follows th' iliction returns." [35]

Some critics go even further. Noting that the Supreme
Court had marked the change in conditions since its earlier
decisions on the question of segregation, former Justice
Byrnes makes severe charges. He does not accept the Court's
determination that the changed conditions are sociological
and psychological in nature. "The only change in conditions," he says, "was that several million Negroes had mi-
grated to the big cities in Northern states and constituted
the balance of political power in several States." [36]

The editor of a leading Southern newspaper agrees, making the blunt assertion that "the Southerner is bitter over
what he believes to be a flouting of the Constitution for political reasons." [37] But what are the bases of these political
attacks?

True, President Eisenhower made campaign promises to
wipe out segregation in the District of Columbia,[38] but it is
unthinkable that the decision of the Supreme Court was a

political maneuver to carry out his pre-election pledges. True also, President Eisenhower nominated Chief Justice Earl Warren to the Supreme Court, the man who was to write the actual decision outlawing school segregation. And while it can be argued that the appointment was political, it was not the appointment of a man pledged to take any particular stand on the question of racial discrimination.

Inherent in the American system of separation of powers is the tradition of an independent judiciary. It is a tradition which has become a part of the thinking of every man who has ascended to the high bench. The nine men may properly be accused of writing opinions to influence the politics of posterity, but their philosophies leave little room for the interplay between Republicans and Democrats.

There are, however, all kinds of "politics." As Mr. Justice Frankfurter explains it: "Since the litigation that comes before the Supreme Court is so largely entangled in public issues, the general outlook and juristic philosophy of the justices inevitably will influence their views and in doubtful cases will determine them. This is saying something very different from the too prevalent notion that divisions on the court run along party lines. Such divisions reflect not former political attachments but convictions of the judges about government, their conception of our Constitution and, above all, their philosophy of the judicial function in general and in the particular context of our Federal system." [39] And, as the late Mr. Justice Jackson observed, "any decision that declares the law under which a people must live or which affects the powers of their institutions is in a very real sense political." [40]. Under these definitions, *Brown* v. *Board of Education* was of course a political decision. But it is unwarranted to challenge the Supreme Court determination as having been motivated by the large Negro vote in New York, Chicago or Detroit.

Chapter 2

NINE MEN

In the final analysis, the school segregation issue was decided by nine men. When the determination of just nine men directly affects the lives and values of nearly twelve million school children—to say nothing of their parents and other interested parties—the unsuccessful litigants and their supporters are understandably tempted to make personal attacks upon the probity of the individuals making that unwelcome decision. But before examining the nature of these assaults on the constitutional philosophies of the nine men under attack, it is essential to comprehend the basis of criticism. Underlying all this faultfinding are conceptions and misconceptions of the judicial function. Any analysis of whether the nine men of today—or the nine men of other eras of American history—were wrong in their decisions depends upon an understanding of what judges are supposed to do.

There is an old quotation much used and abused when these critics go into battle. John Adams' stirring phrase calling for "a government of laws and not of men" [1] is cited time and again when the nine justices are accused of promulgating "unconstitutional" decisions. But there is no such thing as a government of laws and not of men. Laws are only words. They are words fashioned by men. They are words which must be given meaning by other men—men like those on the Supreme Court.

Another ancient rubric beloved by the foes of the Court is that judges are not supposed to make law; their job is to find and interpret law. These critics of judicial lawmaking find comfort in the declaratory theory of Sir William Blackstone, who warned the bench that cases were not to be determined according to the judges' own private judgments. Judges are "not delegated to pronounce a new law, but to maintain and expound the old one," wrote Blackstone.[2]

Where judges are supposed to find the law is never revealed. How judges can possibly interpret law and not make new law in the process is never explained. Where in the Constitution, for example, can one *find* law on the power of a state to tax the gross receipts of a radio broadcasting station? How can the Supreme Court reach the conclusion that the transfer and receipt of electromagnetic radio waves is "interstate commerce" under the Constitution [3] without *making* some new law in the process? Further, since the law is largely made up of decisions, how can a judge possibly decide a case without inevitably making law? [4]

"A generation or two ago, it was thought rather daring to insist that judges make law." [5] Times have changed. Everyone knows that judges make law. "Of course Supreme Court Justices decide cases on the basis of their ideas of policy." [6]

At the other extreme is the oft-quoted and likewise misused statement of Charles Evans Hughes—a statement he was much to regret when he became Chief Justice of the United States twenty-three years later. "We are under a Constitution," said the then New York Governor, "but the Constitution is what the judges say it is." [7]

Much legal discourse has cluttered the pages of the law reviews on the extent to which judicial decision is a reflection of personal viewpoint. It is argued that judges make up their minds with little or no preliminary attention to legal rules, and that later they write opinions making it appear as if the decisions were the result of legal analyses.[8] ". . . the judge really decides by feeling, and not by judgment, by 'hunching' and not by ratiocination," [9] said one scholar. Or: "Approval is here given to the type of judge who looks at the equities of a cause and then searches for precedents to sustain the desired results." [10]

These are not wild statements. They may be only partially true, but they contain truth. They are essential to an understanding of the judicial process. What these observers are prone to forget, however, is that the judge making the decision has spent a lifetime in studying and practicing something called "law." Judges do go to law school. Judges are trained in the reading of cases, and read a great many of them. Judges are nurtured in the traditions of *finding* law and in the doctrine of judicial restraint. The predilections, hunches and equities which guide decision are generally based upon a secure knowlege of the nature and trends of the law. There is a significant difference in kind between the informed "hunch" of the trained lawyer and the rough-and-ready lay concept of equity and justice.

The brilliant legal scholar Benjamin N. Cardozo could find no room in his philosophy for a "jurisprudence of mere sentiment or feeling." [11] He scorned the "doctrine of undisciplined surrender to the cardiac promptings of the moment, the visceral reactions of one judge or another." [12] He, of course, recognized the creative role of the judge and the fact that judges do make law. But he recognized—as do most lawyers—the importance of the reasons given in judicial opinions. He was—and most lawyers are—guided by these reasons.[13] A given judge might decide a given case in a given way because of the stomach-ache which followed an unfortunate breakfast. It is safe to say, however, that most decisions can be reconciled with established precedents more readily than with the concepts of "gastronomic" jurisprudence. "Courts make law," observes Columbia Law Professor Edwin W. Patterson, "but they do not make it out of whole cloth." [14]

Individual criticism of individual members of the Supreme Court is not per se to be condemned. Human beings are subject to prejudice and error. The words of Associate Justice David J. Brewer are as valid today as when uttered fifty-eight years ago: "It is a mistake to suppose that the Supreme Court is either honored or helped by being spoken of as beyond criticism. . . . The time is past in the history of the world when any living man or body of men can be set on a pedestal and decorated with a halo." [15]

Three times before in American history the nine men have been under heavy attack. It happened when John Marshall was Chief Justice; it happened just prior to and during the Civil War; and it happened again in the early days of the New Deal.

Chief Justice Marshall had an enemy in the White House during nearly all of his thirty-four-year tenure on the high court. Thomas Jefferson and Andrew Jackson were his implacable foes. Strife reached such a fever pitch after an 1832 opinion that President Jackson reputedly said, "John Marshall has made his decision, now let him enforce it." [16] Whether or not Jackson actually made that statement, the fact remains that the Chief Executive refused to support the Court. The Supreme Court had ruled that the federal government had exclusive jurisdiction over Indian lands, and that the Cherokees were not within the authority of Georgia law.[17] Georgia refused to accede to the Court's order and put the state act into effect by force.

The second eclipse of the Supreme Court followed the Dred Scott[18] decision of 1857. A Negro slave, Dred Scott, had been taken by his master from the slave state of Missouri to the free territory of Minnesota. Upon his return to Missouri, after having lived for four years in the territory, Scott claimed that his residence had made him a free man and sued for his freedom. Recounting the position of the Negro in history, Chief Justice Roger B. Taney concluded that colored persons were the natural objects of slavery. The Court then denied Dred Scott his freedom and denied Congress the power to abolish slavery in the federal territories.

"The decision was greeted by antislavery papers in the North with derision and contempt," said Charles Evans Hughes. "[T]he widespread and bitter attacks upon the judges who joined in the decision undermined confidence in the Court. False and scurrilous comments upon the traits and character of the judges supplemented hostile analysis of Chief Justice Taney's opinion. . . . It was many years before the Court, even under new judges, was able to retrieve its reputation." [19]

New Deal legislation in the 1930's provided the stimulus for the third great struggle against the Supreme Court. "The Nine Old Men," as they were called by columnists Drew Pearson and Robert S. Allen, proceeded to declare unconstitutional measure after measure designed to rescue the nation's depression-ridden economy. In 1937, President Franklin D. Roosevelt presented his "court packing" plan. Legislation was introduced to increase the number of justices from nine to fifteen, thus enabling the Chief Executive to appoint six "liberal" judges who would outvote the "conservative" majority on the high bench. The plan was rejected, but time settled the problem. Deaths and resignations soon gave Roosevelt his desired appointments, and the appointees promptly ruled judicial support of congressional enactments.

The months since May 17, 1954, have witnessed the fourth major attack on the Supreme Court.

While it is true that the desegregation decision was made by only nine men, it is significant that all nine men were in agreement. The unanimity of the ruling has meant much to the prestige of the Supreme Court—as it has meant much to the Negro.[20]

Was the decision unanimous *on purpose?* Did a bare majority of the justices take a resolute and unyielding stand on the issue? And convince the minority that unanimity was in the best interests of the nation? The answers will never be known. It is unquestionable that a 5 to 4 decision would have added many-fold to the controversy, and that the 1956 Presidential election campaign would have revolved about pledges to appoint a lawyer with expressed views on the issue to the next vacancy on the high bench.

Vital 5 to 4 decisions are not unknown. It was by a single vote that the Supreme Court declared the unconstitutionality of the Child Labor Act.[21] Again by a margin of one, the Court sustained the validity of the National Labor Relations Board.[22] But 5 to 4 decisions are not met with favor. It is common legal gossip that Hughes, as Chief Justice in 1936, planned to vote in favor of the validity of the Agricultural Adjustment Act, and made a last-minute switch to the conservative side when he saw the 5 to 3 alignment against constitutionality.[23]

It is unusual to see a single, unanimous opinion in today's Supreme Court. Not only are dissents common, but also concurring opinions and special dissents. Some legal prophets even foresaw nine divergent opinions on the Brown case, which would have left the central issue in confusion regardless of the majority ruling. And it is precisely because unanimous opinions are so infrequent that the question of "unanimous on purpose" has been raised again and again.

Certainly no one could have predicted unanimity. Professor Patterson has expressed the view that "given a case involving some genuine doubt about labor unions or monopolies or freedom of speech, during most of the past thirty years, and a shrewd counselor could guess how four to six Supreme Court justices would *vote* on the case with a probability value better than even." [24] These are hardly odds for confident legal prophecy.

On May 17, 1954, the Supreme Court consisted of Chief Justice Earl Warren and Associate Justices (in order of their dates of appointment) Hugo L. Black, Stanley Reed, Felix Frankfurter, William O. Douglas, Robert H. Jackson, Harold H. Burton, Tom C. Clark and Sherman Minton. And also to be considered is the late Chief Justice Fred M. Vinson, who sat on the Court during the early deliberations on the school segregation cases.

Of the nine men who decided the case of *Brown* v. *Board of Education,* only two—Warren and Burton—are Republicans. Two of the judges are Southerners—Black of Alabama and Clark of Texas. Reed comes from the border state of Kentucky. Chief Justice Warren is a Californian, while the other five members of the Court are from the North: Frankfurter from Massachusetts, Douglas from Connecticut (though originally from Oregon), Jackson from New York, Burton from Ohio and Minton from Indiana.

Justices Black, Reed, Frankfurter, Douglas and Jackson were named to the Court by President Roosevelt; Justices Burton, Clark and Minton were Truman designees; and Chief Justice Warren was appointed by President Eisenhower. Chief Justice Vinson, a Kentuckian and a Democrat, received his appointment from President Truman.

Black and Douglas, both ardent New Dealers, comprised the strong liberal core of the Court. Chief Justice Warren, who has in recent cases joined the Black-Douglas camp, could only be classified as a middle-of-the-roader in the days prior to May 17, 1954. Both Frankfurter and Jackson were at one time leading members of the Roosevelt "Brain Trust," but that was twenty years ago. Their subsequent judicial pronouncements and scholarly writings preclude definite classification. Onetime New Dealer Reed, Republican Burton and Truman's ex-senatorial associate Minton definitely constituted the conservative wing of the Court. Just where former Attorney General Clark fits into the picture is difficult to analyze. During his years as Chief Justice from 1946 to 1953, Vinson was consistently unpredictable; the conflict between an innate conservatism and years of service to the New and Fair Deals resulted in a variety of legal contradictions.

Classification of the justices of the Supreme Court in terms of liberal vs. conservative, pro-capital vs. pro-union, strong central government vs. states' rights, and such issues, is not always a useful analysis. As Professor Freund has observed, "A topical catalog of decisions or of votes of individual Justices is likely perforce to focus on the winning and losing litigants and the social interests with which they are identified: big business, taxpayers, labor, political or religious minorities, and so on. To rely on any such scheme of analysis is a dubious approach to an understanding of the Supreme Court." [25] Nor can the Supreme Court be understood at any particular time by taking inventory of political affiliations, geographical backgrounds, former clients and business interests and the like.

Yet the fact remains, in Mr. Justice Jackson's words, "that the Court functions less as one deliberative body than as nine, each Justice working largely in isolation except as he chooses to seek consultation with others. These working methods tend to cultivate a highly individualistic rather than a group viewpoint." [26] It is a study of these "highly individualistic" viewpoints which frequently makes it possible to predict how a particular justice will vote on a particular issue at a particular time. This is no idle exercise. The lawyer's function is largely one of prediction. No attorney can guarantee the validity of any document or the outcome of any litigation; all he can do is vouchsafe a probability, based on the study of what judges have said and done in the past.

The issue of public school segregation has been determined, though not its enforcement. Nor has the Supreme Court said its final word on public accommodations, employment, marriage and other family relations or, most important, housing. Understanding why and how the nine men, as individuals, decided the case of *Brown* v. *Board of Edu-*

cation is helpful in understanding the legal aspects of desegregation. More important, it offers insight into the trend of decision which will prevail in the future. Certainly, the view of Senator Eastland that the entire Supreme Court was "brainwashed," is not tenable. The records of the justices are too individual and differentiated to support such a charge. A brief look at those records will demonstrate this point.

Case after case in the recent Supreme Court reports ends with the cryptic phrase, "Mr. Justice Black and Mr. Justice Douglas dissent." And when such dissents are tabulated, they are inevitably recorded on the side of civil rights. So, none of the legal prophets was surprised that Black and Douglas concurred in the school desegregation decision.

The Fourteenth Amendment, with its "equal protection" and "due process" clauses, looms large in the judicial philosophy of Mr. Justice Black. For the major portion of his tenure on the Court, the former Alabama Senator has waged an unsuccessful campaign to convince his colleagues that they should adopt his construction of that Amendment. The first eight amendments to the Constitution—the specific provisions of the Bill of Rights—enumerate the restrictions placed on federal government. The Fourteenth Amendment, on the other hand, provides that *no state* can make or enforce any laws affecting the rights of citizens or their property without according "equal protection" and "due process" of the law. And this amendment does not set forth the restrictions specifically as does the Bill of Rights. The gist of Black's position is that the Fourteenth Amendment incorporates the first eight as restrictions against the states. Attaching such labels as "basic," "inherent" and "fundamental" to some of the limitations on federal authority set forth in the Bill of Rights, the Court has indeed held certain of these restrictions to apply to the states. But the Court has gone only part way in its support of the Black argument.

A portion of Black's concurring opinion in *Rochin* v. *California* [27] best epitomizes this aspect of his philosophy: "I believe," he says, "that faithful adherence to the specific guarantees in the Bill of Rights insures a more permanent protection of individual liberty than that which can be afforded by the nebulous standards stated by the majority [of the Court]. . . . What the majority hold is that the Due Process Clause empowers this Court to nullify any state law if its application 'shocks the conscience,' offends 'a sense of justice' or runs counter to the 'decencies of civilized conduct.' . . . What paralyzing role this same philosophy will play in the future economic affairs of this country is impossible to predict. Of even graver concern, however, is the use of the philosophy to nullify the Bill of Rights. I long ago concluded that the accordion-like qualities of this philosophy must inevitably imperil all individual liberty safeguards specifically enumerated in the Bill of Rights."

In addition to his many judicial utterances against racial discrimination, Mr. Justice Douglas has said much to indicate his position on the school desegregation issue. "The law," Douglas contends, "is not a series of calculating machines where definitions and answers come tumbling out when the right levers are pushed." [28] Thus, he continues, "A judge who is asked to construe or interpret the Constitution often rejects the gloss which his predecessors have put on it. . . . For the gloss may, in his view, offend the spirit of the Constitution or do violence to it." [29] In constitutional law, he believes, "*stare decisis* must give way before the dynamic component of history." [30] Writing two years after the decision of May 17, 1954, he reaffirmed his earlier position on rejecting the views of his judicial predecessors: "[A judge] cannot do otherwise unless he lets men long dead and unaware of the problems of the age in which he lives do his thinking for him." [31] And again: "Throughout American history the Supreme Court has never hesitated to overrule constitutional decisions that did not seem to fit the requirements of the new age." [32]

The best indication of the Black-Douglas position, however, is found in their brief dissents in the preliminaries leading to the May 17, 1954, determination. Both eagerly pressed for decision. Douglas twice and Black once disagreed with their colleagues' ruling to postpone argument. They voiced joint objection on January 28, 1952,[33] when the majority remanded the case to the lower court in order that that tribunal might receive and comment upon a report on a Negro school building program in South Carolina. Both justices took the position that the facts of the report were wholly irrelevant to the constitutional issues presented, and that the case should be set down for immediate argument. On October 8, 1952,[34] the Supreme Court acted to combine all the public school segregation cases for the purposes of argument and decision. Here Douglas rendered his lone dissent, again objecting to the postponement of Supreme Court determination.

It was just seven months after Warren's appointment and eleven weeks after Senate confirmation [35] that he delivered the Supreme Court opinion outlawing public school segregation. There was little or nothing in his public statements that gave a hint of his views on racial discrimination. If anything, his record would have indicated at least a tolerance for segregation. Many observers were surprised by his decision; more were surprised by the strength and vigor of his opinion. Future legal scholars—armed with his determinations since *Brown* v. *Board of Education*—will wonder that his vote could have been in doubt. But they will have the advantage of hindsight.

Now firmly linked with Black and Douglas in the liberal wing of the Supreme Court, Warren, the Chief Justice, bears little resemblance to Warren, the California Governor of only a few years ago. Thrice elected chief executive of the nation's second largest state, Warren consistently displayed his unusual ability to stay in the middle of the road and still get things done. He had served as district attorney of Alameda County; he had spent four years as California's attorney general. During his ten years as Governor he signed more than 10,000 bills into law. But despite his wide range of experience, he was not known as a lawyer. Nor had he had any prior experience as a judge. No one was surprised that the man who had once secured both the Republican and Democratic gubernatorial nominations would be a top administrator in his Supreme Court post. The surprises were reserved for the critics who equated legal knowledge with judicial experience.

Some Southerners foresaw an ally in the new Chief Justice. They knew that he had been involved with race problems in his own state. The race discriminated against on the Pacific Coast is Oriental, not Negro; but similar types of segregation were in force. In the days following Pearl Harbor, Japanese were taken from their homes in California and "relocated," many in internment camps. Warren was attorney general at the time. Records do not disclose personal approval of the discrimination practiced; neither do they reveal Warren as among those concerned about the validity of the program.

The decisions in which Warren earned (or was condemned by) the tag of "liberal" were not unanimous. Quite the contrary. The Chief Justice, himself, delivered the opinion which sustained the Supreme Court of Pennsylvania in tossing out the conviction of Communist leader Steve Nelson under the Pennsylvania Sedition Act.[36] The Pennsylvania Act, in effect, made it a crime to engage in Communist activities. Such activity is likewise a crime under the federal government's Smith Act. Joined by Justices Black, Frankfurter, Douglas, Clark and Harlan, the Chief Justice held that the Smith Act pre-empted the field of antisedition legislation, and thus necessarily superseded the Pennsylvania statute. Reed, Burton and Minton joined in a strong dissent.

Exactly one week later, the Court declared unconstitutional a provision of the New York City Charter authorizing the firing of any city employee who "utilizes the privilege against self-incrimination to avoid answering a question relating to his official conduct." [37] Brooklyn College, operated by the city of New York, was ordered to reinstate Professor Harry Slochower, who had invoked the Fifth Amendment before the Senate Internal Security Subcommittee. Justice Clark spoke for the Court, including the Chief Justice. Reed, Burton, Minton and Harlan dissented. Justice Harlan not only switched to the conservative side but wrote the dissenting opinion.

On June 4, 1956, the Court majority sustained: (1) the action of Wisconsin's State Labor Board which prohibited certain union conduct during the course of a strike; [38] and (2) the action of Cutter Laboratories of California in firing an employee for "just cause" because she had allegedly been a member of the Communist party. [39] Justice Reed delivered the first opinion and Justice Clark the second. Both cases bore the following words: "Mr. Justice Douglas, Mr. Chief Justice Warren, and Mr. Justice Black dissenting."

Brown v. *Board of Education* was a unanimous decision. In the words of University of Chicago Professor C. Herman Pritchett, "A unanimous judicial decision throws little light upon what Walton Hamilton calls 'deliberation in process.' It tells nothing of the conflicts around the judicial conference table, the alternative lines of argument developed, the accommodations and the compromises which went into the final result. A unanimous opinion is a composite and quasi-anonymous product, largely valueless for purposes of understanding the values and motivation of individual justices." [40]

But this is not entirely true. The fact of unanimity, in and of itself, is a factor in understanding the nature of the men who make Supreme Court decisions.

To what extent Warren's "genius for bringing divergent factions together" [41] brought about the unanimity in *Brown* v. *Board of Education* the public will never know. The individual and individualistic views of the nine men are aired behind closed doors in the Supreme Court conference room, and it is there that decisions and compromises are made. Earl Warren is warm and affable. He is a good administrator and a natural leader. He is popular with and respected by his colleagues. But did those factors alone produce unanimity?

Before this question can be answered, it is necessary to examine the judicial approach of two other Supreme Court justices, the late Chief Justice Vinson and Associate Justice Frankfurter.

To understand the Vinson-Frankfurter role, it must be remembered that *Brown* v. *Board of Education* was really three decisions rather than one. Bracketing the historic ruling of May 17, 1954, were the unanimous school segregation determinations of June 8, 1953,[42] and May 31, 1955.[43] The 1953 case was not a decision in the popular sense. All that the nine men did was to ask five questions in order to define and present the issues which would be determined in 1954. Here Vinson may have played a major role. The 1955 decision, on the other hand, was essentially a decree relating to the problems of enforcing the conclusions reached on Black Monday. And this is the decision which reflects the judicial philosophy of Mr. Justice Frankfurter.

There was a significant departure from usual Supreme Court practice in so breaking up the decision in the case. And it is contended that the mere fact of posing the five questions gave definite indication of the will of the Court to outlaw public school segregation.[44] The asking of these questions—plus their nature and phraseology—has led to the proposition that the Supreme Court actually reached its basic decision in June, 1953, fully six months before argument on the questions and a year before Black Monday. If this propo-

sition is correct, Vinson must share the praise or blame for
the unanimity in *Brown* v. *Board of Education*. But even if
the proposition is wrong, the influence of the former Chief
Justice cannot be overstated.

Vinson died in September, 1953, three months after the
1953 decision and three months before the major arguments.
It was he, and not Warren, who presided over the Court during the early deliberations, and it was he who directed the
closed sessions where the five questions were being prepared.
But more than that, it was the Vinson Court, with Vinson
writing unanimous opinions on behalf of the Court, which
set the pattern of decision which was to lead to the major
determination on May 17, 1954.[45]

It is unlikely that unanimity could have been achieved
without the device of breaking the segregation issue into
two separate questions.[46] The first question was Whether?;
the second question was How and When? Postponement of
the second question for a full year afforded the South a
needed breathing spell. Was this a deliberate compromise to
obtain unanimity? Or was it that the nine men, after lengthy
deliberations, decided that this was the most practicable way
to handle their determination?

Credit is also given Vinson for this "compromise." Toronto
Law Professor Edward McWhinney believes that "the five
questions directed to counsel in June, 1953, which helped to
solve the 'remedy' dilemma, bear all the imprints of Chief
Justice Vinson's border-state experience and wisdom." [47] The
Vinson imprint is nevertheless far less prominent than the
label bearing the name of Mr. Justice Frankfurter.

Felix Frankfurter is the most complex of the nine men
of the United States Supreme Court. If some of his colleagues
are unpredictable because they have written so little, the
former Harvard Law Professor presents an enigma because
he has written so much. For many years a teacher of constitutional law, he has written much for the legal journals on

the role of the high tribunal in handling the varied issues which come before it. Much of this commentary is now found in his long and intricate opinions which bear a striking resemblance to professorial lectures. If there is one man on the high bench who defies classification, that man is Frankfurter.

Condemned both as a radical and as a reactionary, Frankfurter has been regarded as a turncoat by some of his early liberal supporters. This is not the same man, they feel, who stood in the forefront of the defense of Sacco and Vanzetti a generation ago. At the same time he has not been accepted by the conservatives, who look with dismay upon his liberal past. He has been characterized as the "Emily Post" of the Supreme Court.[48] *Time* magazine, attempting to explain him to the general public, calls him the judge who "would rather decide a case on statutory law or a legal technicality than on a basic constitutional issue." [49] Reviewing a recent collection of Frankfurter's papers and addresses,[50] New York University Law Professor Edmond Cahn paints quite a different picture: "Felix Frankfurter has awakened and inspired a multitude of creative minds, and it is a public boon to have access to his urbanity and sparkle. . . ." [51] The odd thing is that all these comments are right.

Judicial restraint is the keynote of Frankfurter's philosophy—something which he himself calls "dominating humility." He does not consider the Supreme Court either omnipotent or omnicompetent in all fields of government action. He is loath to disturb existing enactments; he defers to authority outside of the Court. In his own words: "The admonition that judicial self-restraint alone limits arbitrary exercise of our authority is relevant every time we are asked to nullify legislation." [52] He feels the same way about the judicial dictates of the state courts. Dissenting in one case, he voiced impatience with the Court's readiness to review state decisions. "After all," he admonished his colleagues, "this is the

Nation's ultimate judicial tribunal, not a super-legal aid bureau." [53]

In their contention that the Supreme Court rendered a "sociological" decision, desegregation critics have found apparent solace in one of Justice Frankfurter's utterances. Former Justice Byrnes,[54] Senator Eastland,[55] Georgia's attorney general Eugene Cook and Missouri lawyer William I. Potter [56] all quote and argue from the same Frankfurter statement in *Beauharnais* v. *Illinois:* "It is not within our competence to confirm or deny claims of social scientists as to the dependence of the individual on the position of his racial or religious group in the community." [57] This statement, however, was merely a remark in passing which had no bearing on the decision. The Beauharnais case saw Frankfurter writing a majority opinion *sustaining* the constitutionality of *pro-Negro* legislation. It was a case in which the Court affirmed the conviction of one Beauharnais for exhibiting "publications [which] portray depravity, criminality, unchastity or lack of virtue of citizens of Negro race and color and which exposes [sic] citizens of Illinois of the Negro race and color to contempt, derision, or obloquy." Beauharnais challenged the statute under which he was convicted as violating freedom of speech and press. The Supreme Court said "No."

Sympathy for the views held by Southern legal scholars is found in large measure in Frankfurter's dissent in the Barnette case.[58] West Virginia's State Board of Education required public school children to salute and pledge allegiance to the American flag. There were objections. Members of the religious sect, Jehovah's Witnesses, consider the flag a "graven image" and believe that by saluting the flag they are breaking the First Commandment. They charged that the flag salute regulations violated freedom of worship and asked that the rules not be enforced against their faith. The Supreme Court agreed with Jehovah's Witnesses; no one could be compelled to salute the flag. Frankfurter dissented.

His dissent begins emotionally: "One who belongs to the most vilified and persecuted minority in history is not likely to be insensible to the freedoms guaranteed by our Constitution. Were my purely personal attitude relevant I should wholeheartedly associate myself with the general libertarian views in the Court's opinion, representing as they do the thought and action of a lifetime. But as judges we are neither Jew nor Gentile, neither Catholic nor agnostic. . . . As a member of this Court I am not justified in writing my private notions of policy into the Constitution, no matter how deeply I may cherish them or how mischievous I may deem their disregard."

Concluding comments read like excerpts from a brief supporting racial segregation: "I think I appreciate fully the objections to the law before us. But to deny that it presents a question upon which men might reasonably differ appears to me to be intolerance. And since men may so reasonably differ, I deem it beyond my constitutional power to assert my view of the wisdom of this law against the view of the state of West Virginia." [59]

Frankfurter does not think of law in terms of good and bad, right and wrong. Just as he is reluctant to reach decision, just as he is reluctant to overturn the dictates of outside authority, so he is reluctant to voice conclusions without qualifications. The decision of May 17, 1954, was sharp and clear—until the end. And the end was a determination to postpone decrees until further argument was heard on what the Court should do about the enforcement problem. This postponement is a reflection of the Frankfurter philosophy. "Adjudication," he contends, "is not a mechanical exercise nor does it compel 'either/or' determinations." [60] One of the unique characteristics of a court of law is the power to fashion a particular remedy to fit a particular situation in a particular case—to mold the law by way of adjudication rather than merely announce rules. The Supreme

Court escaped the "either/or" dilemma by postponement, by asking the Southern states for help in formulating decrees. This is unmistakably Mr. Justice Frankfurter at work.[61]

In legal philosophy and judicial action, Justice Frankfurter and the late Justice Jackson were closely related. Like Frankfurter, Jackson was conscious of the mandate of judicial restraint and reluctant to pin the badge of unconstitutionality on state and federal enactments. Like Frankfurter's, his opinions and writings were many and varied. Jackson, like Frankfurter, refused to pattern his decisions to meet the confines of a particular judicial pigeonhole. Usually the two men voted alike in the Supreme Court.

A highly successful advocate before embarking upon his career in government service, Jackson wrote his opinions the way he had once written his briefs. "He thought in terms of concrete operation: a good judge should feel responsible for the practicality of his judgments." [62] His decisions are clear and concise and directed to the controversies in issue. Jackson's judicial writings contain little of the wordiness which makes Frankfurter's opinions so subject to interpretation and reinterpretation. He wrote with more candor, and his words left little doubt as to his position on a particular issue.

A clue to Jackson's position on desegregation is found in this commentary on the "equal protection" clause of the Fourteenth Amendment: "There is no more effective practical guaranty against arbitrary and unreasonable government than to require that the principles of law which officials would impose upon a minority must be imposed generally." [63]

When California enacted legislation to stem the Okie migration of the late 1930's, it was made a misdemeanor to bring any "indigent person" into the state. The Supreme Court majority held the statute "an unconstitutional burden on interstate commerce." Jackson concurred with the result, but not the reasoning. The migrants, he pointed out, were United States citizens, and, under the Fourteenth Amendment, "No State shall make or enforce any law which shall abridge the privileges or immunities of citizens of the United States. . . ." He continued with a statement close to the basic legal premise of the NAACP: " 'Indigence' in itself is neither a source of rights nor a basis for denying them. The mere state of being without funds is a neutral fact—constitutionally an irrelevance, like race, creed or color." [64] Under this theory, the "neutral fact" of race could not be made the basis of any classification which might result in discrimination. This position would preclude consideration of the possible "reasonableness" of racial distinctions. And this is the NAACP point of view.

Pro-segregationists take the position that the Fourteenth Amendment was never intended to apply to school segregation. They argued in the Supreme Court—and they are still arguing—that the framers *clearly* contemplated separate educational facilities for whites and Negroes. Wrote Mr. Justice Jackson in a volume published posthumously in 1955: "The legislative history of that Amendment is not enlightening, and the history of its ratification is not edifying." [65] Jackson died on October 8, 1954, less than four months after the historic decision Monday. Whether his words were penned before or after May 17, 1954, is a matter of conjecture. It is unlikely, however, that he reached his personal opinion on the Amendment's background *after* the deliberations in the Supreme Court conference room.

Little was revealed in the writings by or about Justices Burton, Minton, Clark or Reed which indicated a definite stand on the issue of school segregation. Conservatives Burton and Minton were the great enigmas—and there is a complete absence of any legal literature which would warrant the conclusion that they were either pro- or anti-Negro or pro- or anti-civil rights. But while Clark and Reed have been simi-

larly loath to expound their constitutional philosophies via
judicial opinions, the basic character of these men provided
a definite indication of how they might vote on May 17, 1954.

Mr. Justice Clark has been an unfortunate victim of the
barbs of critics of the Supreme Court. He is an easy target.
His appointment to the high tribunal was the climax of a
frankly political career, and he became one of the nine men
only because a close friend was the then Chief Justice and
another close friend had moved into the White House. Tom
Clark, according to one summary, is "still trying to live down
his name as Harry Truman's most patent political appointee
[and] tends (with some notable exceptions) to follow the lead
of the Chief Justice, whether it be Fred Vinson or Vinson's
successor, Earl Warren." [66] But such characterization belies
the qualities of the man.

True, "the Justice has never posed as an intellectual, a liberal, or a brilliant lawyer [yet] he has demonstrated considerable legal talent . . . and his political astuteness and judgment are well recognized." [67] And the "notable exceptions"
to his adherence to the views expressed by Vinson and
Warren are too significant to deny his exercise of independent judgment. The greatest defect in Justice Clark as a jurist
is his disinterest in the complexities of creative jurisprudence, and even judicial philosophy.

Nor does Clark's Texas background provide a key to his
judicial views or racial discriminations. Although he was de-
nounced as anti-Negro in the Senate hearings which confirmed his Supreme Court appointment,[68] Clark had demanded the admission of Negro lawyers to the Federal Bar
Association during his term as president.[69] And Clark filed
a concurring opinion in the 1950 decision which quashed a
criminal indictment because of discrimination against Negroes in selecting grand jury panels.[70]

Before his resignation from the Supreme Court in January,

1957, Kentuckian Reed had spent nearly a score of years writing opinions on virtually every aspect of constitutional law. Generally conservative, his views on the Fourteenth Amendment see him more a supporter of economic interests than of individual rights—save where the Negro is concerned. It is not what Justice Reed has said by way of constitutional analysis which invokes decision in favor of the Negro; it is something personal, more a reflection of background than of judicial philosophy. From the pen of Justice Reed, for example, came the opinion [71] which invalidated legislation requiring all-white primary elections. "Under our Constitution," he declared, "the great privilege of the ballot may not be denied a man by the State because of his color. . . . The United States is a constitutional democracy. Its organic law grants to all citizens a right to participate in the choice of elected officials without restriction by any state because of race." [72]

There have been three changes in the personnel of the High Court since the school segregation decision of May 17, 1954. Justice Jackson died in late 1954, Justice Minton resigned in 1956 and Justice Reed resigned in 1957. President Eisenhower named to their seats John Marshall Harlan of New York, William J. Brennan of New Jersey and Charles Evans Whittaker of Missouri.

All three have ascended to the Supreme Court bench with constitutional philosophies as yet unexpressed. A leader of the New Jersey bar, Justice Brennan donned judicial robes for the first time in 1950, becoming a member of the state Supreme Court two years later. He has had a distinguished career on the bench and has been praised for his scholarship, especially in the field of administrative law. Despite his numerous judicial pronouncements, however, few cases have come before New Jersey's highest court involving basic constitutional issues, and there is no way to gauge Justice Brennan's views on the over-all problems of racial segregation. But whatever may be his personal predilections, the new justice is first and foremost a "lawyer's judge."

One of the leading trial lawyers in his native Kansas City, Justice Whittaker has received three judicial appointments from President Eisenhower in less than three years. He was named to the Federal District Court in 1954 and advanced to the Court of Appeals eleven months later. Like Justice Brennan, he is an experienced business lawyer and more of a legal tactician than a philosopher.

Likewise a veteran at the bar, Justice Harlan also received a Court of Appeals judgeship from President Eisenhower prior to his Supreme Court appointment. And, although he was a member of the unanimous Court which decided the enforcement aspects of *Brown* v. *Board of Education* in 1955, it is also too early in his judicial career to predict his future stands on issues of racial discrimination.

But it cannot be forgotten that the new justice is the grandson of the Justice John Marshall Harlan who raised the lone dissenting voice in the Supreme Court decision of *Plessy* v. *Ferguson,* more than sixty years ago. Said the first Harlan: ". . . in view of the Constitution, in the eye of the law, there is in this country no superior, dominant, ruling class of citizens. There is no caste here. Our Constitution is color-blind, and neither knows nor tolerates classes among citizens. In respect of civil rights, all citizens are equal before the law. . . . The destinies of the two races, in this country, are indissolubly linked together, and the interests of both require that the common government of all shall not permit the seeds of race hate to be planted under the sanction of law." [73]

Such are the men of the Supreme Court which decided the issue of school segregation—and some of their successors. These are some of their views on racial discrimination and on the function of the Supreme Court. These are the men who outlawed public school segregation, and thereby declared unconstitutional the laws of twenty-one states and the District of Columbia. But powerful as these nine men are, they are powerless to act until an Oliver Brown goes to court.

Chapter 3

OLIVER BROWN GOES TO COURT

The Supreme Court possesses no self-starter. It does not—and cannot—take the initiative in uncovering constitutional violations. Despite its formidable power to pass on acts and deeds of chief executives, legislators, judges and administrators, the Supreme Court is powerless to move until an actual case is before it. The Supreme Court is a court of law. As Mr. Justice Frankfurter put the point, "our exclusive business is litigation." [1]

When the issue arises, judicial review of the constitutionality of legislation takes place in the course of ordinary lawsuits. Nothing can happen until John Doe sues Richard Roe. Both Doe and Roe can be plain, simple members of the public. Likewise, either or both can be corporations, unions, school boards or other types of associations; either or both can be federal or state officials—or the United States, or a state itself. The important thing is that Doe must have a real (lawyers call it "justiciable") controversy against Roe, and must go to court to resolve that controversy.

Issues may be large or small at their inception. The case can be one between America's multibillion-dollar steel industry and the Secretary of Commerce, and involve the power of the President to seize the nation's steel mills.[2] On the other hand, a case brought by a bondholder against a railroad on a coupon worth $22.50 upheld the validity of "gold-clause" legislation (providing for payment of debts in paper currency, even though contracts specified payment in gold).[3]

Oliver Brown went to court because the Topeka white elementary school five blocks from his home barred the admission of his eight-year-old daughter. Regardless of the fact that the NAACP used his controversy as an excuse to fight the entire issue of public school segregation, Oliver Brown had a real controversy indeed. *Brown* v. *Board of Education* was the result.

The word "case" is an omnibus term for any action, cause, suit or controversy at law or in equity. It is a question contested before a court of justice. It is an aggregate of facts which furnishes occasion for the exercise of a court's jurisdiction.[4] It is a dispute litigated to decision. It is also a condition precedent to judicial review. And, as recognized and developed in the United States, judicial review is "the principle which sanctions exercise by courts of a power to declare statutes and other governmental action unconstitutional."[5] In brief, then, judicial review is a by-product of the dispute-settling process.

No feature of America's tripartite scheme of government has—in the words of Englishman James Bryce back in 1888—"caused so much discussion, received so much admiration, and been more frequently misunderstood"[6] than the doctrine of judicial review. Writing more than half a century earlier, another commentator on the American scene, Alexis de Tocqueville, pointed out that the doctrine was peculiar to the United States, and observed that "few laws can escape the searching analysis of the judicial power for any length of time. . . ."[7]

"Contrary to an oft-expressed popular opinion," points out Columbia Law Professor John M. Kernochan, "judicial review was neither a sudden innovation nor the work of one man, but rather the culmination of a long development and of many factors."[8] Power to override state judicial decisions and void the acts and enactments of the executive and legislative branches of government, however, stems largely from two constitutional provisions, one act of Congress and one judicial decision. Significantly, there is no *express* statement in the Constitution authorizing the Supreme Court to exercise judicial review.

"This Constitution," reads Article VI, Section 2, ". . . shall be the supreme Law of the Land; and the Judges in every State shall be bound thereby, any Thing in the Constitution or Laws of any State to the Contrary notwithstanding." And, in Article III, Section 2: "The judicial Power shall extend to all Cases, in Law and Equity, arising under this Constitution, the Laws of the United States, and Treaties made, or which shall be made, under their Authority. . . ." So the Constitution is law; and cases arising under the Constitution must be dealt with as law—and law cases are the business of the courts.

Section 25 of the famous Judiciary Act of 1789 [9] gives the Supreme Court power to affirm or reverse state judicial determinations which (1) might declare *invalid* "a treaty or statute of, or an authority exercised under the United States," or (2) which might sustain the validity of state acts which are "repugnant to the constitution, treaties or laws of the United States." Since this act recognized the power of state courts to rule on constitutional issues, and since the Supreme Court was given the power to affirm or reverse state determinations, it would appear that the high court possessed the power of judicial review.

It was not until 1803, however, that judicial review became an integral part of the American governmental structure. In an otherwise unimportant case, *Marbury* v. *Madison*,[10] Chief Justice Marshall of Virginia made the landmark decision of nineteenth-century American jurisprudence. Here is what he wrote: "It is emphatically the province and duty of the judicial department to say what the law is. Those who apply the rule to particular cases, must of necessity expound and interpret that rule. If two laws conflict with each other, the courts

must decide on the operation of each. So if a law be in opposition to the constitution; if both the law and the Constitution apply to a particular case, so that the court must
either decide that case conformably to the law, disregarding
the constitution; or conformably to the constitution, disregarding the law; the court must determine which of these
conflicting rules governs the case. This is of the very essence
of judicial duty. If, then, the courts are to regard the constitution, and the constitution is superior to any ordinary act
of the legislature, the constitution, and not such ordinary
act, must govern the case to which they both apply."

What John Marshall did in his decisions and wrote in his
opinions transformed a collection of judges into the most
powerful judicial body in the history of man.

While Virginia's Marshall had no hesitancy in declaring
an act of Congress unconstitutional, his successors have been
more timid. Decision after decision has come down from the
high tribunal refusing to exercise the power bequeathed by
the greatest of the chief justices. In 1931 Chief Justice
Hughes wrote: "When the validity of an act of the Congress
is drawn in question, and even if a serious doubt of constitutionality is raised, it is a cardinal principle that this Court
will first ascertain whether a construction of the statute is
fairly possible by which the question may be avoided." [11]
Concurring in a 1936 case, Mr. Justice Louis D. Brandeis
had this to say: "The Court will not pass upon a constitutional question, although properly presented by the record,
if there is also present some other ground upon which the
case may be disposed of. . . . [I]f a case can be decided on
either of two grounds, one involving a constitutional question, the other a question of statutory construction or general law, the Court will decide only the latter." [12] More
pointed was the earlier statement of Mr. Justice Rufus W.
Peckham in 1905: "It is not the habit of the Court to decide

questions of a constitutional nature unless absolutely necessary to a decision of the case." [13]

Over and above this general philosophy are the many square holdings that "the jurisdiction of federal courts is limited to actual cases and controversies." [14] The words "cases" and "controversies" are mentioned specifically in the Constitution. These words mean that the Court will consider only suits "instituted according to the regular course of judicial procedure" [15]—suits in which the Court "is called upon to adjudge the legal rights of litigants in actual controversies." [16] By insisting that the litigation must be *actual,* the Court has raised other bars to its own power. The Court will not pass upon the constitutionality of legislation in a friendly, nonadversary proceeding; [17] it will not act at the behest of one who has taken advantage of the benefits of a statute; [18] and it will not invoke judicial review unless the complaining party shows he is injured by the operation of a statute.[19]

Since the Supreme Court does not act unless and until it has a case in issue, the judges can never anticipate a question of constitutional law in advance of the necessity of making a judicial decision. This precludes the rendering of advisory opinions, even at the request of the President.[20] As a result, neither the executive nor the legislative branches of government can ever know whether their acts and enactments are constitutional until *after* they have been promulgated—and *after* someone has been injured by the operation of such acts and enactments—and after the injured party brings a lawsuit.

Limitations such as these result in another restriction whenever the Supreme Court does invoke its power of judicial review. Mr. Justice Stanley Matthews, in 1885, warned that the Court must not "formulate a rule of constitutional law broader than is required by the precise facts to which it is to be applied." [21]

This is amplified by Justice Jackson's statement: "And

when it is all over, the judicial decree, however broadly worded, actually binds, in most instances, only the parties to the case. As to others, it is merely a weather vane showing which way the judicial wind is blowing—a precedent that the Court in a similar case is likely to follow." [22]

It is for this reason that the following words appear in the school segregation brief submitted by one of the Southern school boards: "The judicial power, with which we shall here be much concerned, is not exercised in a vacuum. By this we mean that the question before this Court for decision in this case is the constitutionality of segregation by race in the high schools of Prince Edward County, Virginia." [23] Judicial decisions are limited by the facts of the case presented.

Thus, despite the seemingly all-inclusive language of *Brown* v. *Board of Education,* technically the actual decision applied only to the Negro parties involved in the litigation. This then leads to the question of who the actual parties were in the school segregation cases. The answer must be not only the named plaintiffs, but also those whom they represented.

This leads to further questions. To what extent does the decision of May 17, 1954, apply to school children and school boards not represented on the day that Oliver Brown was before the Supreme Court of the United States? The technical language of the decision spoke in terms of segregation based on race or color. Does the weather vane indicate the nature of decision when school children are segregated on the basis of "scholastic aptitude"? The technical holding and language of the decision is limited to segregation in the public elementary and secondary schools. What of public transportation, public parks, public beaches, public theaters? What of housing? And what of such insignificant, yet annoying, indicia of segregation as the Jim Crow water fountain and the Jim Crow washroom?

FIVE CASES—AND MORE

By a strange accident of alphabetization and chronology, a little-known man named Oliver Brown has become one of the nation's best-known citizens. He was one of the men who went to court. Because he was first in alphabetical order in the case which was first placed on the Supreme Court docket, Oliver Brown has given his name to the most important judicial decision of this century.

Case No. 1 on the Supreme Court docket for the October Term, 1953, bore the simple and unassuming title of *Brown et al.* v. *Board of Education of Topeka et al.* But this was not the only school segregation case decided in the early afternoon of May 17, 1954; and this was not the first—or the last—time that the courts handed down some ruling under that name.

Neither was Oliver Brown the only litigant to bring suit against the Board of Education of Topeka, Kansas. The words *"et al."* on the plaintiffs' side stood for twelve other Negro parents who joined with Oliver Brown in bringing suit. The other defendant was the State of Kansas. Oliver Brown's NAACP lawyers used his battle with the school board to fight for desegregation. All that Oliver Brown really cared about in the first instance was his eight-year-old daughter, Linda Carol Brown. Linda was forbidden to attend the white elementary school five blocks from her Topeka home and had to walk through railroad yards to catch the bus to take her to a Negro school twenty-one blocks away. Early in 1951, Oliver Brown and the twelve other parents had brought suit on behalf of their children in the United States District Court for the District of Kansas "to enjoin enforcement of a Kansas statute which permits, but does not require, cities of more than 15,000 population to maintain separate school facilities for Negro and white students."

Round one in the school segregation battle had begun.

More than three years later, when the Supreme Court ruled in the Brown case that segregation in public education is "a denial of the equal protection of the law," it was actually ruling at the same time on three similar cases from South Carolina, Virginia and Delaware.

It was a long three years between the early arguments in the Topeka courtroom and the decisions of May 17, 1954. It is a long trip up the judicial ladder to Supreme Court opinion, and a great many decisions have to be made en route.

The first decision involving Oliver Brown *et al.* was rendered by a federal district court in Kansas on August 3, 1951.[24] It was a special three-judge court which heard the case. And the reason for the special court was a provision of the United States Code[25] requiring a three-judge determination where the constitutionality of a state statute is first under consideration.

Oliver Brown lost. The court considered itself bound by the "separate but equal" doctrine of *Plessy* v. *Ferguson* [26] and unanimously denied relief on the basis of findings that the Negro and white schools were substantially equal. ". . . the physical facilities, the curricula, courses of study, qualification of and quality of teachers, as well as other educational facilities in the two sets of schools are comparable," said the court. "We conclude that in the maintenance and operation of the schools there is no willful, intentional or substantial discrimination. . . ." At once, NAACP lawyers began preparing the appeal to the Supreme Court.

Six weeks before the first Brown case, another special three-judge court sat in Charleston, South Carolina, to decide the case of ten-year-old Harry Briggs, Jr., and sixty-six other Negro children who had brought suit against the members of Clarendon County's School Board No. 22.[27] Here also, a federal court denied relief, but this was a much harder case. Unlike the Negro schools of Topeka, the segregated schools in Clarendon County, South Carolina, were found to be far inferior to those afforded the whites. This court, too, invoked *Plessy* v. *Ferguson,* but there was a difference. The defendants were ordered to take steps to equalize the public school facilities "promptly," and to report back in six months. Further, the plaintiffs were denied admission to the white schools during the equalization program. This time there was one dissenting voice.

Harry Briggs, Jr., v. *R. W. Elliott* was the first of the school segregation cases to reach the Supreme Court.[28] On January 28, 1952, the Supreme Court decided only that it would not decide the case. The proceedings were remanded to the three judges in Charleston. Seven months had passed since the district court ruling, and the high tribunal was desirous of obtaining the views of the lower court on the six-month progress report of the Clarendon County School Board. Black and Douglas dissented. They contended that the report to the district court was "wholly irrelevant to the constitutional questions presented" and that the Supreme Court should mark the case for argument.

Before the South Carolina court could take the next steps in the Briggs case, a third special three-man district court was convened on March 7, 1952, to decide a similar cause in Virginia. Dorothy E. Davis *et al.* had brought suit against the County School Board of Prince Edward County, Virginia.[29] Plaintiffs asked the court to declare invalid the state's constitutional and statutory provisions requiring segregation or, as an alternative, to require equalization of existing school facilities. Only the alternative request was granted. The court confessed the inadequacy of the school plant provided for Negroes and ordered the county board to pursue "with diligence and dispatch" its already-begun building project. The unanimous decision cited the first Briggs case as legal authority for supporting the constitutionality of Virginia's segregation laws.

Less than a week after the Davis decision, the Briggs case was once again before the district court in Charleston.[30] Obeying the Supreme Court dictates, the federal court in South Carolina duly considered the progress reports on the Clarendon County equalization program, and duly presented its views. The reports were found "to be true and correct," and the school board was praised for having "proceeded promptly and in good faith to comply with the court's decree." The court then reaffirmed its earlier stand and specifically denied the injunction abolishing segregation. This time the decision was unanimous.

The fourth of the cases decided together on May 17, 1954, differed considerably from the other three. It was a case which entered the judicial machinery of a state court rather than the federal courts; and it was a case in which the judgment was rendered for the Negro plaintiffs. It was actually two cases in one: *Belton* v. *Gebhart* and *Bulah* v. *Gebhart*. It became *Gebhart* v. *Belton* and *Gebhart* v. *Bulah* in the state supreme court; it became just *Gebhart* v. *Belton* before the United States Supreme Court.

Action was brought by the parents of the Negro children Ethel Louise Belton and Barbara Bulah *et al.* against Francis B. Gebhart and other Delaware school officials. As in the other cases, the plaintiffs sought to enjoin constitutional and statutory provisions requiring segregation. This time the plaintiffs won.

On April 1, 1952, Delaware Chancellor Collins J. Seitz ordered the immediate admission of Negro students to schools previously attended only by white children.[31] He did so consistent with the "separate but equal" doctrine of *Plessy* v. *Ferguson.* Unlike the Brown situation in Kansas, and like the Briggs and Davis cases in South Carolina and Virginia, the court found that Negro school facilities were far inferior to those of the whites. Instead of ordering a building program as in Briggs and Davis, the Delaware court enjoined school officials from enforcing segregation laws in the schools involved.

Chancellor Seitz's opinion contained the strongest judicial language supporting desegregation up to that time. He argued that "State-imposed segregation in education itself results in the Negro children, as a class, receiving educational opportunities which are substantially inferior to those available to white children otherwise similarly situated." He expressed the personal belief that "the 'separate but equal' doctrine in education should be rejected." He added, however, that the rejection must come from the United States Supreme Court.

The judgment of the Delaware Court of Chancery was affirmed on August 28, 1952, in a unanimous decision by the state supreme court.[32] But the affirmance lacked the vigor of the lower court determination. The supreme court of Delaware gave strong indication that segregation laws might again be enforced if and when school facilities were equalized.

During this period, Spottswood Bolling and others had applied unsuccessfully for admission to a brand-new white high school in Washington, D. C., and their case was pending in the United States Court of Appeals for the District of Columbia Circuit. This case had to be handled differently, because of the wording of the Constitution and the special jurisdiction of the federal government over the District of Columbia.

Seconds after delivering the unanimous opinion in *Brown* v. *Board of Education,* Chief Justice Warren began reading the likewise unanimous opinion in *Bolling* v. *Sharpe.*[33] He pointed out the fact that the Court had just invoked the "equal protection" clause of the Fourteenth Amendment to prohibit the *states* from maintaining racially segregated public schools. But, he continued, "the legal problem in the District of Columbia is somewhat different." It is different for two reasons. Since the District of Columbia is not a state, its laws are made under federal authority. And federal authority is restricted by the Fifth Amendment, rather than the Fourteenth which is applicable only to the states. Further, while both Amendments have due process provisions, only the Fourteenth has an equal protection clause. The question in the Bolling case was whether a statute which violated the equal protection clause might also violate the due process clause.

"The Fifth Amendment, which is applicable in the District of Columbia, does not contain an equal protection clause as does the Fourteenth Amendment which applies only to the states," said the Chief Justice. "But the concepts of equal protection and due process, both stemming from our American idea of fairness, are not mutually exclusive. . . ."

This statement has an additional significance. For the four state cases which made up *Brown* v. *Board of Education* were argued on the basis of the due process clause of the Fourteenth Amendment as well as its equal protection clause. An indication as to why the Supreme Court rested its decision in the *Brown* case upon the equal protection argument is found in Chief Justice Warren's words in *Bolling* v. *Sharpe:* "The 'equal protection of the laws' is a more explicit safeguard of prohibited unfairness than 'due process of law,' . . ." but, he continued, "[W]e do not imply that the two are always interchangeable phrases. But, as this Court has recognized, discrimination may be so unjustifiable as to be violative of due process." Admittedly, the courts apply different criteria in testing constitutionality under these two clauses—and under some fact situations the results would differ depending upon which clause was applied. In *Brown* v. *Board of Education,* however, there is no doubt that the Supreme Court would have reached the same conclusion by following the due process test, rather than the test of equal protection. And, in fact, the Court outlawed discrimination

on the basis of due process in one case and on the basis of
equal protection in the four other cases which were decided
on the same day.

In its first decision [34] at October Term, 1952, the Supreme
Court had on its docket the appeals in the Brown and Briggs
cases. Also before the Court was a statement of jurisdiction
in the Davis case, pointing out the similarity of the three
controversies and asking that all three be argued together.
Judicial notice was taken of *Bolling* v. *Sharpe* in the District
of Columbia, and the Court invited a petition for certiorari
in order that the issues in all four cases might be heard simul-
taneously. Such a petition is one of the procedural devices
by which cases are brought to the Supreme Court for review.
Mr. Justice Douglas submitted a lone dissent against postponing argument.

A month later, on November 10, 1952, certiorari was
granted in *Bolling* v. *Sharpe*,[35] directing the lower court to
submit the case to the high tribunal for review. Certiorari
was granted in *Gebhart* v. *Belton* [36] on November 24, 1952,
bringing all five cases together before the Supreme Court
for the first time. On that same day, the Court requested the
state of Kansas to present its views at the forthcoming oral
argument.[37]

Then came the argument, and then came judicial silence.
It was a significant silence. For many other cases involving
segregation laws—in schools, in transportation and in public
facilities—had already been instituted in the lower federal
courts. All proceedings stopped and all judges and litigants
waited to see what the Supreme Court would do in the five
cases involving Brown *et al.*

One week before the last decision Monday of the 1952
Term, on June 8, 1953, the Supreme Court made its first
significant statement in the school segregation cases.[38] No
judgment was rendered. The 1953 decision was an order as-

signing the case for reargument the following October 12 [39]—
and requesting counsel "to discuss particularly" five questions. The Attorney General of the United States was invited to take part in the argument.

On the surface, all the Court did was to ask the five questions. But the tenor of those questions gave a definite hint
as to the outcome of the controversy.

Three of the five questions were answered in the historic
decision of *Brown* v. *Board of Education* [40] (and in the companion case of *Bolling* v. *Sharpe* [41]), on May 17, 1954. And
a year later, on May 31, 1955,[42] the Supreme Court was to
answer the fourth and fifth questions, relating to enforcement.

These five questions—and their possible answers—guided
the thinking of the Supreme Court in reaching its decision.
Here are the questions:

"1. What evidence is there that the Congress which submitted and the State legislatures and conventions which ratified the Fourteenth Amendment contemplated or did not
contemplate, understood or did not understand, that it would
abolish segregation in public schools?

"2. If neither the Congress in submitting nor the States in
ratifying the Fourteenth Amendment understood that compliance with it would require the immediate abolition of
segregation in public schools, was it nevertheless the understanding of the framers of the Amendment

(a) that future Congresses might, in the exercise of their
power under section 5 of the Amendment, abolish such
segregation, or

(b) that it would be within the judicial power, in light
of future conditions, to construe the Amendment as abolishing such segregation of its own force?

"3. On the assumption that the answers to questions 2(a)
and (b) do not dispose of the issue, is it within the judicial

power, in construing the Amendment, to abolish segregation in public schools?

"4. Assuming it is decided that segregation in public schools violated the Fourteenth Amendment

(a) would a decree necessarily follow providing that, within the limits set by normal geographic school districting, Negro children should forthwith be admitted to schools of their choice, or

(b) may this Court, in the exercise of its equity powers, permit an effective gradual adjustment to be brought about from existing segregated systems to a system not based on color distinctions?

"5. On the assumption on which questions 4(a) and (b) are based, and assuming further that this Court will exercise its equity powers to the end described in question 4(b),

(a) should this Court formulate detailed decrees in these cases;

(b) if so, what specific issues should the decrees reach;

(c) should this Court appoint a special master to hear evidence with a view to recommending specific terms for such decrees;

(d) should this Court remand to the courts of first instance with directions to frame decrees in these cases, and if so what general directions should the decrees of this Court include and what procedures should the courts of first instance follow in arriving at the specific terms of more detailed decrees?"

Chapter 4

INTERPRETING THE CONSTITUTION

Brown v. *Board of Education* was one of a special category of cases in which a high court is called upon to interpret—and thus give meaning to—the words of a constitution or statute. Because so much of the common law tradition is based upon adherence to case law, there is a substantial body of legal theory based on the proposition that statutes do not become law until some judicial body interprets them. This is not so. The Constitution (including its amendments) became law as soon as it was ratified by three-fourths of the states. Statutes become law as soon as they are passed by a legislative body and, in the typical situation, approved by a chief executive. Most constitutional and statutory pronouncements are clear and certain, and their words constitute commands which are obeyed without question. Some words, however, give rise to legal arguments as to their applicability to particular cases which come before a court. As these arguments become translated into a legal controversy, the courts may be required to define the meaning of the constitutional or statutory phrase in issue. That is what happened in the school segregation cases.

The interpretation of words in wills, contracts, statutes, the Constitution, is the essence of the judicial function. As in thousands of cases before, the nine men who heard the arguments in *Brown* v. *Board of Education* were required to give definition to words whose meaning was indefinite. As in many hundreds of cases before, the words in issue were those of Section 1 of the Fourteenth Amendment.

"No State shall make or enforce any law which shall abridge the privileges or immunities of citizens of the United States; nor shall any state deprive any person of life, liberty or property, without due process of law; nor deny to any person within its jurisdiction the equal protection of the laws."

What do these words mean? What were they intended to mean? What have they come to mean? What do they mean today within the specific context of racial segregation in the public schools? These were the basic questions; decision in *Brown* v. *Board of Education* had to await the answers.

Faced with interpreting the constitutional validity of laws requiring or permitting school segregation, the Supreme Court directed its attention to the three generic clauses of the Fourteenth Amendment. Clearly, the "privileges and immunities" provision was inapplicable. As between "due process of law" and "equal protection of the laws," the Court ultimately chose the latter as the basis of decision.

The five questions posed by the nine men in the first important school segregation decision in 1953 were divided into two categories. Questions 4 and 5 were limited to implementation problems. The first three were devoted to the *meaning* of the Fourteenth Amendment. Implicit in those first three questions were three separate and distinct techniques which could be used by the high court in ascertaining the meaning of the generic clauses and their relationship to the desegregation issue. Inherent in each question was a tacit premise upon which the Court could base its decision outlawing school segregation. The very formulation of the questions suggested to some that the Supreme Court had already made up its mind.

Interpretation is not a simple process, and in constitutional law it is doubly difficult. Before the Supreme Court can follow Marshall's dictate that "an act of the legislature, repugnant to the constitution, is void," [1] the nine men must first determine what the Constitution *says* which would make that act "repugnant." Despite their legal learning, the framers of the Constitution did not consistently provide ready guideposts for judicial decision.

The Constitution is, in a legal sense, a statute. True, it is a superior, all-pervasive statute and is not subject to all of the same restrictions as legislative enactments. But it is a statute in the sense that it is promulgated by a "rule-making" authority, and the law which it makes is contained in specific words. Judge-made law, on the other hand, is a by-product of litigation, and the force and effect of such law are found more in what the court does than in what it says.

The basic principle of statutory interpretation is that the court must resolve all questions of language in accordance with the intention of the enacting legislature. When the court believes the language clear, it expresses no doubt as to the wishes of either legislators or constitutional framers. Judges then give effect to such wishes by expressing what they believe to be the *obvious* meaning of the words employed. Lawyers call this the application of the "plain meaning" rule. But there is obviously no plain meaning of such words as "equal protection of the laws."

When words lack "plain meaning" precision, the courts must look elsewhere for legislative intention. But where? In all too many cases, neither the legislators nor framers had any real intention regarding the point in issue. They had not thought about the problem, or at least they had not said anything about it. In many cases they could not have foreseen the nature of the issues which eventually came before the court for decision. Antitrust statutes passed in 1890 [2] could not possibly reflect congressional intent as to the validity of a motion-picture licensing arrangement in the 1930's. [3] Nor could the framers in 1789 have had any intention as to whether wire-tap evidence should be admissible in the federal courts [4] under the Constitution's "unreasonable searches and seizures" clause.[5]

"Interpretation," wrote Mr. Justice Cardozo, "is often spoken of as if it were nothing but the search and the discovery of a meaning which, however obscure and latent, had nonetheless a real and ascertainable pre-existence in the legislator's mind. The process is, indeed, that at times, but it is often something more." [6]

The National Motor Vehicle Theft Act of 1919 made it a federal crime to transport a stolen vehicle across state lines. The term "motor vehicle" was defined to include "automobile truck, automobile wagon, motor cycle, or any other self-propelled vehicle not designed for running on rails." One McBoyle was convicted under this act, and his case came before the Supreme Court in 1931.[7] He had transported a stolen *airplane* from Illinois to Oklahoma. Guilty or not guilty? What was the intention of Congress in regard to airplanes when it enacted motor vehicle legislation?

When courts face this dilemma, they seek the guidance of other statutory language and previous judicial decisions. They employ "maxims of construction," such as "penal laws should be strictly construed in favor of the accused." More important, they seek the intention of framers and legislators by taking an excursion into history.

Why look into the past at all?

"[T]he judicial branch of the Government," Justice Owen Roberts wrote, "has only one duty, to lay the article of the Constitution which is invoked beside the statute which is challenged and decide whether the latter squares with the former." [8]

The Roberts rule has achieved public popularity because it is the essence of simplicity; the Court has merely to compare the words of the statute with the words of the Constitution. Further, the statement has met with wide approval since it epitomizes the public conception of a government of laws, and not of men. There is little chance for the nine men to "make law" if they are restricted to the squaring of language.

Roberts' statement may be discounted somewhat, as a product of the political struggle between the New Deal and the "nine old men." He spoke for the Supreme Court which had previously thrown out as unconstitutional, first, part of the NRA,[9] then the Railroad Retirement Act [10] and finally all of the NRA.[11] Closely following these decisions came the case in which Roberts expounded his constitutional philosophy, using it as the basis for declaring the Agricultural Adjustment Act of 1933 likewise unconstitutional.

Undoubtedly, Roberts' rule of construction was intended as the Court's answer to its critics. The answer was that judicial interpretation is merely a mechanical job of comparison. But to compare phrases or sets of words, the phrases or sets of words must be alike, and the words of the school segregation laws and the words of the "equal protection" clause are not alike. The nine men of 1954 avoided this trap of oversimplification. They had learned their constitutional law at another school. They turned to the lessons of Justice Oliver Wendell Holmes: "The provisions of the Constitution are not mathematical formulas having their essence in their form; they are organic living institutions transplanted from English soil. Their significance is vital, not formal; it is to be gathered not simply by taking the words and a dictionary, but by considering their origin and the line of their growth." [12]

What was said or done during the days immediately before and after the adoption of the Fourteenth Amendment which indicated an intention on the issue of school segregation? This is basically what the Supreme Court asked in the first of its questions. And it received a multitude of answers in the more than two thousand pages of briefs which the attorneys submitted in response. After hours of study and other hours of argument, the Court came to its May 17, 1954, conclusion:

"This discussion and our own investigation convince us that, although the sources cast some light, it is not enough to resolve the problem with which we are faced. At best they are inconclusive."

AN EXCURSION INTO HISTORY

The Fourteenth Amendment originated in the Thirty-ninth Congress, which convened in December, 1865, as the first post-Civil War Congress. There was a Republican Senate and a Republican House, and within the majority party a vicious power struggle between the moderate and radical factions had begun.

Literally only hours after the opening of the session, Representative John Bingham of Ohio, a Radical Republican, submitted a proposed constitutional amendment restricting the power of the states to deny equal protection of the laws or to interfere with the privileges or immunities of any citizen. Bingham's proposal was broadened into a general limitation, and expressly granted Congress power to implement these prohibitions by legislation.

Andrew Jackson Rogers, a Democrat from New Jersey, objected to the "equal protection" clause. "Under this amendment," he contended, "Congress would have power to compel the State to provide for white children and black children to attend the same school, upon the principle that all the people in the several states shall have equal protection. . . ." [13] Bingham and his supporters countered with the argument that except for the grant of power to Congress, the amendment was merely declaratory of existing law. Bingham lost. The proposed amendment was defeated, apparently through fear that future Congresses could not be trusted with the centralized power granted by the implementation clause. But it was not a real victory for Rogers. Although his colleagues had forestalled the approval of the Bingham bill, his school segregation argument played no part in their determination. Those who did not ignore Rogers' remarks on Negro education, greeted them with derision.[14]

In April, 1866, Thaddeus Stevens of Pennsylvania submitted to the Joint Committee on Reconstruction a proposed constitutional amendment which embodied the Radical Republican plan for reconstruction of the South. Stevens' fellow radical, Bingham, offered additions. And what he added included the present language of the privileges and immunities, due process and equal protection clauses. After Bingham's additions had been first struck out and then reinserted, the proposed amendment was reported out of committee.[15]

The most striking aspect of the floor debates which followed was the almost complete absence of discussion of the three Bingham clauses which are now the heart of the Fourteenth Amendment. In one of the few comments on education problems, Senator Howe of Wisconsin called attention to a Florida school statute which he believed would be voided by the Amendment. But his objection was not based upon the fact that segregation of the races was required; Howe objected to the levy of special taxes on Negroes to support Negro schools, while the total population of Florida, whites and Negroes, were taxed to support white schools.[16] Despite Howe's standing as a leading constitutional lawyer, his argument drew no substantial rejoinder; Congress was far more concerned with the problem of Southern representation in the House.

Congress, under the lash of the Republican whips, approved the Fourteenth Amendment without change in the

Bingham language. With this, the Amendment was submitted to the states for approval.

On July 28, 1868, the Secretary of State declared the Fourteenth Amendment ratified by "three-fourths and more of the several states of the Union"—the "three-fourths" including some of the former Confederate States.

The Fourteenth Amendment was initiated by Congress; it had to be ratified by the legislatures or conventions of the states. It is arguable that since the clause in issue—"equal protection of the laws"—originated in the Committee on Reconstruction, the members of that committee would be infallible sources as to the meaning of the clause. On the other hand, since the Amendment was not legally effective until three-quarters of the states had ratified, it is equally arguable that the manifested intent of the states is controlling.

The Court in its 1953 decision sidestepped the problem of determining which intent would control in the event of conflict by requesting evidence as to the thinking of both groups. But another problem was still before the Supreme Court: How is the intention of a group to be determined? And the answer is that intent can be found only in the words and deeds of individual members.

The courts have developed a number of formulas to determine the types of evidence which are relevant in translating these individual understandings into group purpose. Application of these rules, however, is quite another problem. Because the formulas are so intricate and complex, not even the most brilliant jurist can adhere to all the rules and still discover an "intent" which can be labeled conclusive.

The first question, it will be remembered, asked: "What evidence is there that the Congress which submitted and the State legislatures and conventions which ratified the Fourteenth Amendment contemplated or did not contemplate, understood or did not understand, that it would abolish segregation in public schools?"

The nine men were on safe ground when they pinned the "inconclusive" label on the intent of the Congressmen who framed and voted on the Fourteenth Amendment. Though Rogers hit the heart of the issue in his statement on the first Bingham proposal, his low standing with his colleagues precluded serious consideration of his views on school segregation. Howe's high standing with his colleagues did not change the situation when he spoke of the applicability of equal protection to Negro education, because Congress was more interested in other matters.

But this was only half of the story. There were thirty-seven states in the Union when Congress submitted the Fourteenth Amendment for ratification by "three-fourths of the several states." [17] In the almost two years which ensued between submission and ratification, many of those states had given some indication of their understanding of the relationship of school segregation and the Fourteenth Amendment.

Little could be gleaned from the action of the South. The former Confederate States had been placed in an anomalous position, since ratification was part of the price for readmission to the Union.[18] Although in 1869, a year after ratification, the Supreme Court held that the Confederate States had never really seceded,[19] that holding was of no benefit to the South in 1866. The Southern states had no choice but to do the bidding of the Radical Republicans in Congress, and the Radicals required ratification.[20] The intent behind Southern ratification was dictated from Washington. Thus the most effective arguments against desegregation advanced by the South today are *not* based on the attitudes or opinions of the South in 1866, but on the "understanding" of the Northern states as to the effect of the Amendment on segregated schools.

South Carolina argued the "intent" question this way in the December before "Black Monday." "Persuasive evidence," wrote South Carolina's counsel, "that the State legislatures which ratified the Fourteenth Amendment did not contemplate and did not understand that it would abolish segregation in public schools is supplied by those Northern States, which although ratifying the Fourteenth Amendment, nevertheless . . . established separate public schools or continued to operate existing segregated public school systems." [21] Nine states were in this category: New York, New Jersey, Pennsylvania, Indiana, Illinois, Ohio, Kansas, Nevada and Oregon.

Of these nine states, only Indiana and Pennsylvania preserved records of their ratification debates. At the time the Indiana legislature considered the question of ratification, Negroes were entirely excluded from the school system. The Governor, in his message urging approval in 1867, suggested that the state would now be required by the Amendment to provide for Negro education.[22] Two years later, the legislature established a separate Negro school system. Nevada followed a similar course.[23] Both Illinois [24] and Kansas [25] followed the lead of Indiana and Nevada, but with a difference. Both states made provision for Negro education by adopting a "local option" plan which permitted local school boards to rule on the question of separate schools. Topeka chose segregation, and eighty-three years later Oliver Brown went to court.

In New York, New Jersey and Pennsylvania there were segregrated schools before ratification and segregated schools after ratification.[26] Although the debates were never recorded in either New York or New Jersey, the actions of both states would seem to indicate their understanding that the Amendment had nothing to do with schools. Pennsylvania legislators filled the public records with statements that the equal protection clause both did and did not affect segregated schools, but when the debates ended, the state still had separate schools for Negroes.[27] No valid evidence of intent can be obtained from either Ohio or Oregon. These states pursued inconsistent policies with regard to school segregation, never acting specifically on the basis of the Amendment.

Five states outlawed segregation in their educational systems at or about the time of ratification. No conclusions, however, can be drawn from this fact. Three of the five states were in the South (Florida, Louisiana and South Carolina) where Negroes were then in control of the legislatures. Negroes would have provided for nonsegregated education whether or not the Constitution required it. The other two states were Connecticut and Michigan. In the latter, Judge Thomas Cooley delivered the opinion of the Supreme Court of Michigan which invalidated school segregation on the basis of state law.[28] As far as Connecticut is concerned, there was a definite relationship between the ratification of the Fourteenth Amendment and the abolition of segregated schools, but the absence of records renders this evidence likewise "inconclusive."

Nine other states maintained nonsegregated schools at the time of ratification: Maine, Vermont, New Hampshire, Massachusetts, Rhode Island, Wisconsin, Minnesota, Nebraska and Iowa. Some had never known segregation; others had long before abolished the practice. Adherence to a policy of nonsegregated schools by these states was clearly unrelated to their ratification of the Amendment.

Of the remaining fourteen states, four, Delaware, Maryland, Kentucky and Texas, refused to ratify the Amendment. And for the other ten there were on record neither deeds nor words reflecting understanding.

Writing in 1950, John Frank and Robert F. Munro reasoned as follows: "The generalities of the Fourteenth Amendment, as reported from Committee, were voted upon by 218 Congressmen, were discussed in hundreds of speeches and countless editorials in the election of 1866, and were thereafter voted upon by some thousands of state legislators. Even if the times had been calm and conditions static, the general phrases of the Amendment could not have meant even approximately the same thing to all who voted upon them; and in fact, interpretations did diverge widely." [29]

After exhaustive historical research, and correlation of their findings in lengthy briefs, opposing counsel urged a diversity of conclusions. "There is convincing evidence," said the NAACP attorneys, "that the state legislatures and conventions which ratified the Fourteenth Amendment contemplated and understood that it prohibited State legislation which would require racial segregation in public schools." [30] Not so, said South Carolina; ". . . the overwhelming preponderance of the evidence . . ." [31] demonstrates that the states had no such understanding. The United States Attorney General, with whom the nine men agreed, concluded that the evidence (and lack of evidence) was "inconclusive."

Ascertaining the *specific* intent of the framers, however, is not the only technique used in determining meaning. The Court indicated a second method in the second question asked: "[W]as it nevertheless the understanding of the framers of the Amendment (a) that future Congresses might, in exercise of their power under section 5 of the Amendment, abolish such segregation, or (b) that it would be within the judicial power, *in light of future conditions,* to construe the Amendment as abolishing such segregation of its own force?" [32]

In posing the second part of this question, the nine men frankly recognized that they make law, and suggested that the framers might have intended the Supreme Court to implement the *general purpose* of the Amendment at a proper time.

Vague as those words may appear, "general purpose" has tangible judicial significance when applied to the equal protection clause of the Amendment. "[I]t is not difficult to give a meaning to this clause," Mr. Justice Miller stated in the famous *Slaughter-House Cases* of 1873. "The existence of laws in the States where newly emancipated Negroes resided, which discriminated with gross injustice and hardship against them as a class, was the evil to be remedied by this clause, and by it such laws are forbidden." [33] Justice Miller limited "general purpose" to the *then* existing evils. By asking question 2, the Supreme Court took the position that future action could be taken to cure *future* evils.

Question 2(a) asked whether future evils could be cured by Congress; question 2(b) asked whether future evils could be cured by judicial action. The evidence is conclusive that the framers intended Congress to have the power to implement the general purpose of the Fourteenth Amendment in the light of future conditions. They said so in Section 5 of the Amendment: "The Congress shall have the power to enforce, by appropriate legislation, the provisions of this article." That was enough for the Radical Republicans for the moment. "Take what we can get now," Thaddeus Stevens advised, "and hope for better things in further legislation; in enabling acts or other provisions." [34] In Congress and in the states, however, there was silence as to the role the *judiciary* should play in implementing the general purpose of the equal protection clause.

After analyzing both the evidence and lack of evidence on these questions, the 1954 Supreme Court answered, "inconclusive." The nine men then had to ask themselves an even more significant question: Does the absence of specific authority to act constitute an unspoken prohibition against further judicial action? Ex-Justice Byrnes would have answered, "Yes." He argues that since school segregation existed before the Fourteenth Amendment, and since there was no specific intent to outlaw it, the Supreme Court was precluded from declaring segregation legislation unconstitutional. [35] Yale's Professor Alexander Bickel, former law clerk to Mr. Justice Frankfurter, concurs in part. He agrees the evidence indicated that the framers and ratifiers of the Fourteenth Amendment had not intended to outlaw school segregation. "But the relevant point," according to Bickel, "is that the Radical leadership succeeded in obtaining a provision whose future effect was left to future determination. The fact that they themselves expected such future determination to be made in Congress is not controlling." [36]

Byrnes and Bickel, considering the same historical facts, came to different conclusions, in part because they gave different interpretations to the statement of the Supreme Court that the evidence "at best" was "inconclusive." Byrnes saw this as an answer to both questions 1 and 2. Bickel, on the other hand, said that the evidence in 1 and 2(a) was conclusive, and that the Court applied the term inconclusive only to question 2(b). Bickel concludes that since Congress looked to some future implementation, and since it did not prohibit the Court from doing the implementing, the Supreme Court had such power.

Not only do Byrnes and Bickel differ in their conclusions, but they disagree in their reasoning as to what the Supreme Court should have done as a result of the finding of "inconclusiveness."

Following Byrnes's reasoning, "Having decided unanimously that the legislative history was not 'conclusive' that Congress or the States intended it should apply to schools, one would think the Court would have stopped there and upheld the previous decisions of the Court." [37] Following Bickel's reasoning, the absence of any guideposts found in the past "invited a decision based on the moral and material state of the nation in 1954, not 1866." [38]

Whether the Court found as Bickel indicates, or it found that the evidence as to both questions 1 and 2 was "inconclusive," it did not feel itself precluded from giving a meaning to the Amendment not contemplated by the framers. The Supreme Court was now ready to consider question 3.

Chapter 5

INTERPRETATION AND AMENDMENT

The power of amendment is granted to Congress and the people of the states by Article V of the Constitution. It is not a judicial function.

Yet, according to Byrnes, "The Court did not interpret the constitution—the Court amended it." [1] Two lines of reasoning have been developed to support the argument that the nine men unconstitutionally amended a part of the Constitution—the equal protection clause of the Fourteenth Amendment. The first of these arguments limits the scope of judicial interpretation to the meaning which the framers ascribed to the words of the Constitution. It is also contended that since the specific powers of implementation had been given to Congress the Court is precluded from going beyond the specified intent of the framers. The second position is that the Court must not disregard established precedent in construing the Constitution. The conclusion drawn from these arguments is that when the Court found no definite intent expressed by Congress or the states, further exercise of the power to interpret was foreclosed. In other words the Supreme Court had to leave the law as it was.

Senator Ervin of North Carolina, now one of the pro-segregation leaders, is an ardent disciple of Michigan's Judge Thomas Cooley, renowned commentator on constitutional law during the late nineteenth century. He cites Cooley [2] to support his assertion that the Supreme Court imperiled the constitutional structure of American government by going beyond the meaning intended by the framers.[3] Another Cooley disciple was Mr. Justice Sutherland, who in 1934 declared in a dissent: "The whole aim of construction as applied to a provision of the Constitution, is to discover the meaning, to ascertain and give effect to intent, of its framers and the people who adopted it." [4] Justice Sutherland, Senator Ervin and Judge Cooley have all expounded the doctrine of limited interpretive powers which was first developed by Chief Justice Roger Brooke Taney.

"No one, we presume," declared Taney, "supposes that any change in public opinion or feeling, in relation to this unfortunate race, in civilized nations of Europe or in this country, should induce the court to give to the words of the Constitution a more liberal construction in their favor than they were intended to bear when the instrument was framed and adopted. Any other rule of construction would abrogate the judicial character of this Court, and make it a mere reflex of the popular opinion or passion of the day." [5] These are the words of Chief Justice Taney in the Dred Scott case of 1857.

Senator Ervin gives a false impression in stating that "their novel decision was based on an astounding constitutional philosophy." [6] As in so many cases before, the Supreme Court had to choose between conflicting constitutional philosophies. It was John Marshall who advanced the view that the Constitution was continually adaptable to the needs of the time. In *Brown* v. *Board of Education,* the Court followed Chief Justice Marshall rather than Chief Justice Taney on the construction of the Constitution.

Even though he was a follower of Taney's constitutional philosophy, Cooley, as a state judge, when the issue was squarely before him, construed the Michigan constitution as requiring the abolition of segregated schools in that state;

and he did so in the face of a long history of segregated school systems.[7]

On the two significant occasions when the Supreme Court has departed from the Marshall doctrine, severe constitutional crises followed. Taney's departure in the Dred Scott decision hastened the Civil War.[8] Similarly, when Sutherland led the Court majority in restrictive constitutional interpretations on New Deal legislation, the government's hands were virtually tied in coping with depression problems.

The Court itself, both before and after the Dred Scott case, recognized the danger of the Taney doctrine to orderly and effective government. Answering Mr. Justice Sutherland's dissent in the 1934 case, Chief Justice Hughes was quite explicit in declaring: "If by the statement that what the Constitution meant at the time of its adoption it means today, it is intended to say that the great clauses of the Constitution must be confined to the interpretation which the framers, with the conditions and outlook of their time, would have placed upon them, the statement carries its own refutation. It was to guard against such a narrow conception that Chief Justice Marshall uttered the memorable warning—'we must never forget that it is *a constitution* we are expounding—a constitution intended to endure for ages to come, and consequently, to be adapted to the various crises of human affairs.' "[9]

Although the framers of the Fourteenth Amendment offered no guides to the Supreme Court in the exercise of its interpretive powers, they were well aware of the nature of those powers, and their exercise since 1803. They knew of Jefferson's proposal that each generation redeclare its basic law.[10] They could well have predicted the conclusion nearly a century later that "So far as the Constitution is concerned, it has demonstrated again and again its capacity for adaptation to the most challenging new conditions."[11] More important, they recognized that the Supreme Court had assumed the power of redeclaration and adaptation. They knew from the lessons of history since the inception of judicial review in 1803 that new circumstances had given rise to new judicial interpretations, and that those new interpretations had made new law. And they could have foreseen a Supreme Court justice declaring (in the course of decision) that "We should not indulge in the fiction that the law now announced has always been the law. . . ." [12]

"Adaptation" does not just happen; it is a product of the interpretation of words by the nine men, and in many cases, by only five of the nine. Yet the Supreme Court in *Brown* v. *Board of Education* was not unmindful that there are limits to its power to interpret.

The high court pointedly raised this issue in the third question put to counsel in June, 1953: "On the assumption that the answers to questions 2(a) and (b) do not dispose of the issue, is it within the judicial power, in construing the Amendment, to abolish segregation in public schools?"

The 1954 answer to this query is found not in what was said, but in what the Court did: ". . . we hold that the plaintiffs and others similarly situated for whom the actions have been brought are, by reason of the segregation complained of, deprived of the equal protection of the laws guaranteed by the Fourteenth Amendment."

Was this holding a proper exercise of judicial power?

"It is our firm opinion," declared two leading pro-segregationist lawyers, Cook and Potter, "that the United States Supreme Court in *Brown* v. *Topeka* not only usurped the prerogatives of the people by amending the Federal Constitution in violation of Article V relating to amendment, but it pursued its pseudo socio-psychological pattern by usurping the prerogatives of the United States Congress." [13]

This argument is derived from the premise that *only* Congress can implement the Amendment. Section 5 of the Fourteenth Amendment, it will be remembered, provides the following: "The Congress shall have the power to enforce, by appropriate legislation, the provisions of this article." This provision, however, does not necessarily mean that Congress was given the *exclusive* power of implementation.

With *Marbury* v. *Madison,* the Supreme Court established its power to declare legislation void which was not in accordance with the Constitution. And, as Marshall explained in the Marbury case, the Court of necessity must exercise such power in order to decide many of the cases before it. Moreover, the oath which every judge takes to uphold the Constitution creates a duty which compels a court to grant relief against infringement of constitutional rights.[14] It follows that in constitutional disputes, the Court necessarily has the power to implement the provisions of the Constitution in issue, in order to dispose of the "case or controversy" before it. These aspects of the Supreme Court's function add up to the power of judicial review.

The framers of the Fourteenth Amendment were well aware of the Court's assumption of this constitutional power. They knew of the existing repository of powers in the Supreme Court to implement the general declarations of the Constitution. They also knew that the Court exercised those powers. The Supreme Court, in the Dred Scott case, had declared unconstitutional a law which had been on the books since 1820 and which had been repealed in 1856. And Dred Scott was still a live political issue in 1866.

There is nothing in the events surrounding ratification which indicates that Congress or the state legislatures intended to prohibit Supreme Court implementation of the generic rights in the Amendment. Lawyers have a complex set of interacting rules and presumptions to determine intent in such circumstances. Summarized, these rules and presumptions amount to "silence gives consent." In this case the consent of the framers was to the normal functioning of the Court in the settlement of disputes. Nothing was said or done by the framers to preclude necessary Supreme Court adaptation of the Fourteenth Amendment in the normal course of constitutional litigation.

Although the Court has the power to implement the Amendment within the framework of a "case or controversy," it has been ever mindful of the congressional power to implement by rule-making.[15] The problem of reconciling co-existent legislative and judicial powers is not peculiar to the Fourteenth Amendment. On some occasions, the Court has even refused to grant relief against unconstitutional actions, when it found that the legislative branch of government, Congress, also had the power to provide a remedy. For example, Article IV, Section 4, provides in part: "The United States shall guarantee to every State in this Union a Republican Form of Government. . . ." The Court as early as 1849 indicated that the enforcement of this "guarantee" was within the power of Congress, and consequently refused to afford a judicial remedy.[16] Similarly, when state legislatures have refused to redistrict congressional districts as required by the Constitution and acts of Congress, the Supreme Court has refused to order compliance because of the implementation power granted Congress.[17]

Cook and Potter based their thinking on these holdings of the Court when they asserted: "It handed down an implementation decision on May 31, 1955, in spite of the fact that the Fourteenth itself vests in Congress the power of implementation." [18]

This objection purports to apply to the enforcement decision of 1955 only. Logically, however, any criticism of *Brown* v. *Board of Education* must be directed to the decision of 1954 as well as to the implementation decree. The Supreme Court's power to interpret and declare a principle of law derives solely from its powers to grant a remedy. In the usual case, the declaration of such principle and the grant of such remedy take place at the same time. In this case, however, the two were separated by a year, and the decision of 1954 was the necessary preliminary to the enforcement decree. If there is no way for the Court to grant some remedy for the infringement of a constitutional right, there is no power in the Court to declare the law.

Yet all constitutional cases are not the same. Disputes involving the guarantee of a republican form of government and the redistricting of congressional districts—where Congress is given the specific power of implementation—differ considerably from the school segregation cases where Congress is also given implementation authority. And because they are different, these decisions are not precedent for the proposition that if Congress is given implementation powers those powers are denied the Court.

The basis of the "republican form of government" and "redistricting" decisions is that the Court could not grant an effective remedy without requiring a coordinate branch of the government, the legislative, to help enforce the Court's order. Since the legislative body, Congress, had the power in these cases to make up its own mind, it might very well have decided not to help the Court. Then, the Court reasoned, it could not order the legislature to make up its mind in accordance with the Court's determination, because the principle of "separation of powers" would be violated. To avoid violating this basic constitutional principle, the Court decided not to decide anything in the first place—and in effect told the plaintiffs to appeal to the legislature for relief. This is what happened in the "redistricting" and "republican form of government" cases.

But in *Brown* v. *Board of Education,* the plaintiffs were asking for orders requiring state officials to stop refusing to admit them to white schools. These state officials were not coordinate branches of the federal government together with the Supreme Court; only Congress and the President share that position. There could be no violation of the doctrine of "separation of powers" by ordering state officials to admit plaintiffs to white schools.

Thus the Court could grant an effective remedy—the one asked for by the plaintiffs—without congressional assistance; and what it necessarily had to do in deciding whether or not to grant the remedy requested, was to interpret the Constitution. The nine men had to find the meaning of "equal protection of the laws" as the clause applied to school segregation.

Yet the nine men were not without guidance. The equal protection clause was nothing new to them. The Supreme Court had decided cases involving segregation many times before. And its prior decisions contained interpretations which could lead to the decision in *Brown* v. *Board of Education*. Again the Court was to take an excursion into history—its own history—still in quest of meaning. Final decision required an analysis of precedent.

Chapter 6

TURNING BACK THE CLOCK

The roots of the American system of law lie deep in the English past. Many of the settled doctrines of the English common law were transmitted to the New World—complete with Latin labels. In many instances a simple Latin phrase was employed by those learned in the law to describe and invoke well-developed sets of legal rules. Lawyers still use such phrases as a type of professional shorthand: *habeas corpus*, a term employed to describe a proceeding in which a person allegedly confined unlawfully is afforded a court hearing, is a phrase summarizing three hundred years of legal history. *Stare decisis*, like *habeas corpus*, stands for a number of rules and concepts which have taken centuries to develop.

Stare decisis deals with the phenomenon of precedent. "It summarizes," writes Cloyd LaPorte, a New York lawyer, "the doctrine which makes precedent so important in the common law and, literally construed, enjoins upon judges the duty of applying to later cases principles which have been enunciated by them and their predecessors in earlier decisions." [1] But this descriptive phrase does more than describe a method of deciding particular controversies. *Stare decisis* also directs the courts to a source of law by which cases are decided. All courts purport to settle disputes before them in accordance with the law. It is when judges deem themselves bound by their own prior determinations that those prior determinations become the law.

Since the middle of the twelfth century, the English courts

(later joined by most American courts) have been deciding controversies between litigants by reference to the holdings of previously decided cases. Judicial recognition of prior decisions thus translates dispute-settling determinations into law. "A mere series of decisions of individual cases," writes Professor Karl Llewellyn of Chicago Law School, "does not of course in itself constitute a system of law. But in any judicial system rules of law arise sooner or later out of such decisions of cases, as rules of action arise out of the solution of practical problems, whether or not such formulations are desired, intended or consciously recognized. These generalizations contained in, or built upon, past decisions, when taken as normative for future disputes, create a system of precedent." [2] Far more law is made by this process than by the myriad of statutes which flow from Congress and the state legislatures.

In adhering to precedent in the settlement of new disputes, the courts are motivated by a desire for consistency. Like cases should be decided alike. But decisional consistency is only a means to an end, not an end itself. "It is revolting," observed Justice Holmes, "to have no better reason for a rule of law than that so it was laid down in the time of Henry IV." [3]

There are, however, a great many better reasons for deciding like controversies alike than the mere existence of precedent. Courts satisfy the sense of justice of the litigants before them when they make similar judgments in resolving similar disputes. Law is rightfully popular when it is impartially administered. Then, too, the courts save time and energy when they decide new controversies according to previously formulated standards. Moreover, by watching adherence to precedent, potential litigants can assume that the courts will continue to dispose of new controversies in accordance with old decisions. This assumption gives rise to a reasonable expectation of judicial action and gives confidence to those about to undertake corporate and contract obligations and the like. Expectation itself, then, becomes a force militating against departure from previously developed lines of decision.

Because most courts cite precedent without articulating reasons for their adherence to past judgments, it is frequently assumed by non-lawyers that courts must always decide like cases alike. This is not so.

There are pressures which at times require departure from recognized lines of decision. In some cases the parties in litigation actually desire a determination based on the "merits," without regard to what the court may have done in previous disputes.[4] Then, too, times change. Rules formulated in the course of decisions involving the horse and buggy are not always apt in resolving controversies arising out of airplane collisions. Old rules must be altered and new rules brought into being. And the phenomena of change which require renunciation of past decisions, are not limited to matters of mechanics and machines. "Social forces like armies," observed Justice Douglas, "can sweep around a fixed [legal] position and make it untenable."[5] The dead hand of precedent does not always rule the living.

Ex-Justice Byrnes argues that the prior decisions of the Supreme Court in fact governed *Brown* v. *Board of Education,* and that the nine men acted "unconstitutionally" in disregarding that fact. "Ordinarily," he writes, "the Court has been controlled by legal precedents. In the segregation opinion, it could cite no legal precedent for its decision because all the precedents sustain the doctrine of separate but equal facilities. . . . The Supreme Court itself, in six cases decided over a period of 75 years, upheld the doctrine of equal but separate facilities."[6] But South Carolina's Byrnes said "ordinarily," and *Brown* v. *Board of Education* was not an ordinary case.

"In approaching this problem," declared Chief Justice

Warren, "we cannot turn the clock back to 1868 when the Amendment was adopted, or even to 1896 when Plessy v. Ferguson was written."

Why were the nine men unanimously opposed to turning back the clock? What impelled them to say that they *could not* follow *Plessy* v. *Ferguson?*

In deciding whether or not to follow a precedent, the Court must eventually harmonize antipathetical goals. A balance must be struck between values which are inherent in consistency of decision and values which flow from judicial recognition of the changing nature and patterns of society. This is judicial labor at its highest level. The Court begins its work at a much lower plane: the first job is to decide which of the three million cases in the law books can be considered precedent.

Law "cases" are the reports of prior decisions. They consist of judicial determinations and the opinions of the judges setting forth their reasons for decision. Reading these reports is an art peculiar to lawyers, including lawyers who are judges. Their ultimate objective is to determine the state of the law as reflected in these cases. But lawyers know that everything in the cases is not law. The first step in finding the law requires a reading of the reports to ascertain what the other courts did, as distinct from what they said. Law reports are read a second time to determine whether what was said was essential to the action taken. From these readings a "holding" is extracted. And holdings are the basic structural units of case law, which, in turn, forms the basis of the law of precedent. This requires the process of putting holdings together to express principles of law. It must be cautioned, however, that the principles which might be so derived are not applicable to all controversies.

A precedent becomes a precedent only when it is a decision resolving a former dispute similar to the dispute at hand. Thus before a decision becomes a precedent there must be a determination that the underlying controversies are sufficiently alike. Here the courts have the last word. If the court declares there is the required degree of similarity, the prior decisions are said to be "in point." Then the derived principle of law can properly be applied to the new case.

In applying the doctrine of *stare decisis,* the courts often say that they are "bound" by precedent—meaning that they are inexorably governed by prior cases in point. However, this is only what the courts say. All cases in point do not have the same "binding" influence: they are not all entitled to equal weight. The opinion of a state supreme court, for example, is accorded more weight than the opinion of a lower tribunal in that state. A former decision of the United States Supreme Court is, of course, a stronger precedent than the determination of a federal district court. Even within a single court, the opinions of some judges are valued more than the expressed views of other judges on that same bench. Here too, the court which must decide a legal issue has the final word as to the worth and effect of a prior decision.

Every court, including the Supreme Court of the United States, goes through this same routine of turning back the clock to prior decisions—of reading and evaluating what other judges have previously said and done. And no matter how the court settles the dispute before it, the new decision itself becomes precedent, ever ready to breed new precedent as the occasion demands.

This is *stare decisis.*

Like every other common law judicial tribunal, the Supreme Court accepts this doctrine. It has developed a great repository of precedent on the meanings of the general declarations of the Constitution. For example, here is how the Court has handled Article II, Section 8, which grants Congress the power to establish "uniform Laws on the subject of Bankruptcies throughout the United States. . . ." The Court has recognized the authority of a state to enact statutes providing for the liquidation of an insolvent debtor's estate,[7] but a state cannot as part of this liquidation grant a final discharge of unsatisfied obligations. This has become the meaning of the Constitution during the periods when a national bankruptcy act has been in force.[8] Where there have been no federal bankruptcy statutes, the states have been permitted in effect to grant discharges [9] limited only by the rule that these discharges would not unreasonably interfere with the rights of creditors in other states.[10] These decisions give meaning to the skeleton of the Constitution, and themselves become law—the law of the Constitution.

Each of the clauses of the Constitution has its own repository of precedent. And most of the constitutional law relating to discrimination and segregation is found in judicial analysis of the Thirteenth, Fourteenth and Fifteenth Amendments. Here are the prior decisions pertaining to the issues raised in *Brown* v. *Board of Education*.

These past decisions were, of course, guides to future Supreme Court action. But this does not mean that any one decision or group of decisions was necessarily "binding" upon the nine men who were to determine the constitutional validity of school segregation. As Justice Douglas cautioned, "So far as constitutional law is concerned *stare decisis* must give way before the dynamic component of history." [11] As Justice Jackson observed, "constitutional precedents are accepted only at their current valuation and have a mortality rate almost as high as their authors." [12]

DRED SCOTT—RIGHT AND WRONG

The basic precedent in the legal area of racial segregation is the case of *Plessy* v. *Ferguson* which set forth the separate but equal doctrine in 1896. Yet the clock must be turned back even beyond that decision. While the Court as an institution makes history, it is at the same time subject to the forces of history. Thus any inquiry into decisions involving segregation and discrimination must start with the case of *Dred Scott* v. *Sandford*,[13] decided three years before the outbreak of the Civil War. History shaped this decision; the decision itself was history-making; the dynamics of future history made this the most far-reaching judicial determination of the nineteenth century.

Twenty years before the Supreme Court spoke in the Dred Scott case, one Dr. Emerson, a surgeon in the United States Army, returned to his home in St. Louis, Missouri, following four years of duty in Illinois and the northern part of the Louisiana Purchase Territory which is now Minnesota. Returning too was his slave, Dred Scott.

Illinois was a free state. As far back as the Ordinance of 1787, slavery had been prohibited in the territory of which Illinois was part. Missouri, on the other hand, was a slave state. Part of the price it had to pay for admission to the Union was embodied in the famous Missouri Compromise: all of the territory north of the 36° 30' line, drawn through the Louisiana Purchase, was to be "ever free." Scott had resided, along with Dr. Emerson, both in Illinois and in territory north of that line.

Upon his return to Missouri, Scott immediately brought suit for his freedom in the state courts. This was not an unusual procedure. Slaves and ex-slaves frequently asserted their claims to freedom via the legal process. Although these actions were largely prohibited in the deep South, legal arguments of a Negro that he had been born free or had been set free were heard regularly in the courts of Missouri and the other border states. The Missouri courts heard the case and decided that residence in a free territory did not make a slave free.

Shortly thereafter, Dr. Emerson died and Emerson's widow became Scott's lawful owner. Mrs. Emerson then married the well-known Massachusetts abolitionist, Congressman Calvin

C. Chaffee. The Congressman could not, of course, allow himself to be known publicly as a slave-owner, and Scott was "sold" to Mrs. Emerson-Chaffee's brother, John F. A. Sanford of New York (mistakenly spelled "Sandford" in the Supreme Court Reports).

Having been denied his freedom in the state courts, Scott prepared to bring a similar suit in the federal courts. Whether such an action could be brought in the federal courts was still an open question in the 1850's. These courts would hear cases only where there was diversity of citizenship—where the litigants were citizens of different states.

It is an unanswered question of history whether Scott was "sold" to Sanford (Sandford) of New York in order to provide diversity of citizenship. But the fact remains that Scott took advantage of the diversity provision of the Constitution [14] to commence proceedings in the federal Circuit Court for Missouri. He argued that he was a Missouri citizen and that Sanford, of course, was a citizen of New York. Sanford's lawyers readily admitted that Scott was a citizen of Missouri under that state's definition of citizenship. But, they argued, a state could not by its definition of citizenship determine who could bring suit in a federal court. That was solely a matter of federal concern. Therefore, Scott would have to show that he was a citizen of Missouri as defined by the Constitution. But the Constitution at that time had no definition of citizenship—for diversity or any other purpose. Accordingly, Sanford's lawyers contended that the federal meaning of the word "citizenship" as used in the diversity clause could be found only in the intent of the original framers. They asserted that it was clear that the framers did not contemplate granting Negroes the privilege of suing in a federal court.

Since the issue raised was the meaning of "citizen" as it appeared in the Constitution, only the Supreme Court could give a final answer.

Decision by the Court involved far more than the freedom of a single slave and his family. Underlying the legal issues were the political implications of the South's struggle for slavery in the territories. The Union was growing. Some determination had to be made relative to the free or slave status of the territories which would become states. Since a three-fifths vote of Congress was required for admission to the Union, and since a fifty-fifty deadlock existed in the Senate, the Supreme Court remained the only agency of government capable of reaching any kind of decision. As on so many other occasions in American history, the political issue was finally turned into a constitutional question. And a constitutional question is a question of law for the federal courts.

The Missouri Compromise of 1820 had sought to restrict the expansion of slavery in the new territory. And in *Dred Scott* v. *Sandford* the Supreme Court had the ideal case in which to determine the constitutionality of that Compromise.

The strictly legal issues were not complex. First was a matter of technical legal procedure. Did the Court have the power to review the ruling that Scott was a citizen of Missouri? If the Court decided that it had such power, it would have to face the second question, whether Scott was in fact a citizen in the constitutional sense—thus permitting the exercise of diversity jurisdiction. If the Court held that Scott was a citizen, it could then decide whether he was entitled to his freedom. These were the issues argued before the Court in 1856. Chief Justice Taney ordered reargument to avoid rendering an opinion during the presidential campaign of 1856.[15] The long-awaited decision came in 1857.

In his opinion for the Court, Taney wrote that the Negro "had no rights which the white man was bound to respect. . . ."[16] This statement comprised no part of the holding of the case, but it symbolized in the public mind what the Supreme Court said and did. Continued repetition of this phrase provided the basic theme of a vigorous and successful attack upon the prestige of the Court. "Of Taney's opinion," declared the New York *Tribune,* "it will be found to exhibit all the characteristics that have marked his career. It is subtle, ingenious, sophistical and false. It is the plea of a tricky lawyer and not the decree of an upright judge." [17] The law of the case was lost in the maelstrom which engulfed North and South.

All that the Court held was that Dred Scott was not a citizen of Missouri within the meaning of the Constitution, and therefore could not invoke the diversity jurisdiction of the federal courts. Taney's statement as to Negro rights was made in the course of recounting the legal history, as he saw it, of the Negro and slavery.[18] While it might have added to the persuasive force of the opinion in some eyes, the statement was clearly not necessary to the decision. As such that statement was not law.

Taney also said that the Missouri Compromise was unconstitutional, therefore Scott could not have a meritorious claim to freedom merely because he resided in free territory. The case could have been decided on that point, but it wasn't. Taney said further that when Scott returned to Missouri his citizenship claim would be determined by Missouri law—and under Missouri law as Taney read it, Scott could not be a citizen. Neither of these conclusions was necessary to the actual decision of the Court—that no federal tribunal had the power to hear the case at all. And that would include the Supreme Court itself. Every court has, however, the power to determine whether a particular case is within its jurisdiction. Consequently, the Court had jurisdiction to determine its jurisdiction. And having decided that Scott's case lacked the requisite diversity, the Supreme Court was without power to make further declarations of law.

The opinions of the Supreme Court, just like the opinions of all other courts, embody and give expression to the reasons supporting the particular disposition of a dispute. They are not general essays on the law. The power of a court is confined to the settlement of the dispute before it, and only statements necessary to settle that dispute are authoritative. All statements which are not necessary to decision are characterized by lawyers as dicta. While useful for some purposes, dicta are not the repositories of the law which should be applied in future disputes under the doctrine of *stare decisis*. The plethora of dicta which comprise the bulk of Taney's opinion is only entitled to such weight as one lawyer-judge might choose to give to the views of another lawyer-judge.

The Constitution as it stood in 1857 had no provision defining citizenship, state or federal, for any purpose. The Court was free to ascribe its own meaning to the constitutional phrase "Citizens of different States." Unlike the Court in *Brown* v. *Board of Education,* the 6 to 3 majority in the Dred Scott case assumed that it was limited to the construction placed on constitutional words by the framers.[19] And in this respect the Court in Dred Scott was in error, even in its own time.

Dred Scott v. *Sandford,* as a precedent, has long since disappeared as a factor in constitutional law.[20] Nor was Dred Scott himself affected by the decision; he was freed by the Chaffees within three months after Taney delivered his opinion. And the law of the case was changed by the very first sentence of Section 1 of the Fourteenth Amendment: "All persons born or naturalized in the United States, . . . are citizens of the United States and of the State wherein they reside." But the shadow of Dred Scott lay across the entire Reconstruction era, and many of the events of that period are explicable only by reference to the case.

In a series of decisions during and after the Civil War,[21] the Supreme Court made itself unpopular with the Radical Republicans who controlled the national government. Hostility toward the nine men grew so acute that at one point Congress even repealed a statute granting the Court appellate jurisdiction in order to prevent consideration of a certain case.[22] Taney, in particular, was subject to continuing attack during his tenure on the Court. Said the New York *Times:* "Too feeble to wield the sword against the Constitution, too old and palsied and weak to march in the ranks of rebellion and fight against the Union, he uses the powers of his office to serve the cause of traitors." [23] The Court itself was looked upon as a Southern stronghold within the federal government. It was therefore not surprising that in the ten years following the Civil War, it was Congress, rather than the Court, that played the leading role in creating a new status in law for the former slaves. The enactment and ratification of the Thirteenth, Fourteenth and Fifteenth Amendments were all a part of this Congressional endeavor.

Immediately after the adoption of the Thirteenth Amendment came the first major legislative effort on behalf of the Negro. Enumerated in the Civil Rights Bill and Freedman's Bureau Bill of 1866 were the rights to make contracts, to own property, to sue and be sued, to give evidence in the courts and to be free from physical violence. Both acts were vetoed by President Johnson on constitutional grounds, but the House and Senate overrode the Civil Rights rejection. Doubt as to the constitutional power of Congress to enact such legislation under the Thirteenth Amendment led almost directly to the proposing of the Fourteenth.[24]

Because of the constitutional criticisms leveled against the Civil Rights Act of 1866, Congress, in 1870,[25] relied upon the implementation powers of the Fourteenth and Fifteenth Amendments to re-enact the 1866 statute. At the same time, Congress strengthened these Civil Rights provisions by adding criminal penalties, not only for the deprivation of the rights enumerated in the earlier law, but for interference with the newly created right of Negro suffrage.[26]

By 1871, the national legislature added the so-called "Ku Klux Act." This statute imposed civil and criminal penalties upon those who deprived "any person or class of persons of the equal protection of the laws, or equal privileges and immunities under the laws." [27]

The most extensive of the Civil Rights Acts was passed in 1875. Sections 1 and 2 of this enactment required all public inns, theaters, conveyances and other public establishments to make facilities available to "all persons within the jurisdiction of the United States . . ." regardless of race, color or "previous condition of servitude." [28] In large measure, Congress was reacting to discriminatory practices of the South. But it is also true that federal legislation of the Reconstruction period was at times enacted out of motivations other than idealism.

The Radical Republicans had obtained and sought to retain control of former Confederate states either by maintaining captive state governments or by military forces.[29] And the urgency of the radical legislation generated strong feelings in Congress, which, as Justice Frankfurter observed, ". . . caused inadequate deliberation and led to loose and careless phrasing of laws related to the new political issues." [30] Congress had committed cardinal technical sins in legal draftsmanship. Judgment day in the Supreme Court was not long delayed.

Little remains of this Civil Rights legislation today. And the nature of the American Congress during the twentieth century has precluded further anti-discrimination legislation of this type. Yet those Civil Rights provisions which have resisted the ravage of judicial declarations of unconstitutionality are still of considerable significance in the pattern of enforcement flowing from the school segregation cases.

THE JUDICIAL COUP D'ÉTAT

Despite constitutional objections, the Court had refused to consider, on three separate occasions between 1867 and 1869, the validity of Reconstruction legislation.[31] But even before Congress had completed its Civil Rights program, the nine men had begun to limit the scope of the Fourteenth Amendment—the constitutional basis for this legislative action.

Oddly enough, the first major case did not involve Negroes at all. In 1869 the Louisiana legislature granted a charter of incorporation to "The Crescent City Live-Stock Landing and Slaughter-House Company," and, at the same time, gave the company the exclusive privilege of slaughtering animals in and around New Orleans. A lawsuit followed. The unhappy butchers of New Orleans invoked the privileges and immunities, due process and equal protection clauses of the Fourteenth Amendment in their plea for a declaration of unconstitutionality. The Supreme Court, however, held the legislative grant by Louisiana valid. The Fourteenth Amendment, wrote Justice Miller for the majority, was solely intended to protect the newly freed Negroes from discriminations based on color.[32] The butchers could not qualify as members of that protected class. They were accordingly denied the protection provided in the Amendment.

Appearing as one of counsel in the *Slaughter-House Cases* was John A. Campbell, a former Justice of the Supreme Court. He had resigned from the bench when his native state of Alabama left the Union. The right to labor, argued Campbell, is "property" within the meaning of the Fourteenth Amendment. And, he continued, the Amendment was intended to protect not only Negroes, but every citizen of the United States as defined in the Amendment itself. Since the Louisiana statute deprived plaintiffs of the right to work, Campbell concluded that they had been denied a privilege of citizenship, that their property had been taken without due process of law, and they were denied the equal protection of the laws.[33] This argument was much too strong for the Supreme Court as constituted in 1873.

The majority summarily disposed of the equal protection

argument. "We doubt very much," declared Justice Miller, "whether any action of a state not directed by way of discrimination against Negroes as a class, or on account of their race, will ever be held to come within the purview of this provision." [34]

Of more importance to the status of the Negro was the Court's construction of the privileges and immunities clause. This clause was designed to protect "citizens of the United States." But did that mean only national citizenship, *i.e.*, the rights of a citizen in relation to the federal government, or did it likewise encompass state citizenship? The Supreme Court majority flatly rejected Campbell's argument that the clause was designed to throw a mantle of federal protection around all of the privileges which might be ascribed to citizenship, both national and state. Five of the nine men held that only the privileges of *national* citizenship were protected by the clause, and that national citizenship comprehended only such matters as free access to seaports, the right to travel to Washington, D. C., on official business and the like. Following this interpretation, the clause did little to protect the Negro, since rights to share in public education, public transportation, etc., are all incidents of state citizenship.

Four justices dissented. They were persuaded by Campbell's argument that the clause protected the privileges and immunities of state citizenship; they were also convinced that the word "citizens" was not limited to Negroes.

Later, of course, the Supreme Court itself adopted the Campbell philosophy. But it did so by expanding the meaning of the *due process* provision. There has been no substantial change in the restricted judicial interpretation of the privileges and immunities clause since it was first expounded by Justice Miller in the *Slaughter-House Cases*.

The clause has thus been of little significance in the law regarding discrimination and segregation. True, in 1935, Jus-

tice Sutherland spoke for a Supreme Court majority which
expanded national citizenship to include the right "to engage
in business, to transact any lawful business, or to make a lawful loan of money in any state other than that in which the
citizen resides. . . ." [35] But at the time Justice Sutherland
wrote, forty-four cases had previously been before the Court
on claims that state statutes had denied the privileges and immunities protection of the Fourteenth Amendment.[36] And the
nine men had uniformly denied relief. Four years after Justice
Sutherland tried to resurrect this clause, the nine men of the
New Deal Court overruled his holding and relegated privileges and immunities once again to comparative obscurity.[37]
It was not even mentioned in *Brown* v. *Board of Education.*

Two years after the decision in the *Slaughter-House Cases,*
the Supreme Court whittled away the protection afforded
Negroes under the Civil Rights Act of 1870. The case was
United States v. *Cruikshank,*[38] in which the Court refused to
punish private persons who had broken up a Negro meeting.
According to the Supreme Court, interference by private
individuals could only be a crime where the meeting was
held for some purpose connected with *national* citizenship.
Here the assembly had convened to discuss local Louisiana
elections, rather than national elections.

By 1877, it was clear that the grand design of Congress to
enforce enumerated civil rights through civil and criminal
provisions of federal legislation was doomed to failure by an
unfriendly Supreme Court.

"What gave satisfaction to the South and strength to bear
the affliction in which they found themselves was the determination of the Court to maintain the true character of government, and to hold, notwithstanding the excited feeling
growing out of the war, that the existence of the states, with
powers of domestic and local government including regulation of civil rights, the rights of persons and property, was
essential to the perfect working of our complex form of gov-

ernment." [39] In this manner a leading Southern lawyer characterized the Supreme Court decisions in the postwar era.

Congress had intended to enact legislation against discriminatory practices which would be directly operative against each and every person "within the jurisdiction of the United States." [40] But this power was denied in the Cruikshank case. "The Fourteenth Amendment," said the Court, "prohibits a state from denying to any person within its jurisdiction the equal protection of the laws: . . . this provision does not add anything to the rights which one citizen has under the Constitution against another." [41] This ruling thus limited the protections of the Amendment to actions by a state. Congress could impose no legal sanction on individual discriminatory practices unless such individual was acting for the state—what lawyers call acting "under color of state law."

From the low ebb of Supreme Court influence in the generation following the Dred Scott decision, the nine men evolved the state action concept to achieve a judicial *coup d'état* in 1883. In the famous *Civil Rights Cases* of that year, the Supreme Court struck down the all-important sections 1 and 2 of the Civil Rights Act of 1875.[42] These were the provisions which had prohibited discrimination in places of public accommodation—and which had imposed penalties directly against persons guilty of such discrimination, regardless of whether the state was in any way involved.[43]

Justice John Marshall Harlan alone dissented from the Court's judgment. Said Harlan, "Constitutional provisions adopted in the interest of liberty, and for the purpose of securing, through national legislation, if need be, rights inhering in a state of freedom, and belonging to American citizenship, have been so construed as to defeat the ends the people desired to accomplish, which they attempted to accomplish, and which they supposed they had accomplished by changes in their fundamental law." [44]

The Supreme Court, however, has not departed from the

views expressed by the majority in the *Civil Rights Cases.* This position has been affirmed and reaffirmed in numerous decisions since the post-Civil War period. But the doctrine was merely noted in passing in *Brown* v. *Board of Education.* Chief Justice Warren's unanimous Court neither approved nor criticized these prior decisions. Since only state-supported public schools were involved in the decision of May 17, 1954, there was no need for the Court to re-examine the "state action" concept in the same manner as they re-evaluated the "separate but equal" doctrine.

With the demise of the Civil Rights Act of 1875, Congress was to play little part in the further implementation of the Fourteenth Amendment. The Supreme Court, on the other hand, reassumed its role as the dominant branch of the federal government. Oddly enough, the Court emerged from the eclipse of Dred Scott by rendering decisions much in the spirit of Dred Scott.

There were many reasons why the Supreme Court limited the civil rights impact of the Civil War Amendments. The reasons were social, economic and political. The Supreme Court justices appointed after 1872 comprised a new breed of American lawyers. These were lawyers who had represented the developing big business. They were innately conservative, and far more interested in property rights than the problems of civil liberties. As lawyers, they reacted against the Thirteenth, Fourteenth and Fifteenth Amendments as too radical a change in the nation's scheme of government. These judges felt that too much power had been given to the federal authorities. Then too, in an age of rugged individualism, any governmental regulation of personal conduct which restricted freedom of action in business and social matters was itself suspect. "It would be running the slavery argument in the ground," declared Justice Bradley in 1883, "to make it apply to every act of discrimination which a person may see fit to make as to the guests he will entertain, or as to the people he will take in his coach or cab or car, or admit to his concert or theater, or deal with in other matters of intercourse or business." [45] Moreover, the moral indignation aroused by the institution of slavery had largely disappeared from public discussion by 1880.

Charles Warren, historian of the Supreme Court, concluded that the Court's decisions ". . . largely eliminated from National politics the negro question which had so long embittered Congressional debates. . . ." [46] Even before the nine men eliminated the basic issue, national preoccupation had turned from slavery and the Civil War to economic and geographic expansion.[47] The promise of absolute equality for the Negro proved to be an illusion. The Radical Republicans deserted the Negro, so that they could then befriend the emerging corporate giants.

Chapter 7

SEPARATE BUT EQUAL

In 1895, an era of aggressive Negro leadership ended
with the death of Frederick Douglass, a Negro spokesman
and a close companion of the Radical Republicans who
dominated Congress during the post-Civil War period. In
that same year, Negro leader Booker T. Washington delivered a major speech in Atlanta, calling for a new program of
racial coexistence based upon the concept of racial separation. And, in 1895, the Supreme Court docketed the case
which was to establish the "separate but equal" doctrine in
constitutional law.[1]

Homer Plessy, one-eighth Negro and seven-eighths white,
was arrested in Louisiana when he refused to ride in the
"colored" coach of a railroad train as required by the
Louisiana statutes. He then instituted an action to restrain
enforcement of these statutes on the grounds that they violated the Thirteenth and Fourteenth Amendments. The defendant, Ferguson, was the Louisiana judge designated to
conduct the trial of Plessy on criminal charges. Plessy's plea
to prohibit Ferguson's hearing the case was denied in the
Louisiana courts. The Supreme Court affirmed.[2]

As it did in the *Slaughter-House* and *Civil Rights Cases*
the Court brushed aside all arguments based on the Thirteenth Amendment. Debate on the Fourteenth Amendment
raised more difficult legal problems. Unlike the cases which
had involved the power of Congress to forbid discrimination,
Plessy v. *Ferguson* posed the issue of the power of the state

to require racial separation. The state action requirement, which had been read into the Fourteenth Amendment by the Court, had been fully satisfied. Louisiana had acted affirmatively in ordering segregation by race on public carriers. A new problem on the meaning of the Fourteenth Amendment was squarely before the nine men—and the opinion of the Supreme Court comprised the basic precedent for the arguments of the South in *Brown* v. *Board of Education.*

The "object" and purpose of the Fourteenth Amendment, according to the Court, was to secure the "absolute equality of the two races before the law." But, wrote Justice Henry Billings Brown, "in the nature of things it could not have been intended to abolish distinctions based on color, or to enforce social, as distinguished from political equality, or a commingling of the two races upon terms unsatisfactory to either." [3] In reaching this conclusion the Court did not indicate whether or to what extent it had followed the intent of the framers. But this was not important. The majority was obviously seeking to present its own particular viewpoint, and the method of analysis employed would have made such an inquiry irrelevant. Once the justices assumed that "in the nature of things" distinctions based on color could not have been intended to be prohibited, then the actual intent of the framers could play no part in their constitutional interpretation.

Plessy argued that state-enforced segregation stamped Negroes with a badge of inferiority. The high court disagreed, saying that such laws did not necessarily imply the inferiority of either one of the races. Following this point of view, Plessy could suffer no damage as a result of mere separation so long as the facilities furnished were equal to those from which he was excluded.

Counsel for Plessy asserted that if separation by race were held valid, a legislature might enact, with impunity, statutes designed solely to annoy a particular class. Legislation re-

quiring Negroes and whites to walk on separate sides of the
street, or an act requiring a railroad to provide separate cars
for passengers with red, black and blond hair would all be
valid, argued Plessy's lawyer. The Court concluded that
classifications of this type were far different from state-
required segregation.

"[T]he case reduces itself to a question whether the statute
of Louisiana is a reasonable regulation," declared the high
court, "and in respect to this, there must be a large discretion
on the part of the legislature. In determining the question
of reasonableness it is at liberty to act with respect to the
established usages, customs and traditions of the people, and
with a view to their comfort, and the preservation of the
public peace and good order." [4] Implicit in the analysis made
by the Court is the proposition that a legislative classification
based on race alone may be justified under the Fourteenth
Amendment, as long as some court deems it *reasonable*.

The conclusion that the Louisiana statute was reasonable
was based upon the then existing traditions, customs and
usages of the people, evidence of which was found by the
Court in the school segregation statutes passed by the various
states and District of Columbia. Particular reliance was
placed upon the 1849 case of *Roberts* v. *City of Boston*,[5] in
which the Supreme Judicial Court of Massachusetts upheld
school segregation under the state constitution. Charles
Sumner, later a leader among Radical Republicans, had
been attorney for the plaintiff in the Roberts case. He argued
that school segregation violated the Massachusetts constitutional declaration that all men were created free and equal.
According to Sumner's reasoning, "free and equal" meant
that all men were entitled to equal protection of the laws,
and requiring Negroes to attend separate schools deprived
them of that protection. Sumner's argument was the first formulation of the equal protection of the laws concept.

The Court in the Plessy case had ignored the impact of the

Fourteenth Amendment itself on Massachusetts and other states. It did not recognize, as had the Supreme Court of Michigan in 1890, that the Roberts case "was made in the *ante bellum* days before the colored man was a citizen, and when, in nearly half the Union, he was but a chattel." Concluded the Michigan court, "it cannot now serve as precedent." [6] *Roberts* v. *City of Boston* was not strictly a precedent for the Plessy decision, but it was considered as evidence of customs and traditions of the American people. Although *Plessy* v. *Ferguson* did not involve education, there is no doubt that the Supreme Court had bestowed its blessings on state-maintained segregated school systems.

As in the *Civil Rights Cases,* John Marshall Harlan was the sole dissenter. "Our constitution," he declared, "is color blind, and neither knows nor tolerates classes among citizens." And, he continued, "In my opinion the judgment this day rendered will, in time, prove to be quite as pernicious as the decision in the *Dred Scott* case." [7]

With the Plessy decision, the separate but equal formula became the law of the Constitution. *Plessy* v. *Ferguson* is cited again and again as the case which established this doctrine. And yet, oddly enough, there are no words in the Court's opinion which declare that segregation is to be permitted where equal facilities are provided. Such words were to come from later lower court decisions which attempted to give meaning to the Plessy principle. What happened in the Plessy case was that the judges upheld what they believed to be the "reasonableness" of the Louisiana transportation laws without providing guidance for the other courts which had to decide these subsequent segregation cases. The principle propounded by the nine men of 1896—that a state could compel "reasonable" racial segregation—was strictly judge-made law, giving a hitherto unknown meaning to the Fourteenth Amendment. It was basic law, but it left unanswered two critical questions: What are the criteria for measuring equality? What is the proper judicial remedy where inequality is found to exist?

In view of the ultimate holding in *Plessy* v. *Ferguson,* the Court was not required to reach the second question. While logically it should have considered the first question in arriving at its decision, there is nothing in the opinion which shows any attempt to formulate a standard of equivalence. This failure probably lies in the fact that the Court classified the right to ride an unsegregated train and attend an unseggated school as inherently *social.* And the Supreme Court had already concluded that the Amendment was designed to protect political rights only. On the basis of this type of analysis Plessy had no right to invoke the Amendment at all, even if there were in fact inequality.

In view of later decisions on segregation there is no valid distinction between social and political rights where the racial segregation is state-imposed. Regardless of the distinction which might be made by a layman between political and social rights, once those rights are affected by state action they become political in nature. Failure of the Court to grasp this fact has led lawyers as well as laymen to the mistaken assumption that the absence of a state command to separate the races is the logical equivalent of a command to commingle. This in turn has led to the observation that "If one race be inferior to the other socially, the Constitution of the United States cannot put them upon the same plane." [8] The assertion was completely irrelevant. Plessy was merely requesting freedom from a state-imposed requirement that he ride in a separate railroad car; he was not requesting a ruling that whites and Negroes be compelled to ride together. What Plessy was requesting may sound like the same thing as an order to commingle, but it is in reality something quite different. That difference is spelled out in numerous opinions which have been handed down since the Plessy decision. An individual may with impunity choose his social peers by the application of any criteria he desires—color, religion, education, wealth or hair styling. Once the state enters the picture, however, the choice is no longer personal or social. Discrimination becomes a political matter. It follows that a state may not behave as if it were a country club when it enacts laws affecting voting, jury service or public education.

Three years after *Plessy* v. *Ferguson,* the Court faced its first school segregation case, *Cummings* v. *Board of Education.*[9] The Negro plaintiffs had asked for an injunction closing the white schools of Richmond County, Georgia, until a separate school was provided for Negro children. At the beginning of the litigation, plaintiffs contended that under the separate but equal doctrine complete failure to provide a high school resulted in obvious inequality. Then, during the oral argument, the Negro parents asserted for the first time that state-maintained separate schools were unconstitutional. As a matter of technical legal procedure, the contention came too late. "It was said at argument," Justice Harlan responded for the Court, "that the vice in the common school system of Georgia was the requirement that the white and colored children of the State be educated in separate schools. But we need not consider that question in this case. No such issue was made in the pleadings." [10] The nine men then held that the remedy requested was improper, since closing all the schools would not eradicate the wrong, and the suit was dismissed. Thus in its first education case, the Supreme Court not only avoided passing on the validity of separate but equal, but also failed to indicate any appropriate standards for measuring equality.

The 1899 Cummings case was cited by ex-Justice Byrnes in 1956 as the first of six earlier Supreme Court opinions upholding the separate but equal doctrine in public education.[11] Byrnes, however, omits discussion of the very similar case of *Berea College* v. *Kentucky,*[12] decided in 1908. For, in this case, as in the Cummings case, the Supreme Court had before it a question of segregated schools—and in the Berea case, as in the Cummings case, the Court avoided direct consideration of the separate but equal doctrine.

In the Berea case, the Supreme Court had under analysis the "Day Law" of Kentucky, which stated that whites and Negroes could not be taught together in any private school unless that school maintained separate buildings for each race at least twenty-five miles apart. The Court sustained the law on the narrow ground that a corporate charter (and that would include the one held by Berea College) was subject to the reasonable regulations of the legislature which granted that charter. The effect of the ruling was to allow the "Day Law" to stand, without the necessity of reconsidering separate but equal. As in *Plessy* v. *Ferguson,* Justice Harlan registered a dissent.

The second of the cases cited by Byrnes as authority for the validity of the separate but equal doctrine is the important 1927 decision of *Gong Lum* v. *Rice.*[13]

Martha Lum, a Chinese resident of Mississippi, objected to a school board order requiring her to attend a school maintained for members of the colored race. Since there were no separate schools for Mongolians, she contended that she was entitled to attend the white schools. Homer Plessy, who was seven-eighths white, initially argued essentially the same point; he asserted that he should be entitled to the benefits of being white and not subjected to the disabilities of being Negro. In *Plessy* v. *Ferguson,* the Supreme Court avoided decision as to whether Plessy was white or Negro. In the Gong Lum case it accepted the finding of the Mississippi courts that for purposes of the public education laws, all those who were not white belonged to the "colored race."

Legally, Martha Lum might just as well have been Negro. Thus the stage was set for a direct ruling on the validity of separate but equal in public education. Was legislation requiring racially segregated schools unconstitutional as an automatic denial of the equal protection of the laws?

"Were this a new question," wrote Chief Justice Taft, "it would call for very full argument and consideration, but we think that it is the same question which has been many times decided to be within the constitutional power of the state legislature to settle without intervention of the federal courts under the Federal Constitution." [14] The Chief Justice then cited fifteen cases in support of his assertion, but in none of the cases had the Supreme Court spoken.

Speaking for the Court, Taft then referred to the Plessy case as having approved the decision in *Roberts* v. *City of Boston*. This was in large measure inaccurate. The Roberts case, it will be remembered, arose before the Fourteenth Amendment was in existence. And in *Roberts* v. *City of Boston*, the Plessy Court had found not a precedent, but only some evidence of "custom, usage and tradition" which justified the classification by race. On the other hand, the fifteen lower court cases cited by Taft were precedents; they did hold that separate but equal facilities satisfied the re-quirements of the equal protection clause. The Supreme Court of 1927, however, refused to accord those precedents express approval. They merely held that Martha Lum could be classified as colored "*assuming* that the cases above cited to be rightly decided" [15] (emphasis supplied).

While the separate but equal rule did come before the Court again during the first forty years following *Plessy* v. *Ferguson,* it was upheld only in the transportation cases. Certainly, questions as to the constitutionality of the doc-trine were not reconsidered by the Court in the only three school cases which had arisen during that period. Failure to act resulted in the continuation of separate school systems all over the South and in some parts of the North. It was clear that such schools would continue to exist until the Su-preme Court squarely faced the issue. For all practical purposes, the separate but equal concept had achieved *de facto* constitutionality in the field of public education as a minimum constitutional requirement.

But this was the extent of the decisional law as formulated by the United States Supreme Court. There still remained the question of how to measure equality; there still remained the question of a proper judicial remedy when and if inequality was found to exist.

These questions arose again and again as the lower federal courts struggled to reach judgment in subsequent school segregation cases. The federal district judges could not find the answers in the Plessy, Cummings and Gong Lum decisions, and they obviously could not ask the Supreme Court to explain its prior opinions. All that the lower courts could do was to apply the Plessy principle as they understood it— and answer the questions themselves. From the amalgam of their decisions came the expression and amplification of the separate but equal dogma. Yet, despite the number of lower court cases which were to consider the issue of school segregation, the courts were significantly unsuccessful in fashioning definite criteria to measure equality.

In 1912, per capita expenditure for Negro schools was $1.71, as compared to the figure of $15 for all schools.[16] But measurement in terms of dollars and cents alone is not necessarily the best guide in evaluating a state's educational offerings. In the Cummings case, the Court had found no vice in the disparity of expenditures in the dual school system. Nor was it feasible to demand identical school facilities as a requirement of equality, since absolute duplication would be an impossibility. All that the courts could or did say was that separate but equal required "substantial" equality.

Defining substantial equality was itself a formidable task. Even when the issue presented was one of physical inequality in the tangibles—buildings, books and equipment—inconsistent judgments followed.[17] When more subtle standards were argued before the courts—quality of instruction, school supervision and curricula content—even greater divergence of opinion resulted.[18]

Fiscal differences, while easily proved as matters of fact, gave rise to difficult collateral legal questions involving tax incidence and tax classification.[19] Separate but equal raised many more problems than it solved.

The remedy for correcting such inequality was similarly left to the lower courts. The Supreme Court had already indicated in the Cummings case that closing down all the schools was not an appropriate solution. No further guidance was given by the high tribunal as to the proper relief. The lower courts fashioned remedies which varied from ordering immediate admission to white schools to vague directions to educational authorities to equalize the schools.[20]

Writing in 1954, Robert A. Leflar, dean of the Arkansas law school, and Wylie Davis concluded: "It is generally conceded that the experiment, so far as it depended in areas of governmental regulation upon a judicial guaranty of 'separate but equal' facilities for Negroes and other minority races in this country has failed to effectuate the theory underlying it. Until recently," they continued, "the governmental conduct required in public education by the 'separate but equal' rule has seldom been clear, and even when clear, has seldom been forthcoming." [21]

The cases of Plessy, Cummings and Berea were certainly not definitive as to constitutional requirements in public education. In *Brown* v. *Board of Education*, the Supreme Court recognized that the Gong Lum case had not decided the ultimate constitutional question. The plaintiff in that case, observed Chief Justice Warren, "contended only that state authorities had misapplied the doctrine by classifying him [sic] with Negro children and requiring him [sic] to attend a Negro school."

This certainly does not mean that because the first three

education cases did not technically validate the doctrine of separate but equal, the Court in 1954 was forced to decide as it did in *Brown* v. *Board of Education*. Just as the Supreme Court limited its reading of those three cases to restrict them to their technical holdings, so it could have, on the other hand, read them expansively. Counsel for the Southern states urged the broader interpretation.

The Supreme Court might have concluded that after fifty years of failure to declare separate but equal *invalid,* it was too late to raise the argument anew in 1954. John W. Davis urged the Court to adopt this position during oral argument: "[S]omewhere, sometime, to every principle comes a moment of repose when the decision has been so often announced, so confidently relied upon, so long continued, that it passes the limits of judicial discretion and disturbance." [22]

On some occasions such argument has been persuasive. The constitutional doctrine which extended the protection of the Fourteenth Amendment's due process clause to corporations became established in much the same manner as did separate but equal doctrine in the field of public education.[23] In 1937, forty-eight years after corporations first received the benefits of due process, only Justice Black was willing to disturb the legal principles upon which states and incorporated associations had so long relied.[24] Lawyer Davis contended that judicial statesmanship required the Court to accept the settled practices of the South: "And we said in effect—and I am bold enough to repeat it here now—that, in the language of Judge Parker in his opinion below, after that had been the consistent history for over three quarters of a century, it was late indeed in the day to disturb it on any theoretical or sociological basis." [25] John W. Davis, as chief proponent of the Southern argument, was unable to persuade Chief Justice Warren's Court.

Why did the Supreme Court, fifty-five years after its first educational decision in the Cummings case, decide to call for "very full argument and consideration" of the question of the constitutionality of school segregation? A portion of the answer is found in four other opinions of the Court, and in a case decided by the highest court of Maryland. Interestingly enough, all but one of these cases involved segregation in law schools, while the one exception was concerned with separate facilities in graduate education. In each of these five cases the court ordered integration to achieve the requirement of equality.

In 1935 a graduate of Amherst College, Donald Murray, was denied admission to the University of Maryand Law School solely because of his race. In Murray's suit against the University, he was represented by Thurgood Marshall, just two years at the bar. University officials offered Murray a scholarship to attend any law school which would accept him, but he claimed a right to attend the state-supported school in Maryland.

The Maryland Court of Appeals decisively answered the two critical questions involved in the application of the separate but equal doctrine.[26] The first of these questions related to the measure of equality; the second was concerned with the proper remedy.

As to the first problem, the court held that Maryland's offer of an out-of-state tuition scholarship was inadequate as a matter of dollars and cents. Murray would have to bear the costs of living away from home. Further, the Court of Appeals agreed with Murray's other arguments. "And as petitioner points out," said the Court of Appeals in regard to non-Maryland law schools, "he could not there have the advantages of study of law of this state primarily, and of attendance on state courts, where he intends to practice." [27] For these two reasons, the Court concluded that Maryland's treatment of Murray not only constituted a factual inequality, but was below the standard of "substantial" equality required by the equal protection clause.

The opinion was equally decisive as to the proper remedy. "[Since in] Maryland now the equal treatment can be furnished only in the one existing law school, the petitioner, in our opinion," declared the high court, "must be admitted there. We cannot find the remedy to be that of ordering separate schools for Negroes." [28] And Murray entered Maryland Law School.

Not so fortunate was Lloyd Gaines, who sought and was denied admission to the state-supported law school at the University of Missouri. Seven of the nine men of the United States Supreme Court eventually held in 1938 that Gaines must be offered a legal education in Missouri, and that in the absence of a separate equal school there, he had the right to attend the "white" law school.[29] Gaines was never to enjoy the fruits of his victory. He disappeared shortly after the opinion was rendered, and diligent search has failed to uncover his whereabouts.

The Gaines case was the beginning of a revolution in the Supreme Court approach to educational problems. True, separate but equal was not overturned. In fact, the Court was expressly giving content to the "equal" requirement of the formula. But in giving substance to the doctrine, the Supreme Court began to consider the intangible factors obviously present in legal education. "Petitioner insists," wrote Chief Justice Hughes in the Gaines case, "that for one intending to practice in Missouri there are special advantages in attending a law school there, both in relation to the opportunities for the particular study of Missouri law and for the observation of the local courts, and also in view of the prestige of the Missouri law school among the citizens of the State, his prospective clients." [30] And, as had the state tribunal in the Murray decision, the Supreme Court concluded that the offer of tuition in an out-of-state law school could not duplicate these advantages.

Neither the Gaines nor the Murray situations involved a

separate Negro law school within the state. Thus the only effective remedy for Gaines and Murray was the immediate admission to the state-supported law school.

This was desegregation even under the separate but equal formula.

Justice James C. McReynolds and Pierce Butler disagreed with Hughes' analysis in the Gaines case. They suggested arguments which the South was to use in *Brown* v. *Board of Education.* "For a long time," wrote McReynolds in his dissent, "Missouri has acted upon the view that the best interests of her people demand separation of whites and negroes in schools. Under the opinion just announced, I presume she may abandon her law school and thereby disadvantage her white citizens without improving petitioner's opportunities for legal instruction; or she may break down the settled practice concerning separate schools and thereby, as indicated by experience, damnify both races." [31]

In 1950, fifteen years after the Gaines case, Herman Sweatt was denied admission to the University of Texas Law School on racial grounds. Unlike Maryland and Missouri, which offered to educate Negro lawyers in other states, Texas established a separate law school. The equality of this new law school was in issue. By the time that the Sweatt case reached the Supreme Court, it was clear that the legal education cases were directly related to the problems of general public education. "Friends of the Court" appeared on both sides, offering their legal views. In addition to the briefs filed by the parties directly concerned, *amici curiae* briefs in support of Sweatt were submitted by the United States government and by a committee of law school teachers among others. The attorneys general of eleven Southern states prepared prosegregation arguments. It was urged that the Court should repudiate *Plessy* v. *Ferguson* in its application to school segregation; it was also urged that the Court make a specific statement recognizing the principle of separate but equal in all areas of public education.

The Supreme Court, however, was not yet ready to make a clear statement adopting either of these divergent positions. It readily found substantial inequality existed between Texas's white and colored law schools in regard to the "tangibles"—size of faculty, number of library volumes, physical plant and location.[32] "What is more important," declared the Court, "the University of Texas Law School possesses to a far greater degree those qualities which are incapable of objective measurement but which make for greatness in a law school." [33]

The Court had little difficulty in dealing effectively with the formulation of criteria of equality in legal education. As a court of lawyers, it was thoroughly familiar with the aims and objectives of legal education. It could and did speak from its collective experience. No sociologists were needed to remind the Court that, "The law school cannot be effective in isolation from the individuals and institutions with which the law interacts. Few students and no one who has practiced law would choose to study in an academic vacuum, removed from the interplay of ideas and exchange of views with which the law is concerned." [34] So far as the law was concerned, the Court's obvious and undisputed premise was that the professional society in which lawyers circulated was of necessity nonsegregated. There are no colored court systems, nor colored governments. Education for an integrated society must of necessity be nonsegregated to be effective. In the Murray, Gaines and Sweatt cases, the courts ultimately found that integration was the constitutional measure of the states' obligation in legal education.

Two years before the Sweatt decision, the Court had used the Gaines formula in ordering the immediate admission of a Negro applicant to the University of Oklahoma Law

School. In that case, *Sipuel* v. *Board of Education*,[35] the nine men issued a *per curiam* decision (a brief opinion of the whole Court with minimum explanation) noting that the inequality was patent. Since no provision had been made for Negro legal education either in state or out-of-state, immediate admission to the one Oklahoma-supported law school was deemed the proper remedy.

This was not, however, the only *possible* remedy. While the Cummings case had rejected the proposal to close down all schools where inequality existed, the Supreme Court might have ordered the state to provide a separate law school which would meet the tests of the then standard of substantial equality.[36] This could only have been done before the Sweatt decision, since that case pointed out the impossibility of segregated equality in a nonsegregated society. But the Supreme Court would not render such a judgment.

The Court (and the judges of Maryland) held that the rights of the Negro plaintiffs under the Constitution were both "personal and present." And since they were "present," the law could not ask Gaines, Sipuel and Sweatt to await the establishment of new law schools. Immediate admission to existing schools was the only adequate remedy.

On the same day that the Sweatt case was decided, the Court also gave judgment in *McLaurin* v. *Board of Regents*.[37] Following the decision in the Sipuel case, McLaurin had been admitted to the Graduate School of the University of Oklahoma. Desegregation, however, stopped at the point of admittance. McLaurin was assigned a special "colored" seat in each classroom, a special table was provided for him in the library, and he was required to dine in a segregated portion of the school cafeteria. The Supreme Court struck down such discriminatory practices in these words: "There is a vast difference—a Constitutional difference—between restrictions imposed by the state which prohibit the intellectual com-

mingling of students, and the refusal of individuals to commingle when the state presents no such bar." [38]

Justice Brown in the Plessy case had assumed that an absence of a state command to separate the races was the logical
equivalent of a state command to commingle. In deciding the
McLaurin case, however, the Supreme Court erased this assumption from constitutional analysis. Notwithstanding the
McLaurin decision, Senator Ervin still argued in 1956 that
Southerners "realize that if a valid law requiring desegregation should be adopted, they would no longer have the freedom to select their associates. They would be forced to associate by legal formula rather than personal preference." [39]

Despite the far-reaching import of the McLaurin decision
and the law school cases, the Court purported not to disturb
the separate but equal doctrine. "Broader issues have been
urged for our consideration," said Chief Justice Vinson in
Sweatt v. *Painter*, "but we adhere to the principle of deciding
constitutional questions only in the context of the particular
case before the Court." [40] There was no need for the Court
to re-examine separate but equal in order to reach its decisions. This principle of judicial self-restraint is well established. The Supreme Court has often said that it "has no
jurisdiction to pronounce any statute, either of a state or of
the United States, void, because irreconcilable with the
Constitution, except as it is called upon to adjudge the legal
rights of litigants in actual controversies. In the exercise of
that jurisdiction, it is bound by two rules, to which it has
rigidly adhered, one, never to anticipate a question of constitutional law in advance of the necessity of deciding it; the
other never to formulate a rule of constitutional law broader
than is required by the precise facts to which it is to be applied." [41] Professor Freund has characterized this as the most
salient proposition of constitutional law next to Marshall's
dictate on constitutional interpretation.[42]

The Supreme Court in *Sweatt* v. *Painter* did not accede to the demands of Sweatt's counsel to overrule separate but equal. Wrote Chief Justice Vinson, "We cannot agree with respondents that the doctrine of *Plessy* v. *Ferguson* should be reexamined in the light of contemporary knowledge respecting the purposes of the Fourteenth Amendment and the effects of racial segregation." [43] The Court had yet to reach the ultimate question: Is racial segregation in public schools unconstitutional *per se?*

Ex-Justice Byrnes, citing Cummings, Gong Lum and the four decisions of the Supreme Court dealing with law school and graduate education, believed that the Supreme Court had already answered this question. He argued that all six of these cases are authority for the validity of the separate but equal doctrine. But in none of these six cases—nor in the Berea or Murray cases which Byrnes had not considered— was the issue squarely before the courts. In all of these cases, decision was rendered without reaching the specific determination of whether a racial classification was unconstitutional *per se*.

But the specific question was not avoided in *Brown* v. *Board of Education*. The nine men of 1954 had turned back the clock to prior decisions and concluded that separate but equal was ripe for re-examination. Did separation itself result in an inequality which deprived Negroes of their "personal and present" rights as guaranteed by the equal protection clause?

"In the instant cases," declared Chief Justice Warren, "that question is directly presented. Here, unlike *Sweatt* v. *Painter,* there are findings below that the Negro and white schools involved have been equalized, with respect to buildings, curricula, qualifications and salaries of teachers, and other 'tangible' factors. Our decision, therefore, cannot turn on merely a comparison of these tangible factors in Negro and white schools involved in each of the cases. We must look instead to the effect of segregation itself on public education."

The criteria by which the Supreme Court measures constitutional equality had been changed.

Chapter 8

CLASSIFICATION AND EQUAL PROTECTION

All legislation involves classification. As Justice Douglas has pointed out, ". . . one chief task of law makers is to make classifications: graduating taxes according to income, regulating business according to size, protecting people according to age, requiring special health regulations for particular communities, reserving certain lands for specified purposes, restricting land holdings to maximum acreages, requiring some equipment to have safety devices, barring trucks of specified weights from the highways, and so on." [1]

In this legislative process of making classifications, laws necessarily affect different people in different ways. There is scarcely a law which is not unequal; there is scarcely a law which is not discriminatory. Literally construed, the words, "No State . . . shall deny to any person within its jurisdiction the equal protection of the laws," would require all laws to affect all persons equally. But such an interpretation would preclude any classifications, and consequently any legislation.

The problem which the courts face in giving meaning to "equal protection" is to determine which particular types of classification are so unequal and discriminatory as to be within the constitutional purview of that clause. In other words, the Supreme Court must first develop standards and sub-standards of judicial measurement which will be applied when specific legislation is involved in a specific dispute. Some unequal and discriminatory laws will be held valid under the equal protection clause, just as others will be declared unconstitutional.

Brown v. *Board of Education* involved state constitutions and statutes where classification was based solely on race. The specific question before the Court on May 17, 1954, was whether race *per se* is an invalid classification when measured against the equal protection clause.

This was not a new question. It had been argued five times before in the five important education cases decided prior to 1954. Yet the Supreme Court, for various reasons, consistently skirted the issue. The fact patterns in *Brown* v. *Board of Education,* however, demanded the formulation of a definite answer. And, as the nine men proceeded to the task of analyzing the relationship between "equality" and "equal protection," they gave a new meaning to the Fourteenth Amendment.

The words of the Fourteenth Amendment resound with freedom and liberty. And the words of the equal protection clause appear to be an interdict to discrimination. To the non-lawyer, freedom, equality and equal protection are synonymous. This is not the law of the Constitution.

Freedom, equality and equal protection are not absolutes— nor can they be. Like virtually every important word in the legal firmament, they must be ever subject to judicial definition and redefinition as they are applied to specific facts in specific cases. Notwithstanding valiant legislative effort to achieve certainty, all law remains a matter of degree. And, despite the criticism of laymen, there is nothing wrong with legal concepts which cannot be subject to absolute precision.

As Justice Holmes wrote in 1914: "I do not think we need trouble ourselves with the thought that my view depends upon differences of degree. The whole law does so as soon as it is civilized. . . ." [2]

Absolute equality is impossible. And, as the Supreme Court has observed, "The Fourteenth Amendment is not a pedagogical requirement of the impracticable." [3] Nor can one "construe the Fourteenth Amendment as introducing a factitious equality without regard to practical differences that are best met by corresponding differences of treatment." [4]

The nine men of 1954 were well aware of the inherent limitations of the equal protection concept. They knew that "The equal protection clause does not require absolute equality." [5] But the Warren Court also knew that some sort of equality is called for under the mandate of the Fourteenth Amendment.

There is judicial reluctance to derive absolute criteria of equality from the words of the equal protection clause. There is widespread judicial recognition that the state legislatures are the nation's primary lawmaking bodies. Of necessity, these legislatures must have sufficient discretion to deal with familiar local problems in all of their manifold ramifications. The Supreme Court is thus loath to disturb the pronouncements of the state lawmakers.

On the other hand, the Supreme Court has assumed the power to invalidate legislative enactments whenever those enactments violate constitutional requirements. This is part of the accepted pattern of American government. And it fits the logic of that pattern. Each of the three branches is charged with maintaining certain "checks and balances" over the other two in order to preserve the federal system and make "separation of powers" work.

As a practical matter, however, the only way in which the Supreme Court can declare a legislative enactment unconstitutional is by declaring that the legislature has abused its legislative discretion. And in exercising its power to make such a determination, the Supreme Court is itself exercising discretion. This means that legislation is unconstitutional whenever the objectives of that legislation are inconsistent with the standards of just five of the nine members of the Supreme Court. Stated in this blunt manner, it may be argued that the Supreme Court, as the final arbiter, may in many instances be charged with the same abuse of discretion which its members ascribe to certain state legislative pronouncements. This is especially true when the exercise of legislative discretion is long-established and overwhelmingly supported by the general public. And this is one of the arguments of the South.

In analyzing the meaning of equal protection, the Supreme Court had to look beyond the mere words of the Constitution. The answers could not be found in semantics.

It was clear that statutes requiring school segregation were intended to solve part of the problems of racial adjustment in the South. And the Southern lawmakers were obviously the men most familiar with the racial problems facing the people of their states. But there was also present the fact that such legislation created an inferior socio-legal status to which all Negroes were assigned. In light of these facts a meaning of equal protection had to be found.

Decision was not easy. What Justice Frankfurter wrote about the judicial task in due process litigation is applicable as well to equal protection controversies: "To rely on tidy formula for the easy determination of what is fundamental right for purposes of legal enforcement may satisfy a longing for certainty but ignores the movements of a free society. It belittles the scale of the conception of due process. The real clue to the problem confronting the judiciary in the application of the Due Process Clause is not to ask where the line is once and for all to be drawn but to recognize that it is for the Court to draw it by the gradual and empiric process of 'inclusion and exclusion.' " [6]

And, in *Brown* v. *Board of Education,* the Supreme Court "included" non-discriminatory public education under the protection of the Fourteenth Amendment.

The nine men of 1954 strove to act within the framework of prior precedents. While *Plessy* v. *Ferguson* gave Supreme Court acceptance to state-enforced segregation in transportation (and, inferentially, education), the Sweatt and McLaurin decisions denied the validity of racial classifications as applied specifically to state-supported colleges and universities. On May 17, 1954, the Supreme Court had to decide whether the criteria of equality developed in the Plessy case or the criteria developed in the graduate school cases should be applied as the standard of measurement in the primary and secondary school disputes. Whatever decision was reached, the Supreme Court would be damned as inconsistent. Regardless of judicial rationalizations, the Court was bound to violate the spirit of either Plessy or the Sweatt and McLaurin cases.

Plessy v. *Ferguson* had provided the judicial basis for nearly sixty years of decisions permitting separation of the races as long as the tangible facilities were substantially equal. But, as was pointed out by Chief Justice Warren, the clock could not be turned back to 1896. The meaning of "equal" had undergone many changes since that time. In assessing law school and other graduate education in terms of its function in American society, the Supreme Court had rendered later decisions holding that no state could exclude a student from the kind of education which one could obtain in an atmosphere free from state-imposed segregation. Such decisions were not based upon a judicial technique which measured equality in terms of number of school rooms, books or teachers. Intangible factors had been found to be of critical significance in the college and university cases. And, as Chief Justice Warren said for his Court, "Such considerations apply with added force to children in grade and high school." The Supreme Court had chosen to follow one line of precedent by extending the principles of the Sweatt and McLaurin cases, rather than the alternative line of precedent which would bring *Plessy* v. *Ferguson* up to date.

Under the Sweatt-McLaurin analysis, the issue of equality was measured against the probable success or failure of graduate students in meeting the goals of society for which they were being trained. Thus, before the Supreme Court could follow the lines of judicial reasoning in those cases, it had to do something which had never been done before in the public school cases: it had to look to the goals and objectives as well as the methods and content of elementary and secondary education.

"Today," wrote Chief Justice Warren, "education is perhaps the most important function of state and local governments. Compulsory school attendance laws and the great expenditures for education both demonstrate our recognition of the importance of education to our democratic society. It is required in the performance of our most basic public responsibilities, even service in the armed forces. It is the very foundation of good citizenship. Today it is a principal instrument in awakening the child to cultural values, in preparing him for later professional training, and in helping him to adjust normally to his environment. In these days, it is doubtful that any child may reasonably be expected to succeed in life if he is denied the opportunity of an education. Such an opportunity, where the state has undertaken to provide it, is a right which must be made available to all on equal terms."

This language did not necessarily presage the end of "separate but equal" as a constitutional standard. There was still a possibility that the Court might reconcile both lines of precedent by distinguishing as a matter of fact between public school and college education. Yet the words did indicate that, as in the law school cases, the Court would again consider the "intangible" factors. "We come then to the question presented," the Chief Justice wrote. "Does segregation of children in public schools solely on the basis of race, even though the physical facilities and other 'tangible' factors may be equal, deprive the children of the minority group of equal educational opportunities?" The Supreme Court answered: "We believe that it does."

These words marked the end of *Plessy* v. *Ferguson* as a constitutional precedent. And this despite the fact that nothing was said overruling that case. The Plessy case had specifically sustained the validity of racial segregation in public transportation on the theory that the discrimination was both non-political and reasonable. And the Supreme Court of 1896 had said (though not held) that separation by race in the public schools fell into that category. Chief Justice Warren's Court ignored this test. By following and expanding the principles of the Sweatt and McLaurin decisions, racial segregation was held to be inherently unequal under the equal protection clause. Public school segregation is now unconstitutional *per se.*

While the Supreme Court studiously avoided comment on most of the pro-segregation pronouncements of the Plessy case, it rejected by implication the 1896 analysis of the effect of segregation. The Court in *Plessy* v. *Ferguson* concluded that separation by race did not necessarily indicate that either whites or Negroes had been stamped with the badge of inferiority. Chief Justice Warren did not agree: "To separate them from others of similar age and qualifications solely because of their race generates a feeling of inferiority as to their status in the community that may affect their hearts and minds in a way unlikely ever to be undone."

When Southern counsel invoked *Plessy* v. *Ferguson* as a controlling precedent, their argument ran somewhat like this: Legislators must have the power to make statutory classifications. *Plessy* v. *Ferguson* declared that statutory classifications according to race were valid where the rights involved were non-political—as long as the classifications were reasonable. The 1896 case had held that Louisiana's system of segregated public transportation involved social rather than political rights. *Plessy* v. *Ferguson* further held that segregation in transportation was reasonable, based upon the customs and usages of the people of Louisiana. The 1896 Court then said that education and transportation should be subject to the same tests. Ergo, public school segregation is constitutional.

While the Supreme Court might have followed this line of argument and still come to the conclusion that school segregation is unreasonable, it is clear that Chief Justice Warren reached his ultimate conclusion via a different method of analysis. Mention of the "reasonableness" test is conspicuous by its absence in *Brown* v. *Board of Education,* and it is only noted in passing in the companion case of *Bolling* v. *Sharpe.* Yet the "reasonableness" test is important in understanding what the nine men did on May 17, 1954.

While equal protection does not require absolute equality, it does require some kind of equality. The distinction between permissible and prohibited inequality in legislation has been measured by the reasonableness test which recognizes the validity of discriminatory legislation where (and only where) there are real differences between the subjects classified.

Differences between men and women, for example, are real. The Supreme Court had no difficulty in reaching that conclusion to sustain a statute devoted exclusively to regulating the working hours of women. "That woman's physical structure and the performance of maternal functions place her at a disadvantage in the struggle for subsistence is obvious," wrote the Court. "The reason for the decision rests in the inherent difference between the sexes, and in the different functions in life which they perform." [7] This type of legislation was admittedly discriminatory. Yet, since the discrimination was deemed reasonable, it was held not to violate the equal protection clause.

A state legislature may even find real differences between women. Michigan, as part of its alcohol control laws, enacted a statute prohibiting the licensing of female bartenders unless the woman in question was the "wife or daughter of the male owner" of a licensed establishment. "While Michigan may deny to all women opportunities for bartending," the Supreme Court declared, "Michigan cannot play favorites among women without rhyme or reason." The legislature was found to have had sufficient reason for making its discriminatory classification. "Michigan evidently believes the oversight assured through ownership of a bar by a barmaid's husband or father minimizes hazards that may confront a barmaid without such protecting oversight." [8] Again the obvious inequality of treatment did not amount to legal inequality.

In a less rational application of the reasonableness test, the Supreme Court rendered a 5 to 4 decision which upheld the administration of a Louisiana statute providing for the licensing of "State Pilots." Since those pilots were granted the exclusive privilege of navigating seagoing vessels through the Mississippi River to the port of New Orleans, these licenses were eagerly sought. When only relatives and friends of the river boat pilots were permitted to obtain certificates, the otherwise qualified candidates for the positions argued that the statute was administered in a manner which violated the equal protection clause. Reasonableness was found by the Court in the "entirely unique institution of pilotage in the light of its history in Louisiana." [9] The obvious inequality of treatment was thus held to be justified.

While racial classifications were not involved in any of these three cases, the judges had all applied the Plessy principle. For it was in *Plessy* v. *Ferguson* that the Supreme Court for the first time acknowledged the power of a state to make "reasonable" legislative classifications under the Fourteenth Amendment. And while the Plessy decision was necessarily confined to the validity of separate transportation facilities, the constitutional standard of measurement which was formulated in that case became an integral part of the equal protection clause.

Real and substantial differences do exist between men and women which necessitate difference in treatment in order to effectuate some legislative purposes. It is also conceivable that the differences between wives and daughters of tavern owners and other females, and the dissimilarities between relatives and friends of river boat pilots and other pilots, are likewise sufficiently "real and substantial" to justify legislative classifications.

To the South, these decisions provided the basis of its argument that the Plessy doctrine was still the law of the Constitution.

Granting this assumption, the sole question which would then be before the Supreme Court in *Brown* v. *Board of Education* would be whether racial segregation in public education was reasonable. The South argued that it was.

Contending that segregation was justifiable, Virginia cast its argument in the precise mold of *Plessy* v. *Ferguson:* Since customs, traditions and usages of the people of Virginia formed the basis of school segregation statutes, the Virginia legislature had not acted arbitrarily. And since only arbitrary action by the legislature is forbidden by the equal protection clause as interpreted by the Court in *Plessy* v. *Ferguson,* Virginia's segregation statutes were immune to constitutional attack.

This argument was presented in one of the five cases which made up *Brown* v. *Board of Education*—and the lower court agreed: "It indisputably appears from the evidence," said the court, "that the separation provision rests neither upon prejudice, nor caprice, nor upon any other measureless foundation. Rather the proof is that it declares one of the ways of Life in Virginia. Separation of white and colored 'children' in the public schools of Virginia has for generations been a part of the mores of her people." [10]

In the South Carolina case which was a part of *Brown* v. *Board of Education,* Judge Parker found another rational basis for the existence of segregated schools. "The student," he wrote, "is taken from the control of the family during school hours by compulsion of law and placed in control of the school, where he must associate with his fellow students. The law thus provides that the school shall supplement the work of the parent in the training of the child. . . . In formulating educational policy at the common school level, therefore, the law must take account, not merely of the matter of affording instruction to the student, but also of the wishes of the parent as to the upbringing of the child and his associates. . . ." [11] Unquestionably, the choice of parents—white parents—for racially segregated schools was symptomatic of custom and tradition, not only in South Carolina, but throughout the South and in many Northern states as well.

The decisions of May 17, 1954, rejected these asserted justifications for separation of the races. "Segregation in public education," summed up Chief Justice Warren, in *Bolling* v. *Sharpe,* "is not reasonably related to any proper governmental objective. . . ." An even stronger finding is implicit in *Brown* v. *Board of Education.*

The conclusion of May 17, 1954, was the logical result of accepting either of two propositions. After examining the sociological data before them, the nine men may have decided that the harm produced by racial segregation in education outweighed the "way of life" argument. The Court may then have reasoned that the imbalance was so extreme as to brand the judgment of the Southern legislatures unreasonable—and therefore unconstitutional. On the other hand, the Supreme Court may have been convinced that a classification based on race is irrational *per se,* and consequently cannot be justified under any circumstances. There is support for both propositions in the language used by Chief Justice Warren.

Thurgood Marshall argued in support of both propositions when he appeared for plaintiffs in the segregation cases. "Even if the Fourteenth Amendment did not *per se* invalidate racial distinctions as a matter of law," reads the NAACP brief, "the racial segregation challenged in the instant case would run afoul of the conventional test established for application of the equal protection clause because the racial classifications here have no reasonable relation to any valid legislative purpose." [12]

The conventional test is the test of reasonableness, and its application necessitates a balancing of factual information. True, the Supreme Court, as an appellate court, does not hear and examine witnesses in order to obtain facts. "Also, as an appellate court," explains Justice Jackson in his posthumous book, "it properly can act only on the state of facts revealed by the record made in the court below, supplemented sometimes by general information of which it may take judicial notice." [13] And there were ample facts in the record before the Court which might have been considered in the application of the conventional test under the equal protection clause.

Chapter 9

THE NEW EQUALITY

Before the Supreme Court on May 17, 1954, was a mass of factual data on all aspects of the segregation problem. Some of these data were in the records of the proceedings in the lower courts; some were contained in the briefs of opposing counsel; some could be found in the various sociological and psychological treatises which had been called to the attention of the nine men who had to reach decision. Some of these data were already known to these same nine men as a matter of common knowledge.

And the influence of these data on the decision in *Brown* v. *Board of Education* has resulted in a welter of misunderstandings, which has led, in turn, to both unwarranted praise and criticism.

The 1896 Supreme Court made law in *Plessy* v. *Ferguson* when it gave approval to state-imposed racial segregation—qualified only by the limitations that the rights affected be social rather than political and that the classification be reasonable. The 1954 Supreme Court might have followed this conventional test and utilized the data before it to conclude that segregation could not be reasonable. There was some evidence that the 1954 Court did just that. "Segregation in public education is not reasonably related to any proper governmental objective," wrote Chief Justice Warren in the companion case of *Bolling* v. *Sharpe,* dealing with separate school facilities in the District of Columbia.

But discussions of reasonableness stop at this point. It is

clear that the Supreme Court in *Brown* v. *Board of Education* utilized the factual data before them in a different way—a way which had nothing to do with the use of data under the *Plessy* v. *Ferguson* formula.

Thus it was that the Supreme Court made new law on May 17, 1954, reaching decision via a judicial road which neither necessitated nor permitted the specific overruling of the 1896 determination.

The South has criticized this approach of Chief Justice Warren's Court. The South has condemned the nine men for making law, rather than applying the law which was already made in *Plessy* v. *Ferguson*. The criticism, however, is not justified in the legal sense. Since the words of the Constitution are necessarily broad and all-inclusive, they are also necessarily vague. Save in rare instances, they cannot be applied directly. Constitutional decisions involve a two-stage process. Before the Supreme Court can arrive at the ultimate rule of law which finally decides a legal issue in controversy, it must have a constitutional standard to apply. And constitutional standards are themselves rules of law. Since the 1954 Court chose not to follow the standard created in *Plessy* v. *Ferguson,* it was necessarily announcing a new rule of law—a rule of law which, in this instance, was a logical extension of the standards which had been created in the Sweatt and McLaurin cases.

The role of the Supreme Court in formulating a constitutional standard is quite different from the job of applying that standard to test the constitutionality of a statute. Both tasks may have to be performed in a single case. But the process by which the judges perform these functions varies according to the task at hand.

When the Court formulates a constitutional standard, its role is essentially legislative. "Thus," points out Federal District Judge Charles E. Wyzanski, "the focus of inquiry becomes not what judgment is permissible, but what judgment is sound." [1]

In formulating sound constitutional standards, the Court becomes a rule-making body. In that guise it utilizes factual data in much the same way as any other rule-making entity. The Court must consider the nature and scope of the problem at hand; it must compare the possible solutions; it must analyze the foreseeable consequences likely to result from the application of the standard.

"Usually, to be sure," writes Judge Wyzanski, "diligent counsel offer in evidence enough relevant material. But where this has not been done, there have been times when a judge has tended to reach his result partly on the basis of general information and partly on the basis of his studies in a library. This tendency of a court to inform itself has increased in recent years following the lead of the Supreme Court of the United States. Not merely in constitutional controversies and in statutory interpretation but also in the formulation of judge-made rules of law, the justices have resorted, in footnotes and elsewhere, to references drawn from legislative hearings, studies by executive departments, and scholarly monographs." [2]

This formulation of a constitutional standard is the first stage in the two-stage process of constitutional decision. Having formulated the standard, the Court must then consider factual data in the application of that standard. Since the creation of the famed "Brandeis brief" in 1906, lawyers have realized the advantages of using nonlegal as well as legal material in their job of persuading the courts. Louis Brandeis, later Mr. Justice Brandeis, originator of this technique, was one of the counsel who successfully advocated the constitutionality of Oregon legislation regulating the number of hours women could be employed in laundries.

In its opinion upholding the Oregon statute, the Supreme Court observed:

"It may not be amiss, in the present case, before examining the constitutional question, to notice the course of legislation, as well as expressions of opinion from other than judicial sources. In the brief filed by Mr. Louis D. Brandeis for the defendant in error is a very copious collection of all these matters. . . . The legislation and opinions referred to . . . may not be, technically speaking, authorities, and in them is little or no discussion of the constitutional question presented to us for determination, yet they are significant of a widespread belief that woman's physical structure, and the functions she performs in consequence thereof, justify special legislation restricting or qualifying the conditions under which she should be permitted to toil." [3]

Even before the advent of the Brandeis brief, judges could acquire (and be persuaded by) information on pertinent nonlegal materials through a technique called judicial notice. Underlying this technique is the assumption that judges are aware of what is common knowledge, and may refresh recollection by reference to almanacs, dictionaries, encyclopedias and the like. But in some instances the courts have dignified loose statements as facts derived from judicial notice without revealing the source of their "common" knowledge. The Supreme Court did precisely this in *Plessy* v. *Ferguson* when they wrote: "The underlying fallacy of plaintiff's argument is the assumption that the enforced separation of the two races stamps the colored race with a badge of inferiority. . . ." [4] The alleged knowledge in the possession of the Court upon which it could characterize the plaintiff's argument as a fallacy was certainly not revealed.

In constitutional litigation prior to *Brown* v. *Board of Education*, the Brandeis brief was used only in arguments *supporting* the validity of statutes. This was the practical result of the conventional test. It was not difficult to present sociological and economic information to show that there was some rational basis for legislation; it was an almost impossible task to marshal data on the proposition that no reasonable basis could exist.

THE SOCIAL SCIENTISTS TAKE THE STAND

Quoting from the lower court opinions in two of the five cases which were joined for decision on May 17, 1954, the Supreme Court declared that the following statements were "amply supported by modern authority":

"Segregation with the sanction of law, therefore, has a tendency to retard the educational and mental development of Negro children and to deprive them of some of the benefits they would receive in a racially integrated school system." Again: ". . . State-imposed segregation in education itself results in the Negro children, as a class, receiving educational opportunities which are substantially inferior to those available to white children otherwise similarly situated." In "footnote 11" of Chief Justice Warren's opinion, he cited the modern authorities which support this view [5]—authorities in the form of sociological and psychological treatises on the subject of segregation.

The five cases making up *Brown* v. *Board of Education* came before the Supreme Court sitting as an appellate tribunal only after they had first been heard in the trial courts. And it is the duty of the trial courts to determine the facts of disputes before them. The responsibility for producing information from which facts may be established rests on the parties to the dispute. The litigants—meaning the plaintiffs and defendants—generally fulfill this obligation by presenting witnesses, who by their testimony provide the raw material for factual determinations. In the traditional common law case, a jury usually ascertains the facts. The segregation cases, however, were in a special category. They were equity cases on which the litigants had no right to trial by jury.[6]

Trial judges heard the evidence and found the facts from the testimony of witnesses at the trials.

Witnesses ordinarily testify as to their direct knowledge of the events in issue. Where they lack firsthand information, their testimony is excluded from consideration by the judicial application of one or more of the rules of evidence—the hearsay rule, the opinion rule, and the like. Some issues in litigation, however, cannot be resolved on the basis of firsthand evidence. And these issues usually involve matters believed to be beyond the competence of the "fact finders," whether judges or jurors. In such cases, "experts" may be called as witnesses. These experts may give testimony involving their areas of special competence, even though their narration is based on hearsay and inevitably includes the expression of opinion.

Social scientists took the witness stand in the four state cases which were consolidated for decision in *Brown* v. *Board of Education*. They did not give evidence based upon their direct knowledge of the events in issue. As experts, they all testified as to the effect of segregation. They all testified that segregation is detrimental to Negro children.

When the Supreme Court adopted the findings of the lower courts in Kansas and Delaware, it was accepting what these tribunals had adjudged to be the truth in the evidence presented before them. And this meant that the Supreme Court had adopted the findings of the lower courts that the psychological and sociological experts were right in declaring that school segregation had a detrimental effect upon the Negro. In so doing, the nine men were not acting beyond the confines of traditional legal procedure. This was not the same thing as sitting in the library and reading the books written by these same experts. The social scientists had all taken the witness stand. Cross-examination was available to test their qualifications to testify as experts and to point up whatever errors there might have been in the opinions expressed. This is the traditional technique employed by courts and counsel to elicit expert testimony, and care is taken to preserve such testimony in the record which is submitted to the appellate courts.

The offer of this expert testimony raised the first of two basic questions: Were the opinions of the social scientists relevant to the legal issues which had to be decided by the judges?

The answer depends upon the specific issue which was before the court for decision. Since the lower courts were bound by the precedent of *Plessy* v. *Ferguson,* they could only apply the rule of law as established and formulated by that case. The segregation legislation under consideration was based upon a classification scheme, and, as Justice Willis Van Devanter has explained, "When the classification of such law is called into question if any state of facts reasonably can be conceived that would sustain it, the existence of that state of facts must be assumed." [7] Thus to sustain such statutes it need only be shown that some rational basis exists for the classification made. Parties opposing such legislation, on the other hand, must show that the statute is completely arbitrary. Such is the conventional test under the Fourteenth Amendment.

If the constitutionality of racial classifications were to be determined by the traditional *Plessy* v. *Ferguson* formula, the proffered testimony would not be relevant. The social scientists did no more than testify that segregation is harmful. They could not give factual evidence that there were no rational bases for the enactments of the Southern legislatures. The pro-segregation states may have been wrong, but they certainly were not unreasonable. There definitely existed a body of reasoned opinion upon which their action was based. As a matter of law, under the conventional test, sociological data could not have overturned the school segregation statutes.

The lower courts in both Virginia and South Carolina rejected the sociological evidence as irrelevant. And while the Kansas and Delaware courts embodied the experts' opinions in their findings of fact, they clearly indicated that the testimony was legally irrelevant under the Plessy formula.

There was a way in which the Supreme Court could utilize this nonlegal information in reaching decision. The "way" is stated succinctly in a *Michigan Law Review* article by Jack Greenberg, assistant NAACP counsel: "Social scientists' testimony," he writes, "was used in a wholly different and new way in the recent school segregation cases. There, by placing before the Court authoritative scientific opinions regarding the effect of racial classification and of 'separate but equal' treatment, the plaintiffs helped persuade the Court in the shaping of a judge-made rule of law." [8]

The necessary task of informing the judicial mind was not left solely to the intellectual pursuits of the individual judges who were to decide *Brown* v. *Board of Education*. Counsel for the NAACP engaged in an organized, systematic effort to provide the nine men with all of the relevant data they would need to create a new constitutional standard.

And counsel did not confine their references to judicial pronouncements and other legal materials. Nor did they provide nonlegal materials for the limited purpose of showing that the legislative action was arbitrary and capricious as measured by the standard of reasonableness.

Plaintiffs clearly recognized the fact that they were before a rule-making body. In presenting scientific evidence on the effect of segregation upon Negro children, they sought to influence the Supreme Court to create a new constitutional standard. They could have had no other reason for offering such evidence.

Obviously, the Negro plaintiffs were not calling psychologists and sociologists to the witness stand in order to obtain data supporting the validity of school segregation statutes.

Nor could there have been an attempt to pursue the negative approach of the Brandeis brief and show that the state legistures of the South had no rational or reasonable basis for passing school segregation statutes. And in this sense, *Brown* v. *Board of Education* marked an innovation in the purpose for which nonlegal materials were being submitted.

Evaluating the effect of the expert testimony within the framework of the conventional constitutional test, Greenberg had this to say about the social scientists: "If testifying, for example, in support of the constitutionality of legislation, their testimony might suffice to establish the law's reasonableness and hence its constitutionality. If testifying against the constitutionality, as in the school cases, such an isolated thrust would most probably fail." [9]

The new approach of presenting nonlegal material solely to inform the judicial mind bore fruit in the decision reached on May 17, 1954. A new constitutional standard had been formulated: "We conclude," wrote Chief Justice Warren, "that in the field of public education the doctrine of 'separate but equal' has no place. Separate educational facilities are inherently unequal."

A SOCIOLOGICAL DECISION

The relevance of the nonlegal materials in the judicial decision-making process is but the threshold question in analyzing the significance of the sociological and psychological data which came before the Supreme Court in 1953. The far more important question is whether it is desirable for a court to consider such data in reaching a sound, workable rule of law.

There is no way of knowing exactly what role nonlegal materials played in the final determination of the legal issue of *Brown* v. *Board of Education*. But this much is certain: Chief Justice Warren's references to these sociological and psychological data have created strange intellectual companions; a new area of agreement has arisen between leading Southern spokesmen and leading social scientists. While they differ in their estimate of the worth of nonlegal data in arriving at a judicial decision, both groups are convinced that the segregation statutes of twenty-one states and the District of Columbia were overturned solely on the basis of the sociological and scientific authorities before the Court.

Mississippi's Eastland in a speech on *Brown* v. *Board of Education* before the Senate said: "Mr. President, in the long history of this country there has never before been a time when an Appellate Court or Supreme Court of the United States relied solely and alone on scientific authority to sustain a legal decision." [10] In making this statement, Senator Eastland takes the position that the use of such evidence marks the end of constitutional government in America.

Professor Kenneth B. Clark of C.C.N.Y., one of the "modern authorities" cited by the Court, felt that the use of psychological data had a significant impact on the trial courts as well as on the higher tribunals. Wrote Clark just prior to the 1954 Supreme Court declarations: "Proof of the argument that segregation itself is inequality and that state imposed racial segregation inflicts injuries upon the Negro had to come from the social psychologists and other social scientists." [11] Thus, while Clark echoes the Eastland view that the Supreme Court made a sociological decision, he considers such decision a manifestation of judicial enlightenment.

It cannot be questioned that nonlegal materials were considered and cited. But both the Eastlands and Clarks overstate their case. There is little likelihood that the contributions of the scientists and social scientists were the sole guide to the conclusions of May 17, 1954.

As Professor Cahn, a proponent of desegregation, has pointed out, the expert witnesses merely testified to the obvious. "For at least twenty years," he writes, "hardly any cultivated person has questioned that segregation is cruel to Negro school children. The cruelty is obvious and evident." [12] Since the facts of segregation are so well known, they could have been recognized and applied by the Court under the doctrine of judicial notice without the help of the social scientists. The Court had in fact decided the Missouri Law School case without the benefit of any scientific testimony. Then, in *Sweatt* v. *Painter,* the Texas Law School case, the Court had ignored voluminous data compiled by sociologists and based its decision on the knowledge the justices themselves, as lawyers, had about legal education. And it would thus follow that the social scientists cannot be entirely credited (or blamed) for the decisions rendered in the school segregation cases.

Support can be found for this conclusion. The record in the Bolling case, for example, was devoid of expert testimony. Yet the disposition of that District of Columbia case was the same as that of *Brown* v. *Board of Education.* In neither case was mention made of the mass of scientific data which dominates the record of the lower court proceedings in the Brown dispute, or of the statement submitted by 32 psychologists and sociologists as a special appendix to the plaintiffs' brief in the Supreme Court. The Court admitted the influence of nonlegal data only to the extent that it quoted from the lower court opinions in the Kansas and Delaware cases and then said that such statements were "amply supported" by the authorities listed in "footnote 11."

To those who oppose the conclusions of *Brown* v. *Board of Education,* the use of psychological and sociological data is a complete anathema. But even the lawyers who oppose segregation are reluctant to condone the use of such materials for more than limited purposes. Professor Cahn wisely warns that he "would not have the constitutional rights of Negroes— or of other Americans—rest on such flimsy foundation as some of the scientific demonstrations in the records." [13] And, he continues, "It is one thing to use the current scientific findings, however ephemeral they may be, in order to ascertain whether the legislature has acted reasonably in adopting some scheme of social or economic regulation; deference here is shown not so much to the findings as to the legislature. It is quite another thing to have our fundamental rights rise, fall or change along with the latest fashions of psychological literature." [14]

Yet the Supreme Court must and will inform itself about the problems which come before it for decision. And this includes information in nonlegal areas. There is always a danger that the judges will stop thinking as lawyers when they embrace some fashionable psychological theory, just as they once did when they gave blind adherence to the laissez-faire doctrine in economics. Nevertheless, where current economic or psychological thoughts influence judicial decision, as they must, such influence should be exposed and identified.

Chapter *10*

THE COLOR-BLIND
CONSTITUTION

By declaring public school segregation invalid, *per se,* the nine men made new law—but they did not make it out of whole cloth. The new constitutional standard was rooted in sound legal doctrine and based in large measure upon judicial pronouncements which long preceded the judgment in *Plessy* v. *Ferguson.* True, the Supreme Court gave new significance to those pronouncements as it disregarded the conventional test of the Plessy case. But it was also true that *Plessy* v. *Ferguson* had limited the meaning of many of these same cases when it made new law back in 1896.

The Sweatt and McLaurin decisions of 1950 were clearly inconsistent with the spirit of *Plessy* v. *Ferguson.* And even more inconsistent with the Plessy philosophy were the fact findings of the Kansas and Delaware courts which were quoted with approval in Chief Justice Warren's opinion. The 1896 decision denied that segregation stamped the badge of inferiority upon the Negro. The law and graduate school cases pointedly asserted that segregated education was defective because of the handicaps it imposed upon the Negro student. The psychologists and sociologists who testified in the trials which led to *Brown* v. *Board of Education* not only refuted the Plessy conclusion, but declared that state-enforced segregation resulted in a feeling of "inferiority" which necessarily retarded Negro children in the learning process.

The extent to which either the Sweatt and McLaurin decisions or the psychological and sociological evidence in the Kansas and Delaware cases led directly to the rejection of the constitutional standard of *Plessy* v. *Ferguson* is in the realm of speculation.

And while a court can and should make use of nonlegal materials, it cannot be said with certainty that the Supreme Court actually used such data in reaching its 1954 conclusions in *Brown* v. *Board of Education*. Certainly, the sociological and psychological evidence might have guided or reinforced the Supreme Court in making its determination. Certainly, also, there are words in Chief Justice Warren's opinion which suggest that the nine men of 1954 may have been so influenced. Yet this is only a partial explanation of the Supreme Court's refusal to turn the clock back to 1896.

Racial segregation has been embodied in literally thousands of statutes, municipal ordinances and administrative regulations covering virtually every area of activity in which whites and Negroes might conceivably find themselves on a basis of equality. In some instances the rights involved are of lesser importance and have yet to call forth widespread litigation. Laws requiring Negroes to sit together in the balconies of motion-picture theaters is an example of such discrimination. Other discriminatory statutes, ordinances and regulations affect more substantial rights—voting, jury service, etc.—and have resulted in Supreme Court action.

There is an imposing body of judicial authority outlawing racial discrimination on the theory that the particular rights involved are "political" in nature; other Supreme Court decisions have invalidated legislation because of the "motives" which impelled the legislature to enact such statutes. None of these cases is discussed—or even mentioned—in the body of the opinions delivered by Chief Justice Warren on Black Monday. And they have been largely ignored by the many lawyer scholars who have reviewed the legal aspects of *Brown*

v. *Board of Education.* These cases were just not considered important. And this despite the fact that four of them are cited in footnote 5 of Chief Justice Warren's opinion. Their importance to—and their influence on—the decision of May 17, 1954, was only realized after the implementation decree of 1955 and after decisions had been rendered affecting racial segregation in the field of public recreation.

The specific words of the Supreme Court's new constitutional standard warrant repetition. "We conclude," wrote Chief Justice Warren, "that in the field of public education the doctrine of 'separate but equal' has no place. Separate educational facilities are inherently unequal."

These words, *standing by themselves,* might have meant one of three things: (1) that public school segregation is constitutionally invalid because it is "unreasonable"; or (2) that public school segregation is invalid *per se,* but that segregation by race might be constitutionally justified in fields other than education; or (3) that all classification by race is unconstitutional *per se,* and that segregation in public education is thus merely an example of such invalidity.

Did the Supreme Court retain the form of the reasonableness formula and adopt new criteria for the application of the standard? Reasonableness is a factual test. Were the nine men of 1954 now saying that they would balance facts pro and con—substituting their judgments for those of the legislatures—in deciding what is or is not reasonable? Was the decision in *Brown* v. *Board of Education* a determination that legislation is only reasonable if the Supreme Court thinks it is right?

There is some evidence which, by itself, would appear to indicate an affirmative answer. Language in the District of Columbia case of *Bolling* v. *Sharpe* might warrant the conclusion that new criteria for the application of the standard had been developed and that public school segregation was held constitutionally invalid because it is unreasonable.

The Supreme Court pointedly asserted in the Bolling case that public school segregation "is not reasonably related to any proper governmental objective." This would appear to indicate the application of the reasonableness test with new criteria, and the conclusion that racial segregation in education—and only in education—is thus unconstitutional.

Most Southerners believe that there are real differences between whites and Negroes—differences which justify school segregation. Differences there are, of course; for example, there is no questioning the fact that most Negroes have a darker skin pigmentation. But skin pigmentation in and of itself is not a constitutional factor under the equal protection clause.

Few of even the most ardent pro-segregationists today support the viewpoint of the Old South that "the faculties of the Negro, as compared with those of the Saxon, qualified him for a state of servitude and made him unfit for the enjoyment of freedom." [1] Yet Southern legal leaders believe that there are biological "facts" which justify state-enforced racial segregation. They take comfort in the words of the Supreme Court of 1928 permitting discrimination where there is "a difference which is real, as distinguished from one which is seeming, specious, or fanciful." [2]

Judge Brady's "Black Monday" tract presents this argument: "We don't know what happens to the brain of man, but we do know that the negro's brain pan seals and hardens quicker than the white man's. We do know that the negro has, in certain instances, elliptical blood cells, which cause disease. We do know that his skull is one-eighth inch thicker, and we do know he has to have two determiners to have his kinky black hair. We don't know what it takes to make his mind different from our mind. This Supreme Court seeks to set aside all the laws of eugenics and biology!" [3]

Biological differences between whites and Negroes are, of course, meaningless in the legal order when confined to such

factors as hair curl and skull dimensions. Would differences
in blood constitute a constitutional difference under the
equal protection clause?

Medical studies have shown that there are three important
blood diseases. Hemophilia is extremely rare in Negroes. In
pernicious anemia, the rate of the disease among Negroes is
elevated in proportion to the amount of intermixture with
whites. The third disease is sickle–cell anemia, so called because the blood cells are sickle-shaped—and only Negroes are
subject to this malady.[4] But these differences have yet to be
considered a reasonable basis for any legislative classification.
Of more importance is the fact that, in varying percentages,
both whites and Negroes share types A, B, AB and O. And
it is these blood types which cannot be mixed. Physicians
make no distinction between Negro and white blood when
emergency transfusions are required or when plasma is
needed to stock a blood bank.

Were the situation otherwise—if it were impossible for
whites and Negroes to give each other blood transfusions—
then there would be a reasonable basis for discriminatory
legislation affecting white and Negro blood donors and the
operation of blood banks. Then, in the words of the District
of Columbia decision, segregation would be reasonably related to a proper governmental objective. But even then it
would be impossible to conceive of the Supreme Court upholding the validity of school segregation on the basis of such
blood variance. Differences such as these could not serve as
a rational (and hence reasonable) basis for legislative classification for educational purposes.

Writing two years after the decision in *Brown* v. *Board of
Education,* Justice Douglas made statements which would
appear to indicate that the Supreme Court might have applied a reasonableness test in its 1954 determination. Declared this staunch advocate of civil rights in 1956: "There
may even be a need to make a regulation based on race, the

source of the most invidious discriminations man has made. Experience shows that liquor has a devastating effect on the North American Indian and Eskimo. It is, therefore, commonly provided in the United States and Canada that no liquor should be sold to those races. Other regulations based on race may likewise be justified by reason of the special traits of those races, such, for example, as their susceptibility to particular diseases." [5]

If the Supreme Court had adopted the Douglas approach, it would have upheld the constitutionality of school segregation only if it could be shown that Negroes have "special traits" requiring reasonable legislators to keep them separated during their school years. This is admittedly a much more difficult task than that of showing that the Southern "way of life" made segregation reasonable under the conventional test in *Plessy* v. *Ferguson*.

Neither judicial decisions nor judicial commentaries give hint of any differences between whites and Negroes which justify school segregation—or any other type of segregation. And, certainly, differences in skin pigmentation, hair curl, skull dimensions and blood cells do not provide a valid reason for drawing a legislative color line. Justice Douglas' adherence to the unanimous decision in *Brown* v. *Board of Education*—and his two dissents as the lower court cases came up the judicial ladder toward Supreme Court decisions—indicate his firm belief that school segregation is either unconstitutional because unreasonable or unconstitutional *per se*. Yet it is Justice Douglas—and only Justice Douglas among the nine men of 1954—who suggests that there may be some justifiable racial classification in areas other than schooling. His example is the legislation controlling the sale of liquor to Indians.

True, the Supreme Court has upheld the validity of laws imposing criminal penalties on those who sell liquor to Indians. But the cases on this subject involving the selling of alcoholic beverages on the reservations are based upon the specific power of Congress under the Constitution's commerce clause to make laws regulating Indian affairs. Further, the leading case on this subject [6] was handed down in 1865, at a time prior to the ratification of the Fourteenth Amendment and its equal protection clause. Renewed doubts as to the constitutionality of such legislation have been raised in recent years in regard to Indians who have acquired citizenship and have left the reservations. The doubts have, of course, been the result of Supreme Court action affecting the Negro.

Even Justice Douglas' factual assertion that "Experience shows that liquor has a devastating effect on the North American Indian and Eskimo" has been questioned. When the Idaho Supreme Court in 1954 upheld a state statute prohibiting the sale of liquor to Indians, the two dissenting justices had this to say: "The real basis of the majority opinion is that the Indian as a race is more responsive to the baneful effects of intoxicants than any other race resident in our State. This is so because some ancient court has said so, and other courts have accepted the conclusion, all without inquiry or judicial determination. So, by means of mythology and folklore, it has become established beyond further question. Injustice does not become venerable with age." [7]

It would thus appear that legislation making a racial distinction between Indian citizens and other citizens rests on shaky constitutional foundations, just as Negro-white distinctions are at the very least constitutionally suspect.

In and of itself, the Supreme Court decision of 1954 gives no clue indicating that this type of analysis was employed. Certainly there were no words in Chief Justice Warren's opinion spelling out acceptance of the first proposition that public school segregation is constitutionally invalid because it is unreasonable.

The second proposition is that public school segregation

is invalid *per se,* but that segregation by race might be constitutionally justified in fields other than education. Justice Douglas' contention that classification by race might be warranted under certain factual conditions may lend support to the second possible interpretation of the meaning of *Brown* v. *Board of Education.* Again, this could not be the meaning of the decisions of May 17, 1954, unless there was some case in which the Supreme Court might sustain some non-school type of classification by race. What the Supreme Court has done in noneducation cases since *Brown* v. *Board of Education* makes this proposition untenable.

UNCONSTITUTIONAL PER SE

What the Supreme Court did on May 17, 1954, was to adopt a constitutional standard which was devoid of either of the two reasonableness tests and which denied by implication that racial discrimination might be constitutionally justified in fields other than education. The nine men declared that all classification by race is unconstitutional *per se*—and they discussed public school segregation as merely one example of such invalidity.

The conclusion that the Warren Court accepted the third proposition in arriving at its decision is based upon many considerations. The first involves an understanding of Supreme Court cases decided prior to *Plessy* v. *Ferguson* which were relied upon and cited by the 1954 Court in its opinion. A second factor leading to the determination that segregation by race is invalid *per se* is a long line of judicial utterances, made in ever-increasing number since 1941, which take on special meaning when read in light of the pre-Plessy cases. The implementation decision in *Brown* v. *Board of Education* provides the third source of evidence as to what the nine men did on May 17, 1954. And, fourthly, supporting arguments are found in what the Supreme Court has held in segregation cases not involving education following its implementation decree of May 31, 1955.

Reviewing the judicial history of racial segregation since 1866, Chief Justice Warren had this to say: "In the first cases in this Court construing the Fourteenth Amendment, decided shortly after its adoption, the Court interpreted it as proscribing *all state-imposed discriminations* against the Negro race." (Emphasis supplied.) And in footnote 5 of his opinion, the Chief Justice cited four important decisions which support this view.

The first of these is the famous *Slaughter-House Cases* decision of 1873 which, while it did not involve racial discrimination, spoke pointedly on the subject. "[O]n the most casual examination of the language of these amendments," wrote Justice Miller for the majority, "No one can fail to be impressed with the one pervading purpose found in them all, lying at the foundation of each, and without which none of them would have even been suggested; we mean the freedom of the slave race, the security and firm establishment of that freedom, and the protection of the newly-made freeman and citizen from the oppressions of those who had formerly exercised unlimited dominion over him." [8]

Citing three decisions in which the Supreme Court declared the invalidity of practices restricting the right of Negroes to serve on juries, Chief Justice Warren's footnote 5 contains a long excerpt from the best known of these cases, *Strauder* v. *West Virginia,* decided in 1880. "What is this," wrote the 1880 Court discussing the Fourteenth Amendment, "but declaring that the law in the States shall be the same for the black as for the white; that all persons, whether colored or white, shall stand equal before the laws of the States, and, in regard to the colored race, for whose protection the amendment was primarily designed, that no discrimination shall be made against them by law because of their color?" [9]

These words and others quoted by the Chief Justice from the Strauder case were approved in the two other jury decisions.[10]

And, after expressing their approval of the language in these cases which declared racial discrimination unconstitutional *per se,* the Supreme Court of 1954 called attention to the fact that *Plessy* v. *Ferguson* represented a departure from the earlier line of precedent. "The doctrine of 'separate but equal,' " wrote the Chief Justice, "did not make its appearance in this Court until 1896 in the case of Plessy v. Ferguson, . . . involving not education but transportation." The Plessy case, it will be remembered, broke away from the previous precedents by making a distinction between what it called political and social rights. According to the 1896 decision, the three jury cases were correctly decided because they involved a political issue, while transportation and education are only social rights.

Another 1896 decision—one contrary to the spirit of *Plessy* v. *Ferguson*—is quoted with approval by the nine men of 1954 in the District of Columbia case of *Bolling* v. *Sharpe*. Again the Supreme Court gave its support to language that racial distinctions are unconstitutional *per se.* "As long ago as 1896," reads the opinion, "this Court declared the principle 'that the constitution of the United States, in its present form, forbids, so far as civil and political rights are concerned, discrimination by general government, or by the states, against any citizen because of his race.' "[11]

Statements used in some of the Negro voting cases are similar to those found in the jury disputes. "States may do a good deal of classifying that is difficult to believe rational," wrote Justice Holmes in a representative opinion, "but there are limits, and it is too clear for extended argument that color cannot be made the basis of a statutory classification affecting the right set up in this case."[12]

Omens of the Supreme Court's return to the early interpretations of the Fourteenth Amendment are in plentiful
supply. Beginning in 1941 was a long line of judicial utterances declaring (directly or by implication) that racial classifications are invalid *per se*. This was to be expected. Over
the years from 1896 to 1941, the Plessy distinction between
political and social rights had disappeared through disuse.
More significant, the last case in which the Supreme Court
had expressly upheld a segregation law or any other type of
racial classification was in *Gong Lum* v. *Rice,* decided in
1927. Here are a few examples of the resurgence of *per se*
language:

It was in 1941 that Justice Jackson asserted that race,
creed, and color are constitutional irrelevances.[13] Dissenting
in the river boat pilots case in 1947, Justice Rutledge agreed.
"Classification based on the purpose to be accomplished,"
Rutledge wrote, "may be said abstractly to be sound. But
when the test . . . in fact is race or consanguinity, it cannot
be used constitutionally to bar all except a group chosen by
such a relationship from public employment. That is not a
test; it is a wholly arbitrary exercise of power." Justice Rutledge concluded that the Fourteenth Amendment forbids
". . . legislative lines drawn on the basis of race, color, creed
and the like. . . ."[14]

The Jackson-Rutledge assertions are square statements of
the proposition that the Constitution forbids the use of race
as a distinguishing factor in legislation. Further, their statements are unqualified. The application of their principle
would not be limited to the category of political rights; it
would extend to any instance of "state action."

Surprisingly, Justice Black has expressed a milder position
in considering the constitutional status of racial classification. "It should be noted to begin with," declared Justice
Black in 1944, "that all legal restrictions which curtail the
civil rights of a single racial group are immediately suspect.

That is not to say that all such restrictions are unconstitutional. It is to say that the courts must subject them to the most rigid scrutiny." [15] Chief Justice Warren echoed Justice Black's language in the Bolling case by using these words: "Classifications based solely upon race must be scrutinized with particular care, since they are contrary to our traditions and hence constitutionally suspect." This formulation leaves open the possibility that some racial classifications might be justified, if they survive "rigid" judicial scrutiny. But there has yet to be a racial law before the Supreme Court in this area which has so survived modern scrutiny.

Language of Justice Black embodying the *per se* concept even made an appearance in *Korematsu* v. *United States,* a 1944 opinion which upheld federal regulations having strong racial overtones. This was a difficult case to decide; it was one of those hard cases which sometimes make bad law. It was a controversy involving the relocation program in the early days of World War II requiring Japanese—and only Japanese—to move from their West Coast homes to internment camps. Strong argument was made that the regulations were grounded in racial discrimination and that the classification was necessarily unconstitutional as a reflection of racial prejudice.

Justice Black spoke for a slim 6 to 3 majority in declaring the regulations valid. "Our task would be simple, our duty clear, were this a case involving the imprisonment of a loyal citizen in a concentration camp because of racial prejudice . . . ," wrote Black, "Korematsu was not excluded from the Military Area because of hostility to him or his race. He *was* excluded because we are at war with the Japanese Empire. . . ." [16]

Even if the relocation regulations were considered as examples of racial classification, the Korematsu case would still indicate Supreme Court hostility toward any laws affecting race. The classification had barely survived Black's "rigid judicial scrutiny" test. The nine men upheld the relocation program only because they found that the motives of Congress and the Army were free from bias and prejudice against persons of Japanese ancestry. And it is quite evident that nothing short of the demands of wartime security would have sustained such classification.

The language of Black and Warren declaring that racial classifications are treated differently from other classifications is important in understanding what the Supreme Court was saying and doing between 1941 and 1954. Yet the full import of the judicial utterances during this period did not become clear until the *Brown* v. *Board of Education* implementation decision of May 31, 1955.

Strangely absent from the implementation opinion is a word which one would have expected to have found repeated many times. True, it makes two appearances in the footnotes—but those footnotes are merely restatements of questions 4 and 5, originally propounded two years earlier. The word is not conspicuous by its absence. Lawyers have just assumed it was there. And absence cannot be attributed to an error of omission; on the contrary, it was undoubtedly difficult to write the opinion without using that word. The word is "segregation."

Nor did the opinion delivered by Chief Justice Warren employ any verb, noun, or adjective form of the word by way of substitute. There is no "segregate," "segregated," "segregating" or "segregative." "Desegregate" and "desegregation" are also absent. The nine men used a much stronger word in the word "discrimination." Five times it was repeated; and on three occasions the Supreme Court said that public schools should be "nondiscriminatory."

Why did the Supreme Court avoid the word "segregation" in issuing its decrees in the school segregation cases? "Segregation" and "discrimination" have very different connotations. But the analysis of judicial opinions is more than an exercise in semantics. Is there any legal significance in the particular word choice employed in the decision of May 31, 1955?

Even when it was upholding some statutes involving racial classifications, the Supreme Court has consistently struck down "discriminatory" legislation as invalid. In 1886, the nine men declared unconstitutional a municipal ordinance under which Chinese laundrymen were denied licenses to pursue their trade in wooden buildings, while the same prohibition was not enforced against non-Chinese applicants.[17] "Equal protection of the laws," explained Justice Matthews for the Court, "is a pledge of the protection of equal laws."[18] This pledge was found to be violated when, "No reason for [such discrimination] is shown, and the conclusion cannot be resisted, that no reason for it exists except hostility to the race and nationality to which the petitioners belong, and which in the eye of the law is not justified."[19] The Court characterized the vice in this case as that of "discrimination."

Although the "kinship" classification was upheld in the river boat pilots case, Mr. Justice Black declared for the majority that there were some classifications which could have no reasonable relation to a legislative objective. "An example," said he, "would be a law applied to deny a person a right to earn a living or hold any job because of hostility to his particular race, religion, beliefs, or because of some other reason having no reasonable relation to the regulated activities."[20]

And in *Korematsu* v. *United States,* which upheld the wartime relocation of Japanese-Americans, the Court still asserted that "racial antagonism" can never justify the existence of a restriction against a racial group.[21] Black's position, according to an article in the *California Law Review,* requires "a judgment about legislative and executive motive, and apparently turns upon whether the exclusion order is an expression of racial prejudice." [22]

True, most of the statements by the Supreme Court as to the invalidity *per se* of discriminatory legislation have been by way of dicta. Yet such dicta clearly show the difference in the basis of decision between the *Plessy* v. *Ferguson* line of cases and those decisions in which the constitutional vice has been found to be discrimination.

Where the legislative motive is deemed to be racial hostility or antagonism, the resulting statute has been consistently held unconstitutional regardless of the reasonableness of the objective.

An excellent statement of this position is found in the 1948 case of *Takahashi* v. *Fish Commission*.[23] Here the Supreme Court invalidated a California statute which barred the issuance of commercial fishing licenses to persons "ineligible to citizenship," which, for practical purposes, included only resident Japanese. The plaintiff had argued that the statute was the outgrowth "of racial antagonism directed solely against the Japanese, and for that reason alone it was invalid." [24] The majority of the nine reached their decision on other grounds and declared that it was unnecessary to decide this issue. In a concurring opinion, however, Justices Murphy and Rutledge supported the plaintiff's view. Wrote Justice Murphy: "Even the most cursory examination of the background of the statute demonstrates that it was designed solely to discriminate against such persons in a manner inconsistent with the concept of equal protection of the laws. Legislation of that type is not entitled to wear the cloak of constitutionality." [25] Again, if a statute is held to be discriminatory, the Supreme Court will automatically declare it invalid under the Fourteenth Amendment.

The continued repetition of the word "discrimination" in the *Brown* v. *Board of Education* implementation decree of 1955 amounts to more than a choice of words for literary purposes. It is true that all legislation is discriminatory in the broad legal sense. "Discrimination," however, has a special connotation where race is involved—a connotation which is similar to the nonlegal meaning of the word. In cases involving discrimination, reference is made not to the objectives of the legislation, but rather to the motives of the legislators. When the Supreme Court holds that a statute is discriminatory, its conclusion embodies a finding that the legislative scheme was activated by bias and prejudice, and thus for that reason alone the statute violates the Constitution. The conclusion that the nine men had abandoned the conventional test of constitutionality in deciding *Brown* v. *Board of Education* was reaffirmed. In the reflected light of the implementation decree, the full meaning of the decision of May 17, 1954, clearly emerges: laws based upon racial classifications are necessarily discriminatory and discriminatory legislation is unconstitutional *per se.*

Even more compelling evidence of the exact nature of the constitutional standard developed in *Brown* v. *Board of Education* is found in subsequent cases which required the application of the Brown principle to racial segregation outside the field of public education. This is the fourth of the considerations showing that the Supreme Court had declared racial segregation unconstitutional *per se.*

The South dreaded the decision in *Brown* v. *Board of Education.* It has come to dread even more the cases which have extended the impact of the Brown principle to disputes involving parks, golf courses and, especially, bathing beaches.

Racial legislation has strong sexual overtones. Almost every Southern spokesman argues that desegregation will inevitably lead to miscegenation.

Joint use of bathing beaches is a long way from miscegenation, but it certainly does involve the risks of physical attraction. "High in the hierarchy of social segregation and discrimination is the taboo against interracial swimming," [26] writes New York University Law Professor Robert B. McKay. And the reasons given for that statement are taken from Gunnar Myrdal's *An American Dilemma*—one of the books cited in footnote 11 of *Brown* v. *Board of Education,* written by the man condemned by Southern leaders for his allegedly pro-communist leanings. The reasons: "it involves the exposure of large parts of the body," and creates "erotic associations." [27]

In the important case of *Mayor and City Council of Baltimore City* v. *Dawson* in 1955, both the Court of Appeals and the Supreme Court held that Baltimore could not maintain segregated bathing beaches.[28]

The Dawson dispute and two related cases had been consolidated for federal court decision as early as July, 1954.[29] In Dawson and one of the other cases, counsel had stipulated that the facilities involved were equal; in the third case, agreement was reached that the only issue to be argued was the broad question "of the right of the city to segregate the races in public swimming pools." [30] Decision was purposely delayed until *Brown* v. *Board of Education* had been decided in the Supreme Court. And District Judge Roszel C. Thomsen of Maryland then became the first judge to apply the precedent of May 17, 1954, to a noneducation case.

Judge Thomsen conceded that "Brown v. Board of Education indicates that certain claimed rights which may have been heretofore regarded as social matters should now be considered civil rights entitled to constitutional protection." [31] Nonetheless, he concluded that the conventional reasonableness test of constitutionality was still valid and should be applied. Under that test the judge could—and Judge Thomsen did—find that the segregation was justified.

Judge Parker and his Fourth Circuit Court of Appeals (comprising the states of Maryland, North Carolina, South Carolina, Virginia and West Virginia) reversed summarily.

The error of the district court, they pointed out, was a misreading of *Brown* v. *Board of Education.* The lower court had upheld bathing beach segregation "to avoid any conflict which might arise from racial antipathies." The Court of Appeals declared this reason invalid. If the state may not exercise its powers to sustain school segregation where "racial friction may be apprehended from the enforced comingling of the races," reasoned the court, "it cannot be sustained with respect to public beach and bathing facilities, the use of which is entirely optional." [32] Application of the basic *per se* principle of *Brown* v. *Board of Education* rendered this conclusion inevitable. The lower courts had to give force and effect to the Supreme Court judgment of May 17, 1954, and that judgment left no room to consider the relative "reasonableness" of education and swimming.

Education and swimming are certainly two different things. The education of future citizens is undoubtedly more important than seaside bathing, and undoubtedly a much more reasonable and worthwhile government objective. But *Brown* v. *Board of Education* and the bathing beach disputes have one vital fact in common: in both cases there was a state command which created two separate groups of persons—separated by race alone. And where the problem is the validity of that state-created distinction, bathing beaches and school benches have equal status under the Constitution. In both cases the constitutional imperative made classification by race invalid *per se.* Reasonableness of the objective to be achieved by segregation became immaterial.

Other jurists have arrived at this same conclusion. Judge Michael James Manley, a Maryland state judge, spelled out this meaning of *Brown* v. *Board of Education* in a 1955 decision: "[W]here an attempt is made to set up a segregation policy based solely on race or nationality," he wrote, "it cannot be upheld as a valid exercise of the police power. I am of the opinion that in the present state of the law this constitutional inhibition applies to the authority of the State to regulate the liquor industry to the same extent that it is applicable to any other business or public function or service provided by the State for its citizens." [33] Judge Manley then held that the State of Maryland could not create two classes of licensed bars, one for Negroes and the other for whites, even though the owners of such public places could serve whom they chose. The vice lay in the fact that the state sought to classify by race.

The second proposition—that public school segregation is invalid *per se*, but that segregation by race might be constitutionally justified in fields other than education—is logically indefensible. Rejection of the first proposition did not necessarily compel acceptance of the third proposition. The Supreme Court might have adopted the compromise position. And this would appear to be what the Court did in its characterization of racial classifications as "suspect" in *Bolling* v. *Sharpe*. But once the nine men directly applied *Brown* v. *Board of Education* to the question of bathing beach segregation, it became obvious that racial classifications could not be justified in any type of legislative action.

Since the Supreme Court studiously avoided the conventional test of *Plessy* v. *Ferguson*, it is clear that the decision in *Brown* v. *Board of Education* did not rest upon the proposition that public school segregation is constitutionally invalid because it is "unreasonable." This is further borne out by the fact that the evidence before the nine men did not show that school segregation statutes were either arbitrary or irrational. Nor was there a possibility that the Supreme Court was applying new criteria of "reasonableness" under this first proposition. The nine men may have used the available psychological and sociological data to inform themselves in the process of creating a new constitutional standard—but it is clear that these data were not used to determine whether the state legislatures were right or wrong.

By placing judicial reliance on the four cases cited in foot-note 5 which declared racial distinctions invalid *per se*, by emphasizing the discriminatory aspects of school segregation and thus bringing into consideration the cases based upon legislative motive, and by extending the impact of decision beyond the borders of education, the Supreme Court had evidenced its adoption of the third proposition as its constitutional standard. The *per se* formula has again become the law of the Constitution.

Extending the impact of decision from Brown to Dawson, Judge Parker's Fourth Circuit Court of Appeals made pointed reference to the District of Columbia case also decided on May 17, 1954. "The decision in Bolling v. Sharpe," declared the court, "also throws strong light on the question before us for it admonishes us that in approaching the solution of problems of this kind we should keep in mind the ideal of equality before the law which characterizes our institutions." [34]

Fifty-eight years of Supreme Court history had witnessed the gradual attrition of both the holding and dicta of the seven-man majority which once upheld the validity of Louisiana's transportation laws. *Brown* v. *Board of Education*, however, was more than judicial erosion. It was an affirmative statement of a contrary principle of law. The dissenting opinion of Justice Harlan in *Plessy* v. *Ferguson* had become the unanimous view of the nine men of 1954: "Our Constitution is color-blind . . . all citizens are equal before the law." [35]

Chapter 11

IMPACT OF DECISION

The 1954 decision in *Brown* v. *Board of Education* heralded a long summer of argument and counterargument. "Monday morning quarterbacks" dominated the discussion. Their theme was the validity of the Supreme Court decision. Emotion ruled reason as factions alternately lauded and condemned the nine men and their stand on "fundamental freedom." Obscured by the exchange of invective was the simple fact that the case was not yet closed; lawyers on both sides still had work to do.

During the legal battle which resulted in the decision of May 17, 1954, the consideration of appropriate relief was necessarily subordinated to the primary issue: the constitutionality of segregation in public education. "We have now announced," wrote Chief Justice Warren, "that such segregation is a denial of the equal protection of the laws." What the Court did not announce was the ways and means of implementing that decision.

"Because these are class actions, because of the wide applicability of this decision, and because of the great variety of local conditions, the formulation of decrees in these cases presents problems of considerable complexity," said the Chief Justice. He continued: "In order that we may have the full assistance of the parties in formulating decrees, the cases will be restored to the docket, and the parties are requested to present further argument on questions 4 and 5 previously propounded by the Court. . . ." The Attorney General of the United States was again invited to participate, and permission was granted the attorneys general of the Southern states to appear as *amici curiae,* that is, as friends and advisors of the court, rather than as litigants.

Again, the stage was set for a dramatic decision Monday. The various Negro plaintiffs, together with their NAACP lawyers, were already in the case; so were the states of Kansas, South Carolina, Virginia and Delaware. Six other states— Florida, North Carolina, Arkansas, Oklahoma, Maryland and Texas—filed briefs and participated in the oral argument. Another *amicus curiae* brief was filed for the American Veterans Committee, Inc.

Significantly, several of the most violently pro-segregation states—including Alabama, Georgia and Mississippi—played no part in the *amici curiae* arguments. There were many reasons for this omission. To begin with, these states were already pursuing a course of action which ignored the Supreme Court's action in *Brown* v. *Board of Education;* they were violently opposed to any measures which might be interpreted as a recognition of the Court's power to declare segregation statutes unconstitutional. Further, they wished to avoid the possible quasi-legal argument that they would be bound by the implementation decree issued in a case in which they had participated. A third reason for remaining aloof was the fact that their points of view differed in many respects from the position taken by such states as Florida and Texas. Alabama, Georgia and Mississippi knew that the participating South would have to present a united position which would necessarily involve some concessions to principle in order to debate effectively on implementation. All implementation arguments had to begin with the premise that the 1954 decision was law, and Alabama, Georgia and Mississippi were willing to concede nothing.

All five of the school segregation cases were heard together for the decision of May 31, 1955.[1] *Bolling* v. *Sharpe,* the

Washington, D. C., dispute, had been joined with the cases from Kansas, South Carolina, Virginia and Delaware. The various defendants—and the Southern states appearing as *amici curiae*—were not, however, all similarly situated in respect to segregation practices. As the Court observed, "Substantial progress has been made in the District of Columbia and in the communities in Kansas and Delaware involved in this litigation. The defendants in the cases coming to us from South Carolina and Virginia are awaiting the decision of this Court concerning relief."

Again, the Supreme Court sat attentive as counsel debated. For four days—April 11 to 14, 1955—the lawyers argued. Six weeks later, on Monday, May 31, 1955, the Supreme Court rendered another unanimous and historic opinion: the implementation decision in *Brown* v. *Board of Education*.

FASHIONING A REMEDY

Why did the Supreme Court need—or want—this implementation decision? It had already declared unconstitutional the laws of twenty-one states and the District of Columbia requiring or permitting racial segregation in the public schools. Wasn't this enough? The nine men of 1954 were certainly aware of the words of the nine men of 1886: "An unconstitutional statute is not a law; it confers no rights; it imposes no duties; it affords no protection; it creates no office; it is, in legal contemplation, as inoperative as though it had never been passed." [2] True, this statement of seventy years ago is an oversimplification of a very complex problem in the law, but there is no question of its validity as applied to *Brown* v. *Board of Education*. What further action then was required, or desired, before the doors of all Southern schools were to open to Negroes as well as to whites?

"We have here," explained Dr. Ernst Borinski in 1954, "the rather unique situation that the Court hands down a decision in principle but refrains from formulating the decree necessary to implement this decision." [3] The Supreme Court had declared the existence of a right, but had failed to make it possible to enjoy that right. Certainly there was no necessity to await implementation by act of Congress,[4] but the nine men had to take some action to make their expression of principle meaningful. That something might have been the declaration of a "personal and present" right; it might have been a decree ordering the immediate admission of Negro students to what had formerly been all-white schools. The fact that special decrees prohibiting school segregation based on race were delayed a full year—and then permitted to be delayed still further at the discretion of the lower courts—was part of the compromise that marked the Court's handling of *Brown* v. *Board of Education.*

Had a "personal and present" right been declared, the various Negro plaintiffs would have been able to bring suit against the school authorities for money damages for injuries sustained by their children as a result of being forced to attend segregated schools. This remedy was not seriously considered. From the outset, counsel for the Negro children pointed out that a money judgment would not provide adequate relief. The Supreme Court agreed.

Declaration of a "personal and present" right would also have called the Civil Rights Act of the Federal Criminal Code into operation. This makes it a crime for an individual to deprive another of "rights, privileges or immunities" secured by the Constitution.[5] This remedy, too, was neither requested by the parties nor desired by the Court. Threatening several hundred thousand school officials with the stigma of criminal conviction would have discredited the 1954 decision and made a mockery of the enforcement problem. The decision had to be practical as well as just.

In arriving at its implementation decree, the Court directed its attention to questions 4 and 5, originally pro-

pounded in 1953 and asked again in 1954.[6] The assumption
underlying these questions—"Assuming it is decided that segregation in public schools violates the Fourteenth Amendment"—had become a reality. Question 4 was divided into
two parts: "(a) would a decree necessarily follow providing
that, within the limits set by normal geographic school districting, Negro children should forthwith be admitted to
schools of their choice, or (b) may this Court, in the exercise
of its equity powers, permit an effective gradual adjustment
to be brought about from existing segregated systems to a
system not based on color distinctions?"

Question 4 was not a difficult question, at least not on the
surface. To begin with, the nine men received the replies
they wanted from both sides in the dispute. The answer to
(a) was "no"; the answer to (b) was "yes." John W. Davis,
arguing the case for South Carolina, spoke for all concerned
when he said: "As to the question of the right of the Court
to postpone the remedy, we think that inheres in every court
of equity, and there has been no question about it as to
power." [7]

Courts of equity—and that includes the Supreme Court—
are not inflexibly bound to direct any particular form of relief. They have broad power to fashion their own special
remedies to serve what they believe to be the ends of justice
in a specific case. This is not a new rule of legal procedure;
its history goes back at least as far as the fourteenth century.

While most litigants seek pecuniary damages in their lawsuits, such remedy has its limitation as a solution to legal
controversy. Oliver Brown obviously could not have resolved
his dispute with the Topeka Board of Education in terms
of financial remuneration. In lawyer language, Brown had
"no adequate remedy at law." He had to invoke the equity
or chancery power of the courts to obtain the desired relief.

In making its decree, the court of equity *fashions* its
remedy. It gives direct orders to the litigating parties. It may

also impose conditions on their duty to obey. If a litigant is disobedient, he can even be imprisoned for contempt of the equity order.

Yet no court is omnipotent. While equity power far transcends the authority to award money judgments, equity too has its limitations. Equity can grant or deny a divorce decree; it cannot compel man and wife to share the same bedroom. Equity can require an employer to retain an employee under the terms of an employment contract; it cannot compel a man to work for any other man. Equity can declare unconstitutional the laws of twenty-one states and the District of Columbia requiring or permitting public school segregation; it cannot, solely on the basis of that declaration, compel a single white child to attend a nonsegregated school.

Article III, Section 1, of the Constitution provides: "The judicial Power of the United States, shall be vested in one Supreme Court, and in such inferior Courts as the Congress may from time to time ordain and establish." Article III, Section 2, says: "The judicial Power shall extend to all Cases, in Law and Equity, . . ." The Supreme Court sat as a court of equity in *Brown* v. *Board of Education*. Question 4 requested argument on the *extent* of its equity powers.

The "no" and "yes" responses to questions 4(a) and 4(b) were not given without qualification. The Supreme Court had phrased its queries in the alternative. "Would a decree necessarily follow" to admit Negro children "forthwith" to schools of their choice, *or* did the Court have power to fashion "an effective gradual adjustment"? There was general concurrence only in the fact that the Supreme Court had the power it asked about in 4(b).

Although the Department of Justice had argued against school segregation, it found itself in agreement with the Solid South on the issue of the Supreme Court's equity powers. The government summarized the joint point of view: ". . . whatever the difficulties of determining what remedy would be most effective and fair in redressing the violation of constitutional right presented in these cases, we believe there can be no doubt of the Court's *power* to grant such remedy as it finds to be most consonant with the interests of justice." [8] "We conclude, therefore, that the Court has undoubted power in these cases to enter such decrees as it determines will be most effective and just in relation to the interests, private and public, affected by its decision." [9]

Ample precedent was given for this summary and conclusion. Landmark decisions are cited again and again in the various *amicus curiae* briefs, cataloging the instances in which the Supreme Court has granted "reasonable time" in which to comply with its dictates. In the antitrust case of *Standard Oil Co.* v. *United States,* the Court extended the time for executing its decree from thirty days to six months, "in view of the magnitude of the interests involved and their complexity." [10] *Georgia* v. *Tennessee Copper Co.* was a case in which the state of Georgia sought to enjoin various copper companies from discharging noxious gases from their Tennessee plants, destroying orchards and crop lands in plaintiff's territory. Speaking through Mr. Justice Holmes, the Court held the activities of the copper firms unlawful, but added that the injunction would be issued only "after allowing a reasonable time to the defendants to complete the structures that they are now building, and the efforts that they are making to stop the fumes." [11] In *United States* v. *American Tobacco Co.,* a monopoly case, the Court granted six months' time (with a possible sixty-day extension) to effectuate its decrees. During that period, the lower court was "directed to hear the parties . . . for the purpose of ascertaining and determining upon some plan or method of dissolving the combination and of re-creating, out of the elements now composing it, a new condition which shall be honestly in harmony with and not repugnant to the law." [12]

North Carolina conceded the existence of the equity

powers asked about in question 4—with qualifications. The brief of its attorney general, Harry McMullan, cites the same cases and reaches the same conclusion: ". . . in the exercise of its equity powers [the Supreme Court] can permit a gradual adjustment from the existing school system to a system not based on color distinctions." [13] Lawyer McMullan, however, found the legal authorities inadequate.

"This Court's decision on the merits in these cases gives rise to a question of equity power for which no precise precedent has been found," he argued. "The nuisance and anti-trust cases . . . involved huge investments by many people. However, the confusion likely to result from dividing even so vast an enterprise as was the American Tobacco Company pales into insignificance when compared with the uncertainties confronting the people of North Carolina, and other southern states, as a result of the decision. . . . [T]he decrees approved in anti-trust and nuisance cases throw but a flickering light on the problem here. Nevertheless, they do direct attention to the flexibility of equitable remedies and to the fundamental principles which should guide the [Court] in the exercise of [its] unusual powers." [14]

Thus North Carolina admitted the authority of a federal court (question 4(b)) to issue an injunction directing a state school board to desist from denying a Negro child admission to a public school, solely because the child was a Negro. It denied, however, that a federal court (question 4(a)) had authority to require state school boards to perform affirmative duties or to follow specific procedures prescribed by a judicial tribunal. No federal court can "take the assignment of children to specific state school buildings out of the hands of the state school officials and place it in the hands of Negro children," [15] reads the North Carolina brief.

Speaking for the various Negro litigants, the NAACP gave the only affirmative response to question 4(a), contending that the Court should issue a decree compelling the immediate admission of Negro children to the schools of their choice. Yet it did not say "no" to question 4(b) on the extent of the Court's equity powers. "Appellants have no desire to set precise bounds to the reserve discretion of equity," reads the NAACP brief; "They concede that, as a court of chancery, this Court has power in a proper case to mold its relief to individual circumstances in ways and to an extent which it is now unnecessary to define with entire precision." But the "concession" was qualified: NAACP lawyers debated that there was "no equitable justification" for delay; they knew of "no reasons or considerations which would warrant postponement"; they contended that rights established in these cases were "far outside the classes" in which "a balance of convenience has been or ought to be struck." [16] Rightly or wrongly, these arguments carried little weight with the Supreme Court.

Congress has also spoken on this subject. The legislative branch has expressly empowered the Court, in dealing with cases coming before it, to enter "such appropriate judgment, decree, or order, or require such further proceedings to be had as may be just under the circumstances." [17]

The Supreme Court took the position espoused by the South. It denied the necessity of an immediate decree directing "forthwith" admission of Negro children to "schools of their choice." It acknowledged its power to "permit an effective gradual adjustment." Wrote Chief Justice Warren: "Traditionally, equity has been characterized by a practical flexibility in shaping its remedies and by a facility for adjusting and reconciling public and private needs. These cases call for the exercise of these traditional attributes of equity power. At stake is the personal interest of the plaintiffs in admission to public schools as soon as practicable on a nondiscriminating basis. To effectuate this interest may call for elimination of a variety of obstacles in making the transition to school systems operated in accordance with the constitutional principles set forth in our May 17, 1954 decision. Courts of equity may properly take into account the public interest in the elimination of such obstacles in a systematic and effective manner."

ISSUING THE DECREE

Affirmative responses to question 4(b) came as no surprise to the Supreme Court. It already knew that it had the power to permit "effective gradual adjustment." What the nine men sought was *recognition* of this power to smooth the course of compromise. A decree was to be fashioned in the spirit of this compromise: It had to be sufficiently "gradual" to satisfy the proponents of segregation; it had to be sufficiently "effective" to satisfy the proponents of desegregation. The question was "how?"

The "how" question, fifth and last of those propounded in the 1953 decision, was divided into four parts:

"(a) should this Court formulate detailed decrees in these cases;

"(b) if so, what specific issues should the decrees reach;

"(c) should this Court appoint a special master to hear evidence with a view to recommending specific terms for such decrees;

"(d) should this Court remand to the courts of first instance with directions to frame decrees in these cases, and if so what general directions should the decrees of this Court include and what procedures should the courts of first instance follow in arriving at the specific terms of more detailed decrees?"

Question 5(a) was answered with a flat "no" in the briefs and arguments of the government and the various Southern states which appeared in the dispute. The Supreme Court reached the same conclusion. And, with this negative response to 5(a), questions 5(b) and 5(c) became moot. If the

Court was not to "formulate detailed decrees" in *Brown* v. *Board of Education,* there was no need to set forth "specific issues" or to appoint a special master to recommend "specific terms."

While not material in reaching final decision, the suggestion that the nine men appoint a special master is of considerable interest as an adjunct to the power of the Supreme Court to fashion a remedy. The Supreme Court is an appellate tribunal. It is not, with extremely rare exceptions, a trial court. It does not hear witnesses or take evidence. It does not, save in unusual circumstances, ascertain facts. The function of an appellate court is to make determinations of law based upon the facts found in the trial court below. Congress enacted legislation in 1803 specifically forbidding the introduction of new evidence at the appellate level.[18] This law was repealed in 1948.[19] There was no *legal* reason why a special master could not have been delegated to aid the Court by hearing additional evidence and making recommendations. The suggestion, however, met with disfavor. Neither disputants nor *amici curiae* advocated the adoption of this procedure.

By the process of elimination, the Supreme Court had run out of choices. It had to say "yes" to question 5(d). The government had strongly urged the adoption of the 5(d) remedy. And grudgingly the Southern states lent their support to this last suggested mode of implementation.

The Supreme Court had reached its final decision in *Brown* v. *Board of Education:* It remanded the five cases to the lower courts for further action.

In making its implementation decree, the Court expressed its appreciation to the parties, the United States government and the various states which had appeared to argue the issues involved. "These presentations," wrote the Chief Justice, "were informative and helpful to the Court in its consideration of the complexities arising from the transition to a system of public education freed of racial discrimination."

Regardless of the courtesies, however, the nine men had given little heed to the specific proposals advanced.

Counsel for the Negro appellants had declared themselves "unable, in good faith, to suggest terms for a decree which [would] secure effective gradual adjustment because," they contended, "no such decree will protect appellants' rights." [20] They took the position "that no reason has been suggested and none has been discovered by us that would warrant denying appellants their full rights beyond the beginning of the next school year." [21]

It was apparent from the very start, however, that the Court would deny the NAACP plea for direct action. The answers to question 4 had already precluded the necessity of a decree providing that Negro children "should forthwith be admitted to schools of their choice." Once the alternative of "effective gradual adjustment" had been accepted, there was little chance that the nine men would formulate their own detailed orders. And, in the unlikely event that specific decrees would be formulated, it was evident that such decrees would not call for immediate desegregation.

The NAACP position was based largely on the language in *Sweatt* v. *Painter,* the case involving the admission of a Negro to the University of Texas Law School. "It is fundamental," the Court had said, "that these cases concern rights which are personal and present." [22] Thurgood Marshall and his fellow attorneys placed much emphasis on the words "personal" and "present." They argued that each appellant had the "personal" right to grow up in a democratic society without the impress of state-imposed racial segregation in the public schools. They took the position that the rights were "present" because they would be "irretrievably lost if their enjoyment was put off." [23] They pointed out the simple fact that children can attend elementary and secondary schools only while they are children. They might have re-

minded the nine men that daughter Linda was only eight
years old on the day that Oliver Brown went to court, but
that she would be celebrating her twelfth birthday in 1955.
NAACP proposals were immediately countered. The "personal and present" argument was treated sympathetically in
the government brief, but only for the space of a single page.
"For these plaintiffs," summarized the Department of Justice, "the remedy of immediate admission to non-segregated
schools is an indispensable corollary of the constitutional
right, for to recognize a litigant's right without affording him
an adequate remedy for its violation is to nullify the value
of the right." [24] The very next words in the brief, however,
were "on the other hand."

Distinguishing *Sweatt* v. *Painter* and similar cases on the
facts, the government noted that each of these suits involved
higher education, and that each had but one plaintiff. "It
is one thing to direct immediate relief where a single individual seeks vindication of his constitutional rights in the
relatively narrow area of professional and graduate school
education, and an entirely different matter to follow the
same course in the broad area of public school education
affecting thousands of children, teachers, and schools," [25]
wrote the Justice Department.

The Supreme Court needed little convincing on these
points. The nine men were well aware that justice delayed
is oftentimes justice denied. And they were determined to
do what they believed to be justice. Yet they were admittedly
overwhelmed by the immensity of the enforcement problem.
Implementation could have been effected in 1954: specific
decrees could have been issued at that time; or the Supreme
Court could have ordered the lower federal courts to render
such decrees. But the Supreme Court chose the course of
compromise and delay. It had already adopted procedures
which necessarily resulted in such compromise and delay.
Questions 4 and 5 had been propounded for counsel back in

1953. On May 17, 1954, the request was repeated, and was introduced by such descriptive terms as "wide applicability," "great variety" and "considerable complexity."

Additional delay was forecast for the decision Monday of May 31, 1955.

While the Supreme Court followed the Department of Justice recommendations as to delay, it completely ignored two other government suggestions. No mention was made of the proposal to integrate "on a school-by-school" basis; there was no discussion of the plan of "integration on a grade basis"—a plan to integate the first grades immediately and to continue grade by grade through elementary school.

It was with reluctance that Florida and Arkansas gave affirmative answers to question 5(d), which asked whether the cases should be remanded to the lower federal courts for further action. What Florida really advocated was "a period of gradual adjustment . . . with broad powers of discretion vested in local school authorities to determine the administrative procedure." [26] The basic Arkansas position was that "the Court should leave the problem of integration of the races in public schools to Congress for appropriate legislation." [27] Other states in the South supported both of these positions.

The Supreme Court had nullified pro-segregation argument at the outset by the simple expedient of framing questions which limited responses to "yes" and "no." Obviously, the Southern states would be opposed to a decree providing for the immediate admission of Negro children to nonsegregated schools. In order to avoid this, they had to recognize the equity power of the Court to effect a "gradual adjustment." But even though the Southern states recognized this power, they were still opposed to having the Supreme Court formulate detailed decrees directing desegregation. When John W. Davis appeared before the Court to argue the issues of implementation, he said: "Your Honors do not sit, and cannot sit, as a glorified Board of Education for the state of South Carolina or any other State." The Supreme Court agreed.

What the nine men ignored was Mr. Davis' next sentence: "Neither can the District Court." [28] Having no other implementation alternative, the Supreme Court finally issued its order remanding the cases to the lower tribunals for further action.

The very framework of the questions propounded two years before had made this implementation decision inevitable. And since those questions had been propounded at least two years before, it is certain that the Court had at least half made up its mind by the decision Monday of June 8, 1953. There is much truth in the assertion of Mississippi lawyer Wall that the nine men were "not looking for advice or counsel" from the state attorneys general who argued in the case, "they were looking for somebody to agree with them." [29]

In remanding the cases, the Court, pursuant to question 5(d), had to give "general directions" and indicate the procedures to be followed by the courts below "in arriving at the specific terms of more detailed decrees." Wrote the unanimous Supreme Court: "While giving weight to these public and private considerations, the courts will require that the defendants make a *prompt and reasonable* start toward full compliance with our May 17, 1954, ruling. . . . [T]he cases are remanded to the [lower courts] to take such proceedings and enter such orders and decrees consistent with this opinion as are *necessary and proper* to admit to public schools on a racially nondiscriminatory basis *with all deliberate speed* the parties to these cases." (Emphasis added.)

Again dwelling on "varied local school problems" and "variety of obstacles," the Court assigned to school authorities "the primary responsibility for elucidating, assessing and solving" the extended problems of desegregation. "Courts,"

wrote Chief Justice Warren, "will have to consider whether
the action of school authorities constitutes good faith implementation of the governing constitutional principles." Continuing the outline of "general directions," Warren added:
"Courts of equity may properly take into account the public
interest in the elimination of . . . obstacles in a systematic
and effective manner. But it should go without saying that
the vitality of these constitutional principles cannot be allowed to yield simply because of disagreement with them."

In fashioning the specific terms of its remedy, the Supreme
Court employed a variety of phrases which are not readily
subject to judicial definition. This was perhaps a prerequisite for some measure of Southern co-operation in enforcement. But it is the generality of these phrases which makes
Mr. Justice Jackson's prophecy seem likely—that the outlawing of school segregation would be followed by "a generation of litigation." [30]

DECIDING FIVE CASES

By the time of the implementation decision of May 31,
1955, much had happened in all five of the cases which had
come before the Supreme Court. Desegregation had begun
in the District of Columbia, Delaware and Kansas without
the benefit of an enforcement decree. Virginia and South
Carolina, on the other hand, took advantage of the one-year
gap between decisions to make legal plans for further delays.

Bolling v. *Sharpe,* the case which had arisen in Washington, D. C., had been before the Court a year previously on
a dismissal of the complaint on motion. In its companion
opinion to *Brown* v. *Board of Education* on May 17, 1954,
the Supreme Court held that "racial discrimination in the
public schools of the District of Columbia is a denial of the
due process of law guaranteed by the Fifth Amendment to
the Constitution." [31] Washington, D. C., authorities immedi-

ately put into effect a plan to desegregate public schools in
the District. Shortly thereafter, suit was brought to enjoin
this program. On November 22, 1954, the United States District Court for the District of Columbia rendered judgment
in *Sabine* v. *Sharpe* [32] upholding the school officials and desegregation. The court dismissed plaintiffs' contentions that
no plan could be put into effect until after the final implementation decision of the Supreme Court. Desegregation had
become a reality in the nation's capital.

Gebhart v. *Belton,* the Delaware action, differed considerably from all the other cases. In the cases which had come
to the Supreme Court from Kansas, Virginia and South Carolina, the decision of May 31, 1955, was a step forward on the
road toward desegregation. In *Gebhart* v. *Belton,* however,
the Supreme Court decree had the opposite effect. This was
because the lower courts in Delaware—and only in Delaware—
had previously ordered the immediate admission of Negro
children to what had formerly been all-white schools, and
the two-stage decision of the Supreme Court had the effect
of delaying that admission.

When the case had come before the Supreme Court in
1954, Delaware was the only one of the four states which
did not argue to sustain the validity of its school segregation
laws; the sole contention which was advanced by the state
was that the state courts erred in ordering *immediate* admission. When the case was heard by the Supreme Court in
1955, Delaware had changed its position, and the brief of its
attorney general indicated agreement with the immediate
admission decree previously handed down by the state tribunals.

What delayed desegregation in Delaware were these words
in Chief Justice Warren's opinion: "The judgment in the
Delaware case—ordering the immediate admission of the
plaintiffs to schools previously attended only by white children—is affirmed on the basis of the principles stated in our

May 17, 1954, opinion, but the case is remanded to the Supreme Court of Delaware for such further proceedings as the Court may deem necessary in light of this opinion."

No decision was necessary in *Gebhart* v. *Belton* to supplement the Supreme Court's 1955 implementation decree, and the case never came before the Delaware courts again. But there was another Delaware action in which the state court had the opportunity to express its interpretation of *Brown* v. *Board of Education*—an interpretation which delayed the course of desegregation. After the decision of May 17, 1954, and before the decision of May 31, 1955, *Steiner* v. *Simmons* [33] was appealed to Delaware's highest tribunal. It was a case involving eleven Negro children who had been admitted to a white high school in early September, 1954, and dropped from the rolls before the end of the month. Enrollment was admittedly canceled solely because of race and color. Ten of the pupils filed suit to compel readmittance. The judge in the lower court issued a preliminary injunction, holding that he had the duty of preserving "the legal status quo that he found to exist prior to their expulsion." The Delaware Supreme Court reversed, denying the right to readmission.

Delaware phrased the question this way: "Did the Board of Education of the Milford Special School District have the right to admit these Negro children? If it did, they have the right to remain there. If it did not, they have no legal status which the [court below] was required to protect, and they were not entitled to remain there."

The conclusions of the Delaware high court, handed down on February 8, 1955, were as follows:

"I. The opinion of the Supreme Court of the United States in the Segregation Cases has the present effect of nullifying our segregation laws, but the opinion does not require *immediate* desegregation of the public schools. Until the mandate of the Supreme Court of the United States is received, the state *may* take immediate steps toward desegregation; it is not compelled to do so at the moment.

"II. The State Board of Education of this State, during the past summer, promulgated regulations directing the local boards to submit plans looking to gradual integration in the public schools. These regulations require the approval of the State Board of any such plan, and forbid attempts at desegregation without such approval. They have the force of law throughout the State. The Board of Education of the Milford School District disregarded these regulations, and in admitting the Negro pupils to the school acted without authority of law." [34]

The United States Supreme Court implementation decision of May 31, 1955, followed three months later, giving further approval to decisions permitting gradual desegregation.

The Kansas courts also followed a course of delay. During the summer of 1955, the various plaintiffs in the original case of *Brown* v. *Board of Education* sought the formulation of decrees by the Kansas federal court in accordance with the Supreme Court's mandate. A hearing was held on whether the Board of Education of Topeka had fully complied. Topeka's school superintendent admitted that the plan adopted for the school year 1955-56 did not fully accomplish desegregation, but contended that a good-faith effort had been made toward that end. The lower federal court agreed in a decision rendered October 28, 1955.[35] The Topeka plan was approved. The court retained jurisdiction over the case, however, pending the issuance of final decrees at the time of full compliance.

The Virginia courts took advantage of the opportunity to delay action when, on July 18, 1955, another decision was rendered in *Davis* v. *County School Board of Prince Edward County*.[36] The school authorities were "restrained and enjoined from refusing on account of race or color to admit to any school under their supervision any child qualified to enter such school." But, the court continued, the injunction is to go into effect only after the school board makes "necessary arrangements . . . with all deliberate speed." Plaintiffs had asked for immediate desegregation. The court took the position that its refusal "to require such adjustment and rearrangement to be made in time for the September, 1955, school term is not inconsistent with the public interest or with the decision of the Supreme Court." As in the Kansas case, the court retained jurisdiction for further action.

By far the most bitterly fought of the five original actions was the South Carolina case of *Briggs* v. *Elliott,* which was the first of the suits to reach decision and the first to reach the Supreme Court. It dominated public attention because segregation is so much more prevalent in South Carolina than it is in Kansas, Delaware, the District of Columbia, or even Virginia. It was the case in which the lower court sought to forestall Supreme Court decision at the outset by ordering and supervising action to equalize white and Negro school facilities. And it has been the case involving personalities. When America's leading constitutional advocate, John W. Davis, spoke before the Supreme Court, he did so as counsel for the state of South Carolina. The other outstanding personality in *Briggs* v. *Elliott* is Federal Circuit Judge John J. Parker.

Senior federal judge in the United States, Parker was appointed to his present post on the United States Court of Appeals, Fourth Circuit, in 1925. He was appointed to the United States Supreme Court by President Hoover in the spring of 1930, but the Senate refused to confirm the appointment. Ironically enough, Judge Parker's defeat came at the hands of the NAACP, which, together with the A. F. of L., made claims that Parker was anti-Negro and antilabor. Only those who know him well can testify as to the truth of such charges. Such alleged prejudices are certainly not revealed in his judicial utterances. Above all, Judge Parker is a good lawyer. He is perhaps the outstanding jurist of the South. Other Southern judges take heed of his words and are guided by his views.

Judge Parker wrote the opinion in the first Briggs decision in 1951 which had upheld school segregation under the authority of *Plessy* v. *Ferguson*. When the Supreme Court decided not to hear the case in 1952 and remanded it to obtain the views of the lower tribunal, Judge Parker again wrote the opinion. After the implementation decision of 1955, Judge Parker presided over the court when the third Briggs decision was handed down at the state level. There was no individual opinion rendered by the special three-judge court in the third Briggs case; the decision was *per curiam*, "by the court." This means that the opinion was written by the whole court, rather than by any single judge. There is no doubt, however, that the opinion emanated from Judge Parker and that it is all the more significant because Parker was the presiding judicial officer.

The third Briggs case was decided on July 15, 1955, three days before the Virginia decision in *Davis* v. *County School Board of Prince Edward County*. Significantly, the essential parts of the decrees in the two cases are the same, word for word. The South Carolina school board was likewise enjoined from discriminatory practices *after* it makes "necessary arrangements . . . with all deliberate speed." Jurisdiction was retained for entry of further orders.

More significant were the court's words on the meaning of *Brown* v. *Board of Education*. These words are introduced by a paragraph which has been quoted time and time again by Southern groups which are supporting desegregation efforts. It reads: "Whatever may have been the views of this court as to law when the case was originally before us, it is our duty now to accept the law as declared by the Supreme Court."

What is the law as declared by the Supreme Court? Here are Judges Parker, Dobie and Timmerman on the subject:

"Having said this, it is important that we point out exactly what the Supreme Court has decided and what it has not decided in this case. It has not decided that the federal courts are to take over or regulate the public schools of the states. It has not decided that the states must mix persons of different races in the schools or must require them to attend schools or must deprive them of the right of choosing the schools they attend. What it has decided, and all that it has decided, is that a state may not deny to any person on account of race the right to attend any school that it maintains. This, under the decision of the Supreme Court, the state may not do directly or indirectly; but if the schools which it maintains are open to children of all races, no violation of the Constitution is involved even though the children of different races voluntarily attend different schools, as they attend different churches. Nothing in the Constitution or in the decision of the Supreme Court takes away from the people freedom to choose the schools they attend. The Constitution, in other words, does not require integration. It merely forbids discrimination. It does not forbid such segregation as occurs as the result of voluntary action. It merely forbids the use of governmental power to enforce segregation. The Fourteenth Amendment is a limitation upon the exercise of power by the state or state agencies, not a limitation upon the freedom of individuals." [37]

These are the five cases. Technically, they were the only five cases decided by the Supreme Court on the historic decision Mondays of May 17, 1954, and May 31, 1955. But the Supreme Court had done more than decide just five cases. It had created a precedent.

Chapter 12

BROWN BECOMES A PRECEDENT

In evaluating the influence of *Brown* v. *Board of Education*, consideration must be given to words which are all but hidden in the Supreme Court's opinions. Consideration must also be given to words left unsaid.

The Supreme Court reached decision in five specific cases involving a specific number of Negro plaintiffs and a specific number of school boards and officials designated as parties defendant. For example, *Briggs et al.* v. *Elliott et al.* was not limited to suit between Harry Briggs, Jr., and R. W. Elliott. The *"et al."* which appears after "Briggs" in the title of the case is a shorthand method of designating the other sixty-six Negro children who were plaintiffs in the action. R. W. Elliott was chairman of the board of trustees of School District No. 22 of Clarendon County, South Carolina. The *"et al."* after "Elliott" in the case represents the other members of the board who were named as defendants. When the special three-judge federal court of Parker, Dobie and Timmerman "ordered, adjudged and decreed" on July 15, 1955, they were specifically enjoining the specific defendants in the specific case from permitting racial discrimination in the schools under their supervision. The Supreme Court holding in *Brown* v. *Board of Education* obviously affected the rights and duties of the Negro children and the school officials who were listed as plaintiffs and defendants in the five cases. But what was the meaning of the decision beyond this point?

Probably the narrowest interpretation of the effect of a

judicial declaration of unconstitutionality is found in an 1887 opinion of West Virginia's Supreme Court of Appeals. Said the court: "When, in the course of determining the rights of the parties to a particular suit or controversy, the court finds it necessary to ascertain whether or not a statute is unconstitutional, the court must necessarily pass upon that question; but in doing so it does not annul or repeal the statute. . . . [T]he decision affects the parties only, and there is no judgment against the statute. . . . The parties to that suit are concluded by the judgment, but no one else is bound." [1]

Yet *Brown* v. *Board of Education* has and will have an influence which goes far beyond such a restricted interpretation. Far more persons are affected by the decisions than Brown, Briggs, Bolling, Belton, Davis and the more than a hundred other Negro children designated by the *et al.* The question, however, is "how?"

How does the decision affect Negro pupils in the public schools of District No. 22 of Clarendon County, South Carolina, who were *not* parties to the action?

How does the decision affect other school children and other school boards in South Carolina?

How does the decision affect Negro children and public school authorities outside of Kansas, Delaware, South Carolina, Virginia and the District of Columbia?

How does the decision affect school segregation in public colleges and universities?

How does the decision affect private schools?

How will the decision be applied to transportation, public accommodations and housing?

CLASS SUITS

In its 1954 decision outlawing school segregation, the Supreme Court employed the following language: ". . . we

hold that the plantiffs and others similarly situated for whom
the actions have been brought. . . ." Two sentences later,
the Supreme Court gave its reasons for postponing implementation until the following year. The opening words were:
"Because these are class actions."

Authority to institute class actions is granted by the Federal Rules of Civil Procedure.[2] Paraphrasing the provisions
of Rule 23(a)(3), the complaints in the various actions had a
paragraph similar to the one in the original Brown case before the federal district court. It read: "Plaintiffs bring this
action on their own behalf and also on behalf of all citizens
similarly situated and affected, pursuant to Rule 23(a) of the
Federal Rules of Civil Procedure, there being common questions of law and fact affecting the rights of all Negro citizens
of the United States similarly situated who reside in cities in
the state of Kansas in which separate public schools are maintained for white and Negro children of public school age,
and who are so numerous as to make it impracticable to
bring them all before the Court." [3]

The five cases were indeed class actions. As such, the decisions rendered in *Brown* v. *Board of Education* affected not
only the plaintiffs involved in the litigation but also others
in the same "class"—those similarly situated. This was recognized by the Supreme Court. The question was the extent
to which the decisions recognized the constitutional right of
some "other" Negro children—or all Negro children—to attend racially desegregated schools.

The various complaints appear to restrict the words "similarly situated" to Negro pupils residing in the same states in
which the actions were brought. The NAACP position, on
the other hand, was that all Negro pupils who were required
to attend segregated schools were "similarly situated," and
that the decrees for the plaintiffs in the five cases were, at the
same time, decrees in favor of all Negro school children.

While the various suits met the requirements of a class action under Rule 23(a)(3), it does not necessarily follow that the decrees in the cases should be extended to all members of the "class." It is arguable that the decisions should be limited to those who individually identify themselves with the proceedings, either as original complainants or as later "intervening" plaintiffs. Yale Law Professor James William Moore, one of the drafters of the Federal Rules, discusses this question in his comprehensive work on federal practice. He believes that 23(a)(3) is "an invitation to joinder," rather than a "command performance," and that the decree "binds only those actually before the court." [4] A number of cases support this view, holding that in a class action based upon the existence of a "common question of law or fact," relief is limited to those who come before the court.

One of the government briefs, however, points out that these cases have generally involved actions for damages. "The consideration that damages will vary from plaintiff to plaintiff has apparently been a practical consideration in inducing the holding that the effect of the decision will be confined to those who come into the proceeding," said the Department of Justice. "In 'common question' cases in which relief of an equitable nature is sought, the courts have manifested a greater disposition to extend the benefits of the decree to absent members of a successful plaintiff class." [5]

One of the cases cited by the government in support of this position was a class action against public school authorities in California to compel the admission of five named plaintiffs and some five thousand other Mexican children "similarly situated." The court gave injunctive relief, restraining discriminatory practices not only against the plaintiffs but against "pupils of Mexican descent in the public schools of defendant school districts." [6]

In another representative action,[7] suit was brought to compel the admission of Negroes to a municipal junior college in Kentucky. The court entered judgment on behalf of the

named plaintiffs. Ten months later, two Negroes who had
not been complainants in the original action sought to intervene, that is, become parties to the action; they argued that
they too had been denied admission solely because of race.
The defendant contended that the action was not a proper
class suit because "the persons constituting the alleged class
[were] not so numerous as to make it impractical to bring
them all before the court." The defendant maintained that
the motion to intervene was not "timely." The federal court
rejected these arguments, and permitted plaintiffs to intervene.

Federal Rule 24(b)(2) provides: "Upon timely application
anyone may be permitted to intervene in an action . . .
when an applicant's claim or defense and the main action
have a question of law or fact in common." The timeliness
of the motion is a matter for the discretion of the court,
based upon considerations of "whether the intervention will
unduly delay or prejudice the adjudication of the rights of
the original parties."

Various courts have interpreted this rule in various ways.
There is authority for the proposition that the right to intervene is cut off prior to trial; there are cases which hold that
the right still exists a reasonable time after judgment.[8] No
motions to intervene were brought in the five cases which
made up *Brown* v. *Board of Education,* but it is reasonably
certain that they could have been granted. Intervening
parties would certainly not "delay or prejudice" the determination of the issues or the rights of the original litigants.

The reason why no additional parties have sought to intervene is simply that the actions have been recognized as class
suits in the important South Carolina and Virginia decisions.
The implementation decisions in *Briggs* v. *Elliott* and *Davis*
v. *County School Board of Prince Edward County* [9] contained
decrees phrased in nearly identical language. The defendants
in both cases were enjoined from refusing on account of race

to admit to any school under their supervision "any child qualified to enter such school." The decrees were not restricted to the plaintiffs in the actions; other Negro children in the same school districts were afforded the same relief. Others "similarly situated" were given the same rights as the Negro children who had brought suit back in 1951 and 1952. The decrees, however, said nothing about other school boards and other school officials. Nor could they. No other school authorities were involved in the disputes, and the plaintiffs obviously could not have obtained the relief they sought from boards of education in other districts.

The effects of *Brown* v. *Board of Education* were of two types. The plaintiffs (and members in plaintiffs' class) and the defendants who were parties to the litigation were immediately bound by the decision of the Supreme Court. This direct consequence of a judicial judgment is referred to by lawyers as the "law of the case." And the law of the case in *Brown* v. *Board of Education* was a command to the school officials in the Briggs and Davis disputes to proceed with all deliberate speed in ending the practice of segregation in the schools under their jurisdictions.

For other Negro plaintiffs to obtain similar relief, other legal actions against other school authorities would be necessary. In this situation, of course, the law of the case would be inapplicable; there would be no direct Supreme Court order to the lower tribunals. In the subsequent cases, the courts would be bound by the indirect, precedent effect of *Brown* v. *Board of Education*. Several new cases arose in South Carolina and Virginia following the decrees in the Briggs and Davis cases, and the courts consistently followed the precedent of May 17, 1954, in resolving the controversies between other Negro children and other school boards.

OTHER SCHOOLS AND OTHER CASES

There have been differing reactions to the Supreme Court's decisions in the twenty-two jurisdictions which, prior to May 17, 1954, permitted or required racial segregation in the public schools. Segregation was never a major issue in Arizona, Kansas, New Mexico and Wyoming—the four states which merely *permitted* its practice—and it has, for all practical purposes, disappeared. And desegregation is now the rule in the District of Columbia.

Affirmative action to curtail racial discrimination in the public schools has also been taken by the courts in Arkansas, Delaware, Kentucky, Maryland, Missouri, Oklahoma, Tennessee, Texas and West Virginia.

In 1955, a federal court in Kentucky [10] ordered the admission of Negro pupils to certain county public schools by February, 1956, and decreed that integration be made effective at the elementary school level by the opening of the 1956-57 term. In January, 1956, a federal district judge in West Virginia issued orders in two cases,[11] providing in substance for the admission of as many Negro students "as there is room to admit" during the 1956 spring term—and a complete end to segregation by the opening of the new school year the following September. And in January, 1956, Federal Judge Robert L. Taylor decreed [12] that a "definite" and "reasonable" date for the desegregation in Tennessee's Clinton High School was the fall term of 1956. It was this last decision which marked the beginnings of a series of riots, court actions in response to riots and riots in response to court actions which dominated the headlines through 1956 and 1957.

The same type of result—via a different legal procedure—was achieved in Arkansas and Maryland. On June 25, 1955, the directors of the Hoxie School District in Arkansas made an official finding that all administrative obstacles to integration had been removed. They proceeded to put their desegregation plan into effect. Such organizations as White America, Inc., White Citizens Council of Arkansas and Citizens Committee Representing Segregation in the Hoxie Schools objected. School authorities brought suit in the federal court seeking to enjoin these groups from interfering with their desegregation program. A preliminary injunction was issued in October, 1955,[13] and made permanent ten weeks later.[14]

In Maryland, the pro-segregation faction brought suit [15] against the school officials. A group of Baltimore citizens petitioned the Superior Court of Baltimore City in 1954 for an order compelling the board of school commissioners to continue its former race segregation policy. The petition was denied. Holding that the 1954 decision was binding as to the unconstitutionality of separate schools, the court ruled that the board was acting within its authority in commencing desegregation.

These decisions, however, tell only one part of the story. These are decisions from Kentucky, West Virginia, Arkansas and Maryland. These are cases which have received, and which will receive, judicial approval in Delaware, Missouri and Oklahoma. These are cases which affect the border states and the states which have Northern and Western traditions mixed with their Southern attitudes. They must be accepted for what they are; the dictates of judges who are giving commands to those who, in large measure, are willing and able to give obedience. These are not cases which control the course of decision in the strong pro-segregation states of the deep South.

The states of Alabama, Georgia and Mississippi, joined by South Carolina, Virginia and Louisiana, have been actively engaged in a legal delaying action against desegregation. Despite this legal battle, however, there were some decisions from the deep South showing compliance with the rulings in *Brown* v. *Board of Education*. The implementation decrees in the Briggs case from South Carolina and the Davis case from Virginia had prohibited the defendant school boards from making racial restrictions in their admission policies. Even more important was the Louisiana case of *Bush* v. *Orleans Parish School Board*,[16] decided in early 1956—the first case to rule on an obvious, admitted attempt to avoid the consequences of *Brown* v. *Board of Education*. The decree in the Louisiana case enjoined the Orleans Parish School Board from requiring or permitting racial segregation in the schools under their supervision, "from and after such time as may be necessary to make arrangements for admission of children to such schools on a racially nondiscriminatory basis with all deliberate speed as required by the decision of the Supreme Court."

The conflict between personal emotion and legal responsibility rings out in the words of the opinion: "The problems attendant desegregation in the deep South are considerably more serious than generally appreciated in some sections of our country. The problem of changing a people's mores, particularly those with an emotional overlay, is not to be taken lightly. It is a problem which will require the utmost patience, understanding, generosity and forbearance from all of us, of whatever race. But the magnitude of the problem may not nullify the principle. And that principle is that we are, all of us, freeborn Americans, with a right to make our way, unfettered by sanctions imposed by man, because of the work of God." [17]

Another significant post-implementation decision was the one handed down on Columbus Day, 1955, by the Supreme Court of Texas. The case was *McKinney* v. *Blankenship*.[18] In the background of the action was an order of the board of trustees of the Big Springs School District integrating white and Negro students in grades one through six in the elementary schools. Various Big Springs residents and representatives of a Dallas group brought suit against the school board and other state officers. The attorney general of Texas intervened and aligned the state *against* the school board. Plaintiffs sought a declaratory judgment sustaining the validity of provisions in Texas's constitution and statutory code which required segregation in the public schools. They also sought to enjoin state expenditure of "public free school funds" for any but segregated schools.

In reaching decision, the nine-judge court concurred [19] in a statement which should have great influence in extending the scope of *Brown* v. *Board of Education* beyond the five jurisdictions involved in the actual litigation. Said the Texas Supreme Court: "At the threshold of our consideration of the issues in this case we are met with the argument that since the constitutional and statutory provisions requiring segregation in Texas schools were not before the Supreme Court in the Brown case they were not condemned and we should hold them valid and enforceable. That proposition is so utterly without merit that we overrule it without further discussion, except to say that Section 2 of Article VII [*sic*] [20] of the Constitution of the United States declares: 'This Constitution and the laws of the United States which shall be made in pursuance thereof, * * * shall be the supreme law of the land; and the judges in every state shall be bound thereby, anything in the Constitutions or laws of any state to the contrary notwithstanding.' " [21]

Dividing the challenged constitutional and statutory provisions into parts, the Texas court ruled them unconstitutional only to the extent that they required racial segregation in the public schools. Such clauses as "impartial provision shall be made for both races" were declared to retain their validity. Having reached this conclusion, the court held that no funds of the school district were being expended in a manner inconsistent with the *valid* provisions of the constitution and statutes, and refused to enjoin appropriations for desegregated schools.

Federal district courts in Texas have shown less reverence for *Brown* v. *Board of Education.* In *Bell* v. *Rippy,*[22] Negro school children in Dallas sought judicial action to compel enrollment in any one of a number of white schools which had denied them admission. Decision was reached on September 16, 1955, nearly four months after the Supreme Court issued its implementation decrees.

Denying the requested injunction, the district court employed some surprising language: "It appears from the facts, of which the court has judicial knowledge, that the premises, conveniences, teaching, and efficiency for the colored student is furnished by the same Texas and Independent School funds as are furnished to the white students. The number of schools for the colored population is a slightly higher percentage than that furnished for the white population.

"All of the law as declared by the various courts, appellate and trial, in the United States, are agreed upon the proposition that when similar and convenient free schools are furnished to both white and colored that there then exists no reasonable ground for requiring desegregation. . . .

". . . the direction from the Supreme Court of the United States required that the officers and principles of each institution, and the lower courts, shall do away with segregation after having worked out a proper plan. That direction does not mean that a long time shall expire before that plan is agreed upon. It may be that the plan contemplates action by the state legislature. It is not for this court to say, other than what has been said by the Supreme Court in that decision." [*Sic.*]

No "plan" was presented to the court; none existed; none was requested. Despite these facts, the opinion concluded: "To grant an injunction in this case would be to ignore the equities that present themselves for recognition and to determine what the Supreme Court itself decided not to determine. Therefore, I think it appropriate that this case be dismissed without prejudice to refile it at some later date."

Another Texas case, *Jackson* v. *Rawdon*,[23] was brought as a class action by three Negro students seeking immediate enrollment in the Mansfield rural district high school at the edge of Fort Worth. To begin with, the federal court held that a class suit was "indiscriminate if not improper" since only twelve colored students could possibly be involved. Much was made of this fact, the court taking it for granted that the other nine Negroes did not wish to bring suit at that time. Activities of the local school board—"studying articles in magazines and papers; holding numerous meetings; passing resolutions and appointing a committee to work on a plan for integration," conferring with plaintiffs, making arrangements for the Negroes to attend a Fort Worth school and providing a bus to transport them to and from the school—were held to constitute a "good-faith effort toward integration." The court pointed out that plaintiffs had already begun the fall term at the Fort Worth high school and concluded that an injunction compelling immediate admission to the rural school would be unjust to all parties concerned.

Appearing between parentheses in the opinion was a rather startling observation: ". . . school board composed primarily of farmers, agents of the State of Texas (whose segregation laws were not voided by the state Supreme Court until the opinion of October 12 and mandate issued October 28, 1955, after the opening of school on September 2, 1955) struggling with . . ." [24]

October 12, 1955, was the date the Texas Supreme Court rendered its decision in *McKinney* v. *Blankenship*. Was it the view of the federal court in Texas that the action in the *McKinney* case was *necessary* to declare the unconstitutionality of Texas's school segregation laws? In its implementation decision in 1955, the United States Supreme Court said it had already declared "The fundamental principle that racial discrimination in public education is unconstitutional." And it then proceeded with the statement that "all provisions of federal, state or local law requiring or permitting such discrimination must yield to this principle." Was this not a sufficient declaration of the unconstitutionality of Texas's school segregation laws? Had it become the duty of the highest tribunal in every state to rephrase and reapply the mandate of *Brown* v. *Board of Education* to its own constitution, statutes and ordinances? Was racial segregation in the public schools of Texas a proper course of action under the authority of valid law until the state's highest tribunal ruled otherwise on October 12, 1955?

The parenthetical observation in *Jackson* v. *Rawdon* is not good law. School segregation laws in the state of Texas had become invalid long before October 12, 1955—sixteen months before, to be almost exact. Yet the observation served as a reminder of the difference between the declaration of a "right" and the framing of a "remedy" to give effect to that "right." *Brown* v. *Board of Education* was not a decision *in vacuo;* it had declared unconstitutional *per se* all statutes requiring or permitting racial segregation in the schools. But it left to other tribunals the responsibility of determining which education laws rested on a discriminatory classification, and whether any education laws still existed under which public funds could be used to maintain a public school system. *McKinney* v. *Blankenship* was not necessary to declare the unconstitutionality of pro-segregation laws, but it was far from an idle judicial exercise.

As was to be expected, neither of these two federal district court decisions was long to remain the "law of the case." Both *Bell* v. *Rippy* and *Jackson* v. *Rawdon* were soon before the United States Court of Appeals for the Fifth Circuit—the circuit which reviews federal district court judgments in the states of Alabama, Florida, Georgia, Louisiana, Mississippi and Texas. And both of the lower court decisions were reversed. *Bell* v. *Rippy* (with the name of the case changed to *Brown* v. *Rippy*) [25] was remanded to the district court for an immediate hearing to determine whether the Dallas school authorities were proceeding toward desegregation with all deliberate speed. An even stronger decision was rendered by the appellate court in *Jackson* v. *Rawdon*.[26] This case was remanded to the lower tribunal with specific instructions governing the future action of the Mansfield Independent School District. There is only one high school in Mansfield, Texas, and the district court ruled that refusal of the school board to admit the plaintiffs on account of their race or color was unlawful.

While the decisions of May 17, 1954, and May 31, 1955, were solely concerned with public education at the primary and secondary school levels, the influence of *Brown* v. *Board of Education* could not help but extend to disputes involving racial discrimination in the colleges and universities. The two-stage decision in *Brown* v. *Board of Education* gave approval to the idea of delay. Southern lawyers were to argue this approach in the higher education controversies.

The important case in this area is *Florida, ex rel. Hawkins* v. *Board of Control*,[27] which had been held for consideration by the Supreme Court until its May 24, 1954, decision. Litigation involved a group of Negro students who had sought and been denied admission to the College of Law of the University of Florida. Suit was predicated on the fact that the university is a tax-supported institution—and on the contention that enrollment had been refused solely on racial grounds. The Supreme Court granted certiorari, vacated the judgment of the Florida Supreme Court, and remanded the case "for consideration in the light of the Segregation Cases decided May 17, 1954 . . . and conditions that now prevail." [28]

When the Hawkins litigation was first before the state courts in 1950 and 1951, admission was denied on the basis of the separate but equal doctrine. Reaffirming the principle of *Plessy* v. *Ferguson,* the Florida position was stated in these words: "There was available to him adequate opportunity for legal education at the Law School of the Florida A. & M. University, an institution supported by the State of Florida for the higher education of negroes, and . . . although the facilities were not identical, they were substantially equal and were sufficient to satisfy his rights. . . ." [29]

The remand order of the United States Supreme Court was a clear invitation to Florida to apply the lessons of *Brown* v. *Board of Education* to cases involving colleges and universities. On October 19, 1955, the seven judges of the state's highest tribunal again reviewed the Hawkins dispute and unanimously agreed that it was their "inescapable duty" to follow the decisions in the Brown cases. They even struck down the pro-segregation argument that "the adverse psychological effect on Negro children on which the case of *Brown* v. *Board of Education* . . . rested would have no application to the petitioner who is a college graduate and 48 years of age." [30] The Florida Supreme Court, at least in principle, had opened the doors of its state university to all qualified students, regardless of race. But this did not mean that a decree would be granted ordering the immediate admission of Hawkins to the law school.

The Board of Control of the University of Florida urged delay. Arguing in the language used by Chief Justice Warren in the Brown cases, the school authorities made pointed use of such phrases as "grave and serious problems," "serious conflicts" and "numerous adjustments and changes." Here, they struck a responsive chord. Five of the seven Florida judges found in the implementation decision of May 31, 1955, a way to postpone desegregation and avoid *Sweatt* v. *Painter* and the other college and university cases decided by

the Vinson Court in 1948 and 1950. They took the view that
there was no duty to order Hawkins' law school admission
"immediately or at any particular time in the future." On
the contrary, the majority asserted that "the clear import of
this [1955] decision—and, indeed, its express direction—is
that the state courts shall apply equitable principles in the
determination of the precise time in any given jurisdiction
when members of the negro race shall be admitted to white
schools." A commissioner was designated to serve as special
master in taking testimony for the court, to help determine
an effective date for the admission of colored students to the
law school.

Two judges registered protest. They saw no need for delay.
Their conclusion: If Hawkins had the necessary qualifications, "he should be admitted to the College of Law of the
University of Florida under the same rules and regulations,
and upon the same conditions, that a white person would be
admitted."

Concurring with the majority in all but the issue of delay,
the dissenting justices spoke with much stronger language in
applying the dictates of the Brown decisions to college and
university cases. The limited technical holding of May 17,
1954, was raised as a straw man, only to be knocked down
again. "While it might be suggested," began the dissenters,
"that the principle . . . is not binding upon us, under the
facts of the case at bar, because the cause in which the principle was stated involved grade and high schools and not institutions of higher learning, we think that a close analysis of
the opinion in the Brown case, and of the decisions upon
which the Court bottomed its conclusion, make it plain that
the principle was meant to apply to public schools at all
levels." And in support of this position they cited *Sweatt* v.
Painter and the other graduate school cases decided prior to
1954.

"While it is elementary," said the dissenters, "that the

opinion and judgment dated May 31, 1955, is binding only upon the parties that were actually involved in the cases in which it was entered, it cannot be doubted that in the rendition of its opinion and judgment the [Supreme Court] laid down certain principles and rules which we must follow in the instant case in determining the nature of the relief that should be afforded. . . ." [31]

Five months later, *Florida, ex rel. Hawkins* v. *Board of Control* [32] was again the subject of Supreme Court decision. The nine men expressed their displeasure with the majority view of the Florida tribunal—and with the vagueness of their own instructions to the state court nearly two years before. "Accordingly," read the Supreme Court's *per curiam* order of March 12, 1956, "the mandate of May 24, 1954, is recalled and is vacated." The Court clarified its decisions in *Brown* v. *Board of Education:* ". . . we did not imply that decrees involving graduate study present the problems of public elementary and secondary schools." Again the case was remanded. This time the instructions were clear: "As this case involves the admission of a Negro to a graduate professional school, there is no reason for delay. He is entitled to prompt admission under the rules and regulations applicable to other qualified candidates."

Florida, ex rel. Hawkins v. *Board of Control* is thus an amalgam of *Sweatt* v. *Painter* and *Brown* v. *Board of Education.* In *Sweatt* v. *Painter* and the other college and university cases decided prior to 1954, the "separate" facilities provided for Negroes were admittedly not "equal," in terms of faculties, libraries and physical plants. And because of this admitted inequality, the Supreme Court ordered the immediate enrollment of Negroes in schools of their choice without the necessity of overruling the *Plessy* v. *Ferguson* principle.

In *Brown* v. *Board of Education,* the Supreme Court ruled that "separate" facilities in the public elementary and high schools were "inherently unequal." In the unanimous view of the Warren Court, inequality exists regardless of efforts to equalize the faculties, libraries and physical plants of white and Negro elementary and high schools. The Hawkins case extended this principle of *Brown* v. *Board of Education* to the field of higher education, making segregation unconstitutional *per se* in *all* public schools.

The right declared in *Brown* v. *Board of Education,* however, was not an immediate right as in *Sweatt* v. *Painter* and the other higher education cases. The Supreme Court decisions of May 17, 1954, and May 31, 1955, sanctioned reasonable delay in elementary and high school desegregation because of the "considerable complexity" of the problems involved. The final word of the Supreme Court in the Hawkins case, however, followed the principle of *Sweatt* v. *Painter* in declaring that in higher education "there is no reason for delay."

Chapter *13*

TREND OF DECISION

Brown v. *Board of Education* was not long confined to the legal pigeonhole labeled "school segregation." Overriding the contentions of Southern counsel, the various courts—including the Supreme Court—have refused to limit the mandates of May 17, 1954, and May 31, 1955, to specific holdings and specific facts. Within two years after "Black Monday," a score and more of judicial decisions had recorded the wide swath which the Brown case had cut in other areas of racial segregation: in transportation, housing, parks and recreational facilities. The reasoning of *Brown* v. *Board of Education* had signaled the end of racial discrimination by law in the United States.

Some of this was inevitable. Education is not restricted to the classroom. Public school integration automatically calls for the desegregation of extracurricular activities connected with the learning process. It also calls for an end to the separation of whites and Negroes on their way to and from, as well as within, the schoolhouse. Desegregated schoolrooms represent but lip-service compliance while school buses remain segregated—and especially when limited transportation may be kept limited as a practical means of thwarting integration decrees.

South Carolina's Byrnes sees "practical difficulties" flowing from a broad interpretation of the desegregation decisions. "Today," he argues, "high schools in the South are more social institutions than in the past. There is a cafeteria where all students lunch together. There is a gymnasium where students of both sexes engage in various sports. Athletic contests, as a rule, are held at night. Students, following the team, travel in school buses. When the races have been accustomed to separation in buses, who can assure there will not be serious consequences." [1]

Regardless of "practical difficulties," however, there is no serious legal argument that *Brown* v. *Board of Education* is limited to the schoolroom, or even the schoolhouse. The nine men made that clear when they reaffirmed the language used in the higher education cases four years before. "[I]n finding that a segregated law school for Negroes could not provide them equal educational opportunities, this Court relied in large part on 'those qualities which are incapable of objective measurement but which make for greatness in a law school.' . . . [I]n requiring that a Negro admitted to a white graduate school be treated like all other students, [the Court] again resorted to intangible considerations: '. . . his ability to study, to engage in discussions and exchange views with other students, and, in general, to learn his profession.' Such considerations apply with added force to children in grade and high schools." So wrote Chief Justice Warren on May 17, 1954.

Exactly one week after "Black Monday," the Supreme Court rendered three *per curiam* decisions extending the effect of *Brown* v. *Board of Education* beyond the borders of public school segregation. Two of those cases were in the field of higher education; [2] the third was concerned with the use of golf courses, swimming pools, athletic facilities and an amphitheater in the city parks of Louisville, Kentucky.[3] All three of those decisions were duly recorded on the same page of the official *United States Reports*. All three contained the identical forty words and six numbers. All three remanded the controversies in issue to the lower courts "for consideration in the light of the Segregation Cases decided May 17, 1954 . . . and conditions that now prevail."

While no subsequent decision was rendered in the Kentucky parks case, the omission is not significant. Other courts and other cases have opened public parks, public golf courses and public beaches to members of the colored race, all on the authority of the school segregation opinions. It has happened in Georgia, Texas and Virginia, as well as in Maryland, Tennessee and, of course, Kentucky.

The landmark case in this area is the bathing-beach dispute of *Mayor and City Council of Baltimore City* v. *Dawson,*[4] affirmed by the Supreme Court on November 7, 1955. The action, based on the "separate but equal" doctrine of *Plessy* v. *Ferguson* and two lower court decisions dealing directly with public recreation, had originally been dismissed in the federal district court.

In his studied analysis of segregation in public recreation, Professor McKay explained the lower court determination in these words: "Principally in reliance on the fact that these cases had not been overruled expressly or by necessary implication in the [Brown] decision, District Judge Thomsen upheld the continued practice of segregation in state and municipal recreation. In thus preserving the validity of the 'separate but equal' doctrine in this area, he noted that the practice of segregation may be continued where (1) there is a proper governmental objective; (2) the regulation is reasonably calculated to achieve that objective; and (3) the separate facilities are 'substantially equal, inherently as well as physically, or the field of governmental activity in which the classification on segregation is made is so unimportant that no substantial rights under the Fourteenth Amendment are involved.' "[5]

Plaintiffs appealed—and here is what the Fourth Circuit Court (comprising the states of Maryland, North Carolina, South Carolina, Virginia and West Virginia) said on March

14, 1955: "Our view is that the authority of these cases was swept away by the subsequent decisions of the Supreme Court. . . . It is now obvious . . . that segregation cannot be justified as a means to preserve the public peace merely because the tangible facilities furnished to one race are equal to those furnished to the other. The Supreme Court expressed the opinion in *Brown* v. *Board of Education* . . . that it must consider public education in the light of its full development and its present place in American life, and . . . must also take into account the psychological factors recognized at this time, including the feeling of inferiority generated in the hearts and minds of Negro children, when separated solely because of their race from those of similar age and qualification." Then came the even more significant statement:

"With this in mind, it is obvious that racial segregation in recreational activities can no longer be sustained as a proper exercise of the police power of the State, for if that power cannot be invoked to sustain racial segregation in the schools, where attendance is compulsory and racial friction may be apprehended from the enforced comingling of the races, it cannot be sustained with respect to public beach and bathhouse facilities, the use of which is entirely optional." [6]

Squarely before the Supreme Court were two widely divergent interpretations of the meaning of *Brown* v. *Board of Education*. By reversing the court of appeals (thus agreeing with the district court) the nine men would have been making a distinction between school segregation and other types of racial classification. They would have been saying, in effect, that school segregation statutes are unconstitutional only because they are "unreasonable"—or that school segregation is invalid *per se,* but that segregation by race might be constitutionally justified in fields other than education.

But the Supreme Court did not reverse Judge Parker's court. On November 7, 1955, the nine men specifically af-

firmed the decision of the court of appeals and the interpretation of *Brown* v. *Board of Education* contained in that
decision. All racial classification had been held unconstitutional *per se.*

Within a year, four similar decisions were handed down
in Virginia, Texas, Kentucky and Tennessee.

Also taking the position that the " 'separate but equal' doctrine was abolished by the United States Supreme Court in
the recent school segregation cases," a federal district court
in Virginia used this language: "Furthermore, the 'separate
but equal' doctrine as applied to the enjoyment of public
beaches and bathhouses maintained by public authorities
was abolished by this Circuit in *Dawson* v. *Mayor and City
Council of Baltimore City.* . . . It follows that state parks,
even where 'separate but equal' facilities exist, are governed
by the same general principles. The recent decisions merely
show the *inevitable trend* to be followed by any District
Judge obligated by the oath of his office to uphold the Constitution and laws of the United States. Such an oath is paramount to the aims, desires and criticisms of any individuals,
regardless of race. . . . Certainly it is true that if members
of the Negro race are to be granted relief in swimming pool
cases, there is even more logical reasoning in affording like
remedies to Negro citizens in state park cases." [7]

Citing the Dawson case, together with a Florida decision
which is not important to this discussion,[8] and the action of
the Supreme Court in remanding the Louisville, Kentucky,
parks dispute, a Texas federal court had this to say: "It is
true that the School Segregation Cases expressly overrule
Plessy v. *Ferguson* only insofar as it applied to the field of
public education, but it seems clear to me that [these other
decisions] are strong indications that *Plessy* v. *Ferguson* will
not, and should not, be held to be controlling in the public
recreational field. If the provisions for equal tangible facilities in the field of public education do not eliminate intan-

gible or psychological discrimination in the field of public education, how can it reasonably be said the equality in tangibles in the field of public recreation eliminates psychological factors so clearly involved in segregation based upon the color of a man's skin? It can, of course, be argued that the intangibles are less effective in the public recreational field than in the field of public education, but that is to say that a little discrimination is to be condoned, but a great deal should be condemned. If the reasoning in the School Segregation Cases concerning psychological factors is sound as it relates to public education, then it must necessarily apply to the field of public recreation." [9]

Based on the authority of the Dawson case, the court of appeals of Kentucky [10] and a Tennessee federal district court [11] ordered desegregation in public parks and public golf courses respectively. Only the Tennessee tribunal qualified its decision by "allowing a reasonable time for defendants to make the necessary arrangements to comply." By so doing, the Tennessee court was willing to recognize the "personal" constitutional right of the Negro plaintiffs, but, following the strict holding of *Brown* v. *Board of Education*, refused to say that the right was also "present." Accordingly, until a "reasonable time" had elapsed from decision date, the Fourteenth Amendment would not become effective in forbidding the exclusion of Negroes from Tennessee's public parks.

These cases represented comparatively easy victories for the desegregation forces. Not so the Georgia dispute of *Holmes* v. *City of Atlanta*. Four decisions were handed down in the course of litigation. On July 8, 1954,[12] the federal district court found that municipal golf courses had not been furnished for the colored, and ordered the city to permit Negroes to share existing facilities on a "substantially equal basis." Segregation was to be permitted. In the Brown case, according to the court, "the doctrine of 'separate but equal'

was rejected only as it applied to public education." The
decision was affirmed [13] by the United States Court of Appeals
for the Fifth Circuit nearly a year later, on June 17, 1955.
The Supreme Court said "no." On November 7, 1955,[14] the
nine men vacated the judgments below and ordered the district court to enter a decree in conformity with the Dawson
decision. Compliance was effected on December 22, 1955,[15]
when the lower court enjoined "any distinction on account
of race or color" on the Atlanta golf courses and "further
ordered that this judgment and decree take effect immediately." Thus the federal court in Georgia—unlike the federal
court in Tennessee—made the constitutional right involved
both personal *and* present.

Before the nine men could act in the Georgia golf course
controversy, a housing dispute had come before the federal
district court [16] sitting in Savannah. Relying in substantial
measure upon the decision of the federal court in Atlanta,
the Savannah tribunal denied the plaintiffs' plea for admission to a white public housing project. Reasoned the court:
". . . the Three (3) colored housing projects in Savannah
are equal in kind to the Three (3) white housing projects in
Savannah," and "the legal doctrine of separate but equal
facilities is still the law of the land and controls this case." [17]

Contrary decisions of two types have been rendered in Missouri [18] and Michigan.[19] Both courts cited *Brown* v. *Board of
Education* as authority for their determinations—but with a
difference. Missouri relied upon the Supreme Court mandate
of May 17, 1954, in immediately enjoining St. Louis housing
authorities from segregating tenants on the basis of race;
Michigan cited the decrees of May 31, 1955, as precedent for
permitting Detroit housing authorities to proceed with "all
deliberate speed" in the transition from segregation to integration. While no further decisions have as yet been reported
in the Savannah dispute, it seems unlikely that the appellate

tribunals will allow the present judgment to stand. The Dawson bathing-beach case has set too strong a precedent.

Save for the lower court decisions in Georgia, the judicial opinions since May 17, 1954, have reflected a clear, steady trend toward total desegregation. Yet there was some technical legal support for the Georgia position. *Brown* v. *Board of Education* was a case involving school segregation, and school segregation only. It did not overrule *Plessy* v. *Ferguson*. It could not. *Plessy* v. *Ferguson* was a case involving public transportation, not public schools. The nine men said only that "separate but equal" as set forth in *Plessy* v. *Ferguson* "has no place" in public education.

Discounted, discredited or studiously avoided in every discrimination controversy which came before the Supreme Court in the two and one-half years following *Brown* v. *Board of Education,* the case of *Plessy* v. *Ferguson* still remained a barrier in the path of total desegregation. Southern lawyers— and a few Southern judges—refused to recognize the fact that *Brown* v. *Board of Education* had declared all racial classifications unconstitutional *per se,* and attempted to limit the impact of that decision to cases involving the public schools.

Since only in a transportation case could the nine men overrule the "separate but equal" doctrine of *Plessy* v. *Ferguson,* the legal profession watched with interest as bus cases from South Carolina and Alabama began the course of trial and appeal which would lead to Supreme Court decision.

The cases were *Flemming* v. *South Carolina Electric and Gas Company* and the famous Montgomery, Alabama, case of *Gayle* v. *Browder.*

The Flemming dispute was the first to reach the courts. A Negro woman sued a bus company for damages because a bus driver made her change her seat in accordance with South Carolina's segregation laws. Federal District Court Judge George Bell Timmerman, Sr., dismissed the action,[20] contending that the state statutes complained of were valid

under *Plessy* v. *Ferguson*. The appeal arrived for decision
before the Fourth Circuit Court of Appeals on July 14, 1955.
A *per curiam* opinion was rendered,[21] reversing the lower
court action and remanding the case for further proceedings
in accordance with the judgment of the appellate tribunal.
Judge John J. Parker presided. Wrote the court: "We do
not think that the separate but equal doctrine of *Plessy* v.
Ferguson . . . can any longer be regarded as a correct statement of the law. That case recognizes segregation of the races
by common carriers as being governed by the same principles as segregation in the public schools, and the recent decisions in *Brown* v. *Board of Education* . . . which relate to
public schools, leave no doubt that the separate but equal
doctrine approved in *Plessy* v. *Ferguson* has been repudi-
ated. That the principle applied in the school cases should
be applied in cases involving transportation, appears quite
clearly. . . ."

This decision was immediately appealed to the United
States Supreme Court. In April, 1956,[22] however, the Supreme Court ruled that the appeal had been prematurely
brought, and refused to hear the case until it had been reconsidered in Judge Timmerman's court.

Six weeks later, while the Flemming case was still before
Judge Timmerman, came the first opinion in *Gayle* v.
Browder. A special three-judge district court heard the case
and concluded—with one judge dissenting—that Judge Parker's court was right. "We cannot in good conscience," wrote
the majority, "perform our duty as judges by blindly following the precedent of *Plessy* v. *Ferguson* . . . when our study
leaves us in complete agreement with the fourth circuit's
opinion in *Flemming* v. *South Carolina Electric and Gas
Company* . . . that the separate but equal doctrine can no
longer be safely followed as a correct statement of the law.
In fact, we think that *Plessy* v. *Ferguson* has been impliedly
though not explicitly overruled, and that, under the later

decision, there is now no rational basis upon which the separate but equal doctrine can be validly applied to public carrier transportation within the City of Montgomery." [23]

While the Alabama authorities were preparing their appeal to the Supreme Court in *Gayle* v. *Browder,* Judge Timmerman spoke again in the Flemming case.[24] Again Judge Timmerman found a way to avoid the application of *Brown* v. *Board of Education* to the South Carolina bus dispute. Again the action was dismissed. Reiterating the fact that *Plessy* v. *Ferguson* had not as yet been specifically overruled by the Supreme Court, he declared that the separate but equal doctrine must have been valid law in South Carolina up until the time that Judge Parker's Fourth Circuit Court of Appeals ruled otherwise. Thus, reasoned Judge Timmerman, since the segregation complained of occurred before the Court of Appeals decision, and since "I do not understand that the Court of Appeals intended to make its reversal of the Plessy case retroactive," the defendant could not be "liable in damages for acts done which were at the time of their doing perfectly lawful." [25]

While it is unlikely that this argument will carry much weight with the Fourth Circuit Court of Appeals, Judge Timmerman's reanalysis of the facts raises more difficult questions for the appellate tribunals. The basic fact pattern underlying *Flemming* v. *South Carolina Electric and Gas Company* varies considerably from the vast majority of cases which have challenged statutes and regulations requiring racial classifications. This was not a suit seeking the admission of Negroes to formerly all-white schools, beaches or buses; this was a civil action for damages under the Federal Civil Rights Acts for injuries sustained as a result of segregation practices. In the first decision rendered in the case, Judge Timmerman asserted that the bus driver had done no wrong, even if he was "acting under color of state law," since the state law was constitutional. Once the Court of Appeals de-

clared the state law unconstitutional, however, Judge Timmerman reconsidered the facts in the litigation before him.
There are no dividing lines in the buses which are maintained in the City of Columbia, South Carolina. White passengers are required to occupy the forward area of buses and
Negroes are required to sit in the rear. How far back white
passengers will sit and how far forward Negroes will be permitted depends upon the relative number of patrons of each
race. On the particular day that Mrs. Flemming was ordered
to the rear of the bus, no white passengers were sitting behind her and none were standing in the aisle seeking seats.
On the basis of these facts, Judge Timmerman came to the
conclusion that "the bus driver was not acting under color
of state law to enforce racial segregation on his bus, whatever
other evil motive he may have had for ordering plaintiff to
change her seat." [26] As a result, Mrs. Flemming would have
no right of action against the bus company based on the enforcement of an unconstitutional statute. Whatever right she
may have would be merely a common-law action against the
bus driver.

Gayle v. *Browder* [27] came before the Supreme Court for
final decision on November 13, 1956. As was to be expected,
the nine men unanimously affirmed the opinion below—the
opinion which declared invalid the state statutes which had
required racial segregation on the buses of Montgomery,
Alabama. As was to be expected, they based their determination on the precedents of *Brown* v. *Board of Education,* the
bathing-beach dispute of *Mayor and City Council of Baltimore City* v. *Dawson* and the Georgia golf course case of
Holmes v. *Atlanta.*

The New York *Times* characterized the decision as having
"placed a headstone at the grave of Plessy v. Ferguson." [28]
And this despite the fact that the Supreme Court had studiously avoided mentioning the 1896 determination by name.
No opinion was written in *Gayle* v. *Browder.* The decision

was rendered *per curiam* merely noting the affirmance. Yet the case must stand as a specific restatement of the *per se* meaning of *Brown* v. *Board of Education* and as a specific rejection of the Plessy concept in the transportation field. *Plessy* v. *Ferguson* may not have been overruled by name, but it was overruled all the same. The "separate but equal" doctrine has finally become a constitutional nullity.

Chapter 14

PATTERNS OF COMPLIANCE

"Private and public opinion as to the desirability of de-segregation in the community" provides no legal basis for delaying a prompt start toward the admission of children to the public schools without regard to race or color, said the United States Court of Appeals in the Mansfield, Texas, High School case.[1] But what the judges did not say was that the law as now expressed does not change that same private and public opinion on the subject of desirability. The law is one thing; enforcement of the law by judicial process is something quite different; and willing compliance with the law is something else again.

Twenty-two American jurisdictions still had school segregation laws on their statute books on the day that Oliver Brown first went to court. And while the Supreme Court could declare those laws unconstitutional, it could not change the people who made those laws. The "way of life" which Virginia espoused before the Supreme Court of the United States existed in the South both before and after the decision of May 17, 1954. Yet, there was a difference. Once the highest court in the land concluded that racial discrimination was against the law, a concerted effort was begun to bring about the end of separate facilities for whites and Negroes. Two years later came the survey report of Harold C. Fleming, assistant director of the Southern Regional Council: "There is no longer a Solid South of segregation." [2]

Southerner Fleming based his conclusion on the 1,100 in-

stances of newly practiced desegregation which he had discovered in the seventeen Southern and border states (and
the District of Columbia) since May 17, 1954. And, observed
Fleming, "virtually all of them took place smoothly and har-
moniously." [3]

This is only half the story. Despite the many "progress"
reports published in the Northern newspapers, the second
anniversary of the Supreme Court's decision marked little
more than a beginning of desegregation. *Look* magazine's
National Affairs Editor, William Attwood, aptly described
the situation when he said in 1956 that "there seems to be
good reason to predict that integration will be the pattern of
the future." But he qualified the remark by adding, "If by
the future we mean not the next few months, but several
years hence." [4]

The balance sheet at the opening of the school year in September, 1956, was singularly unimpressive. Only 723 of the
10,000 school districts of the South—4,000 of which had potential Negro pupils—had been desegregated. Further, in the
eight states which represent the heartland of the South, the
schools remained wholly segregated at the primary and secondary levels.[5] On the day following the 1954 decision, President Eisenhower announced that the District of Columbia
would immediately become the nation's showplace in public
school integration.[6] On the other hand, two years later, Mississippi was still proceeding on the theory that desegregation
could—and would—be avoided.

The South is more than just another American region. It
is also a state of mind. More precisely, it is a collection of
states of mind, united by common customs and traditions—
including racial segregation. Yet there are significant variations in these states of mind, and reactions to the mandate
of *Brown* v. *Board of Education* necessarily differed. No
one—least of all the nine members of the Supreme Court—
expected the same reaction in the sparsely settled hill country

of West Virginia and in the heavily populated delta lands of
Louisiana. There were bound to be differences between the
urban South and the rural South; dissimilarity was inevitable
between an Alabama nurtured in the traditions of slavery in
the cotton fields and an Oklahoma pervaded by the Western
customs common to oil and cattle country.

Recognizing these differences, the Supreme Court provided legal elbowroom for reconciliation to its decision outlawing segregation. "Full implementation of these constitutional principles may require solution of varied local school
problems," wrote the Chief Justice in 1955. "School authorities have the primary responsibility for elucidating, assessing,
and solving these problems; courts will have to consider
whether the action of school authorities constitutes good
faith implementation of the governing constitutional principles. Because of their proximity to local conditions and the
possible need for further hearings, the courts which originally heard these cases can best perform this judicial appraisal."

Headlines in the American press during the opening of the
new school year in September, 1956, gave a distorted picture
of the patterns of compliance. Even the staid New York
Times dwelt overlong on its description of "actions of violence and the unleashing of malevolent moods." "Men,
women and children with wrathful faces," the *Times* reported, "have shouted epithets and obscenities and even
danced in the street to express their delight at thwarting the
purpose of a neighbor. In some instances these scenes have
been framed by the glistening bayonets and khaki uniforms
of militiamen called to preserve law and order." [7]

This was an accurate account of some of the events surrounding desegregation in the schools of Clinton, Tennessee;
Mansfield, Texas; Sturgis and Clay, Kentucky; and, to a
lesser extent, Texarkana, on the Arkansas-Texas border.

There were identifiable reasons for the violent opposition to desegregation in those five communities—in spite of the fact that Tennessee, Texas, Kentucky and Arkansas were among the nine Southern and border states which had made the first substantial strides toward integration.

Desegregation at Clinton, a town in eastern Tennessee, represented the southernmost attempt at integration up to that time in the Old South east of the Mississippi River. At Mansfield, the judicial decree ordering the admission of Negroes to the town's one high school was the first such action in eastern Texas, home of 90 per cent of the state's Negro population. Yet these were not the significant factors underlying the outbreaks of violence.

More important was the fact that in each instance only a handful of Negro pupils, from two to fifteen, were involved in the classroom mixing. Still more important was the fact that, with the exception of Texarkana, the events occurred in small rural communities.

Contrary to Southern contentions, the degree of resistance to desegregation is not the result of the relative percentage of Negroes in a given school area. Southerners argue that districts with a high ratio of Negroes face more and greater problems than districts with few Negroes—and that, as a result, desegregation is difficult if not impossible where the Negro population is high. There is some support for this position. Desegregation has proceeded at a faster pace in the border state of West Virginia, where there is only one Negro to every seventeen whites, than in Mississippi, where nearly half of the population is Negro. It is also true the Negro ratio is high in all of the eight states which remained wholly segregated at the primary and secondary school levels as late as the end of 1956. These states are Alabama, Florida, Georgia, Louisiana, Mississippi, North Carolina, South Carolina and Virginia. Further, in three of those states—Louisiana, North Carolina and Virginia—it has been possible to admit some Negroes to state-supported colleges because the percentage "qualified" for higher education remained small.

A study of the patterns of compliance, however, reveals more significant factors underlying the acceptance or rejection of the Supreme Court's mandate. Maryland is moving fast toward total integration; Florida is resisting desegregation at every turn. In Maryland there is one Negro for every five whites in the total population; in Florida the proportion is one to four. In the District of Columbia, school authorities faced the task of integrating 57,243 Negro and 42,612 white pupils [8]—a population ratio comparable to that of Alabama, Georgia, Louisiana, Mississippi and South Carolina. And violence over desegregation was confined to small towns in Kentucky, Tennessee and Texas where only a few Negro students were involved. Certainly the opposition to desegregation cannot be analyzed in terms of population figures.

There are more important factors which have measured the extent of Southern compliance: preconditioning, urbanization and education.

Segregation was fast disappearing as a way of life in the District of Columbia even before *Brown* v. *Board of Education* and its companion case of *Bolling* v. *Sharpe*. Public transportation had long been integrated. Restaurants in the city of Washington were put on a nonsegregated basis by a Supreme Court decision in 1952 [9] which held that a "forgotten" ordinance passed in the District in 1873 was still valid. The ordinance had made it a crime for any "keeper of a place of public accommodation" to refuse service to any "well-behaved and respectable person or persons." [10] Other public places in the District of Columbia ceased segregation practices after the Supreme Court's 1952 decision, and racial discrimination soon came to an end in public housing and professional societies.[11] To a lesser extent, substantial inroads had been made against segregation practices in Delaware,

Kentucky, Maryland, Missouri and West Virginia prior to the Supreme Court decision of May 17, 1954.

While there was considerable legal resistance to desegregation in these states (and in the District of Columbia), there was a significant absence of the emotional intensity which characterized the opposition in the deep South. And both before and after the federal district courts rendered their implementation decrees, school desegregation in the border states moved rapidly toward realization. The "education" of the people in those states—an education of preconditioning— had created community attitudes which encouraged rapid integration of the school systems.

Desegregation in Delaware, Maryland, and Missouri came first in Wilmington, Baltimore and St. Louis—the large urban centers. This was to be expected; it was due, in part, to the preconditioning process. Negroes had been admitted to labor unions on an equal basis and labor unions, virtually nonexistent in the rural areas, were an important part of the way of life of urban dwellers. There were also economic reasons behind the community acceptance of desegregation in the large cities. Cheap labor—which in the South means Negro labor—is far more important in rural regions than in the urban centers where skilled labor is at a premium. The demand for skilled labor automatically creates a demand for better educated labor, regardless of race or color. And this lessened the "cultural" opposition to desegregated schools. More important, as hundreds of thousands of Negroes were added to the skilled labor force, it was quite natural for them to work side by side with whites in the performance of the same or similar tasks.

Urbanization has other special characteristics which encouraged rapid strides toward integration. To begin with, the city dweller lives in a more complex society than his rural counterpart and therefore is more responsive to change. Then again, the urban citizen is more amenable to changes in the law than are the residents of rural areas. Judges, police officers, members of school boards and other representatives of government are strangers to the people of the cities and it is seldom that the impersonal authority they represent is questioned. In the smaller communities, on the other hand, local officials are friends and neighbors whose judgment is frequently subject to challenge when it does not reflect community attitudes. And, in most instances, the people of the cities are better informed than those in the rural areas.

Commenting on the 1,100 examples of desegregation which he had discovered, Southerner Fleming wrote: "The common notion that desegregation just can't work in the South is plainly contradicted by the findings." [12] Summing up the status of desegregation two years after Supreme Court decision, William Attwood, of *Look,* observed: ". . . in those states which have started to desegregate the schools, people are learning that compliance with the law does not lead to 'mongrelization' or even enforced social mixing." [13]

These and similar findings have dominated virtually every report on the patterns of compliance. And, regardless of their personal feelings toward the Negro, Southerners who have been apprised of these findings have shown a willingness to comply with the law as expounded by the Supreme Court of the United States. An indispensable prerequisite to a desegregated South seems to be an informed South. Unfortunately, however, most of the factual information on desegregation has been confined to the newspapers of the large urban centers.

It is in the largest commercial and industrial center of the deep South, for example, that Southerners have expressed the strongest protests against continuing racial discrimination. Editor Ralph McGill of the influential Atlanta *Constitution* spoke for large segments of urban Southern opinion when he said: "The world . . . has moved on. Segregation

by law no longer fits today's world. . . . Segregation is on
its way out, and he who tries to tell the people otherwise does
them a great disservice. The problem of the future is how
to live with the change." [14]

Just as Baltimore, St. Louis and Wilmington were the first
communities in the border states to bring about an end to
racial separation in the public schools, so it will be the large
cities of the South that will lead the way to total desegregation. The trend was already apparent by the second anniversary of *Brown* v. *Board of Education*. In Louisville, Kentucky, a city with a basic Southern heritage despite its border-
state location, integration was successfully carried out in all
of the public schools, from kindergarten through high school.
In Texas, the first state in the deep South to admit Negroes
to formerly all-white schools, desegregation began first in
San Antonio.

In San Antonio, in El Paso and in more than one hundred
other Texas school areas, integration moved smoothly and
peacefully during 1955 and 1956. True, there were some disturbances in Texarkana. But violence occurred only in the
small town of Mansfield—a town which was conspicuously
lacking in preconditioning, urbanization and information
about the basic issues of desegregation.

The absence of any of the characteristics of urbanization
was even more striking in Clay and Sturgis, Kentucky, and
in Clinton, Tennessee. Both Clay and Sturgis are located in
the backwoods, mountain area of Kentucky where feuding
is not yet uncommon and where disagreement leads quickly
to violence. In Clinton, desegregation had begun quietly
until white supremacist John Kasper of New Jersey reached
the community and stirred up dissension. Mob rule ended
quickly, however, due not only to the intervention of the
National Guard, but also to the prompt action of the citizens who preferred desegregation to lawlessness. It is note-
worthy that when the local judge swore in a band of forty

special deputies to restore order, one of the volunteers was the lawyer who had led the unsuccessful legal fight against integration.

Despite the ever-present threat of another Mansfield, another Clinton, or another Clay and Sturgis, the main battles against desegregation will be fought in the courtrooms. Southern leaders are seeking legal means to thwart the patterns of compliance. This is not only the approach of the Southern moderates, it is also the approach of Mississippi's Senator Eastland,[15] spokesman for the White Citizens' Councils throughout the South. "Acts of violence and lawlessness have no place," declared Eastland. "Violence hurts the cause of the South. It is imperative that we be looked upon with favor and have the best wishes of the average American."

Senator Eastland and his followers still want a fight. He believes that "the antisegregation decisions are dishonest decisions." But he insists that "the fight we wage must be a just and legal fight."

And thus the South has taken up a legal battle—a battle which has introduced (and reintroduced) into the American scene a whole new vocabulary of strange words and ordinary words with strange meanings. It is a legal battle which has been and will be fought over such legal concepts as "interposition," "nullification," "divestment," "psychological aptitude," "free choice" and "with all deliberate speed."

"WITH ALL DELIBERATE SPEED"

No words in the school segregation cases have created more confusion or caused more comment than the simple phrase, "with all deliberate speed." Yet, vague as these words may appear, they were not tossed carelessly into the 1955 opinion just to improve literary style or sentence structure. On the contrary, as Justice Minton told the press shortly before his retirement, these words were the result of "long and careful

consideration." [16] Embodied in the phrase "with all deliberate speed" is a definite rule of law. But it is a peculiar rule
of law in that it is designed to permit so much flexibility in
its application. It is a rule which causes decisions to vary
from court to court and from case to case. And it was for
precisely this reason that it was employed in *Brown* v. *Board
of Education*. "With all deliberate speed" was utilized as a
term of art, empowering the lower courts to adjust the impact of the decision in light of local governmental conditions.

On May 31, 1955, the Supreme Court remanded all five
cases to the lower courts for further action. Since the prior
decision of the Delaware Supreme Court had already ordered
desegregation, the nine men merely instructed the state tribunal to take such further proceedings as it might "deem
necessary in light of this opinion." In the other four cases,
however, the United States Supreme Court issued different
instructions. The federal district courts were directed to require the school board defendants to "make a prompt and
reasonable start toward full compliance with our May 17,
1954, ruling." And the district courts were further ordered
"to take such proceedings and enter such orders and decrees"
as were necessary to accomplish this end. But the mandate
was qualified. "Once such a start has been made," wrote Chief
Justice Warren, "the courts may find that additional time is
necessary to carry out the ruling in an effective manner." It
is at this point that the lower courts were given the leeway
to act "with all deliberate speed."

Acting with all deliberate speed necessarily requires a factual determination as to local governmental conditions. But
this does not mean that these words are without definite
metes and bounds. The only reason why the phrase remains
the subject of confusion and comment is because the lower
courts have failed to give their reasons for assigning various
dates as the starting points for desegregation.

It was from the case of *Virginia* v. *West Virginia*,[17] an opinion by Justice Holmes in 1912, that the nine men of 1955 found the language and meaning of "with all deliberate speed." Following a Supreme Court determination that West Virginia owed a sum of money to Virginia, the latter state sought an order compelling immediate payment. The motion was denied by a unanimous Court. Holmes wrote: ". . . a State cannot be expected to move with the celerity of a private business man; it is enough if it proceeds, in the language of the English Chancery, with all deliberate speed." [18] In *Brown* v. *Board of Education*, as in *Virginia* v. *West Virginia*, the Supreme Court concluded that it was unreasonable to expect immediate action from state officials where those officials did not control all the state processes necessary to achieve full compliance. By permitting local school authorities to move with all deliberate speed, the implementation decision of May 31, 1955, gave time, in Chief Justice Warren's words, to "consider problems related to administration, arising from the physical condition of the school plant, the school transportation system, personnel, revision of school districts and attendance areas into compact units to achieve a system of determining admission to the public schools on a nonracial basis, and revision of local laws and regulations which may be necessary in solving the foregoing problems."

While Justice Holmes and the 1912 Supreme Court denied the *immediate* right of Virginia to recover the monies owed by West Virginia, the payment still had to be made. Delay was permitted only because a legislative act was required to appropriate the sum necessary to satisfy the debt, and the actions of the state legislature were not under the control of the defendant state. Although the 1955 Supreme Court granted a period of transition in which to effect desegregation, the nine men took pains to point out that "the vitality of these [previously announced] constitutional principles cannot be allowed to yield simply because of disagreement with them."

With monotonous regularity, the federal district judges throughout the South have been rendering opinions either parroting or rephrasing the language of the Supreme Court without explaining the factual basis for their decisions. An example is the Arkansas decision of 1955: "In the course of the opinion the [Supreme] Court recognized that local school authorities have the primary responsibility for solving the problems that arise from the constitutional principles announced in the first opinion, and stated that the [lower] courts will have to consider whether the actions of school authorities constitute good faith implementation of the governing constitutional principles. The [Supreme] Court also stated that in fashioning and effectuating the decrees that the court should be guided by equitable principles but emphasized that the plaintiffs and others similarly situated should be admitted to public schools as soon as practical on a nondiscriminatory basis, and that the courts should require the school authorities to make a prompt and reasonable start toward full compliance with the ruling of May 17, 1954." [19] Then the federal court in Arkansas, ostensibly following this language, announced that an injunction against the defendant school authorities would be delayed until "the earliest practicable date."

The court attempted to explain its delay by once more parroting Chief Justice Warren. Additional time was deemed necessary "because of the lack of school finances, the crowded conditions of the present facilities and the necessity to readjust the system that has been followed for decades. . . ." [20] Nowhere in the opinion, however, did the court indicate how much money would have to be obtained how soon before Negro children would be admitted to the schools on a nondiscriminatory basis. Nowhere in the opinion are there any words indicating how soon the present, crowded facilities should be expanded. No standard was set as the measure of "with all deliberate speed."

Even the extreme cases lack definition. A federal district judge in West Virginia issued orders in two cases [21] in January, 1956, providing for the admission of as many Negro students "as there is room to admit" during the 1956 Spring Term, and an end to racial segregation by the fall. A federal district judge in Texas, on the other hand, dismissed a suit despite the fact that the local school board had not even begun to prepare a desegregation plan.[22] In neither case did the court explain (or even outline) the factors which led to its application of the "with all deliberate speed" mandate.

As late as the end of 1956, the only guidance given to the district courts was found in a decision of United States Court of Appeals for the Sixth Circuit.[23] It involved a suit by Negro children against the school authorities in Hillsboro, Ohio, not far from the Kentucky border. Here the judges were specific; they outlined the factual considerations which governed their decision.

Four important factors were considered by the court in its January, 1956, opinion: (1) that racial segregation had been effected by the defendant school board which gerrymandered the school districts *after* the *Brown* v. *Board of Education* opinion of May 17, 1954; (2) that the new schoolhouse which was being built to relieve crowded conditions would not be finished until January, 1957; (3) that the decision was being rendered in the middle of a school year; and (4) that seven of the twenty-four Negro plaintiffs were not then attending any school.

To begin with, the court ordered the immediate admission of the seven to the school nearest their homes—on a nondiscriminatory basis. With all deliberate speed—at least in Ohio—means that no delays will be permitted where any racial group is totally without schooling. As far as the other seventeen were concerned, the court declared their right to attend previously all-white schools, but cautioned that an order to that effect would have to await the beginning of the new school year in September. Directing immediate desegregation in the middle of the term, the court wrote, would "cause dislocation and hardship out of proportion to the purpose to be served." [24]

The new schoolhouse would not be available for use until January, 1957, and admitting additional students in September would lead to overcrowding. Admitting students in the middle of the academic year in January would disrupt the curriculum. The judges concluded that overcrowding was the lesser problem. With all deliberate speed called for desegregation by September, 1956. Further, the court concluded that September, 1956, would work no hardship upon either school board or community. School segregation by law was new to the locality, and there was no necessity to change habits or uproot and rewrite generations of statutes requiring racial discrimination. And finally, since all of the gerrymandering had been done by the defendants then before the court, there was no need to call upon any other state officials in order to achieve full compliance. The factors which Justice Holmes considered in giving West Virginia further time to pay its debt to Virginia were no barrier to judicial action where only the school board (and not a state legislature) was involved. The final result was that the court of appeals had defined some of the borders of the "deliberate speed" rule.

Two types of decisions are needed to give full effect to the Supreme Court mandate of May 31, 1955. The first type of decision requires an express statement of the federal district courts as to the actual basis of their decisions: they must set forth the extent to which their decisions are influenced by the extent of the area subject to dispute; the availability of facilities; and the condition of the local laws. The Ohio decision of the Sixth Circuit Court of Appeals must be supplemented by similar decisions in the courts of appeals which have jurisdiction over the lower federal courts in the deep South. These district courts must have further guides in de-

termining the length of time necessary to add new class-
rooms, provide new school buses and rewrite old statutes and
regulations with all deliberate speed.

The second type of decision is considerably more complicated than the first. It would make federal district court decrees directly binding upon school boards which were not
parties to the litigation in which those decrees were rendered. The court would be required to give more weight to
the first decision involving desegregation at the schools in
a state. Such a decision would partake of and expand some
of the basic concepts of "law of the case," *stare decisis,* and
class suits. In expanding the principle of law in the case, the
court would bind not only the immediate parties to the dispute, but all persons in a similar *legal* position. These persons, of course, would be the members of all other school
boards in the state. *Stare decisis* would be extended in the
same manner. Normally, before this doctrine is applicable,
there must be a judicial determination that the second case is
"similar" to the first in its facts. The court making the second
type of decision, however, would apply the "precedent"
merely on a finding that the same law was in issue, the law
being any statute or constitution of the state permitting or
requiring segregation in education.

As a result of the nature of the Supreme Court's implementation mandate of May 31, 1955, no school board is at
present subject to an enforceable legal obligation to desegregate the public schools in its district until it is before a federal district court as party defendant in a legal suit. This bar
to the speedy enforcement of school desegregation cannot be
hurdled as the law now stands. Thus a decision employing the
traditional concepts of law of the case, *stare decisis* and class
suits would proceed in this manner:

Assume that suit has been instituted against the members
of school board X to desegregate the schools in X district.
In rendering a decree ordering integration, the federal dis-

trict court would necessarily fix a date for desegregation to begin. The time interval between the date of the decree and the date when Negroes would be admitted to formerly all-white schools would then be the measure of "deliberate speed" for the school board actually before the court.

Now, assume that a second suit has been instituted in the same federal district court (or another federal district court in the same state) to compel school board Y to desegregate the schools in Y district. And assume further that X and Y districts are similar in all important respects. It would naturally follow that the lawyers defending the second suit would argue that school board Y was entitled at least to as much time to bring about desegregation as was given to the school authorities of district X.

The federal district court could render such a decree. The federal district court could also re-evaluate the factual bases of the difficulties to be encountered in accomplishing desegregation and set another time interval as the measure of "deliberate speed" in the second case. These are the types of decisions which were rendered during the first two years following *Brown* v. *Board of Education* and neither gave full effect to the Supreme Court's implementation mandate of May 31, 1955.

What the federal district court could do in the second case to speed the course of desegregation would be to hold that the time interval measuring deliberate speed began at the date of the decree in the first case—and not at the date of the decree in the second case.

By rendering such a decree, due notice would be given to all school boards throughout the state that the duty of making a "prompt and reasonable start toward full compliance" had begun with the first case—as soon as the federal district court obeyed the Supreme Court mandate to make a "judicial appraisal" of "local conditions" in the state. It would follow that the law of the case as expressed in the dispute involving school board X would be extended to the suit involving school board Y. And the first determination would establish a precedent as to the validity of the state law in question. Consequently, the federal district court would develop a new species of class action by holding that the decree rendered against school board X was, at the same time, a decree against all school boards similarly situated.

As a result of the extension of the law of the case, and of *stare decisis,* the decree in the class suit would then bind the members of all school boards in the state. The common question of law decided would be the state law itself, and not the application of the law by a particular local school board. The federal district court would then issue a decree based upon the validity of the state law requiring or permitting segregated education.

In so doing, the federal district court would be acting directly against the school segregation laws in effect in the particular state prior to the *Brown* v. *Board of Education* decision of May 17, 1954. It would be reaffirming the fact that those laws were no longer in force for any purpose. Such a decision would be a judicial reminder of what the Supreme Court actually held in *Brown* v. *Board of Education.* The essential "local conditions" to which the nine men referred were not local school board practices. It was the existence of state constitutions and statutes, either requiring or permitting school segregation, which constituted the "local conditions" to be remedied. A decision of this type, directed against the laws which were held unconstitutional, would lead to a more rapid realization of the Supreme Court's mandate than did the early implementation decrees of the district courts—decrees which were directed only against local community attitudes as reflected by local school board practices.

By setting the date of the first federal district court decree as the critical point for measuring "with all deliberate speed," the courts would be making it legally unprofitable for school boards to delay action until they are actually in litigation.[25]

Glimmerings of a sympathetic judicial attitude toward this approach are to be found in a 1956 federal district court decision in North Carolina. The case was procedural in nature. The school board defendant had petitioned for a special three-judge court to hear the case on the theory that none of North Carolina's segregation laws had as yet been declared unconstitutional and that only a special three-judge tribunal could consider this issue. The petition was summarily denied. The court considered the question of the constitutionality of North Carolina's segregation laws settled even though no specific decision had been rendered on that point.

"The validity of that part of the North Carolina Constitution requiring separate schools for the two races is no longer the subject of legal controversy," the court wrote. "Nor is any statute—state or local—or order of a board compelling segregation in the public schools, a legal controversy now. Every judge in the land, state and federal, is required under oath to uphold the Constitution of the United States as the supreme law of the land. In the administration of the law by the courts every judge is likewise bound by the Constitution as last interpreted and construed by the Supreme Court of the United States. If that court is not the final authority in legal proceedings, then where shall we look for the meaning of the Constitution. It is binding on this court and will be faithfully followed to the best of the ability of this court as now constituted. . . . If, then, the state constitution or statutes or orders require that separate schools for the races must be maintained, it follows as the night the day that, being in conflict with the Constitution of the United States as defined by the Supreme Court, they are to that extent, null and void. No three-judge court is necessary to make that declaration."[26]

The underlying premise of this decision is that all laws

requiring segregation automatically became null and void as a result of the Supreme Court's determination of May 17, 1954. And this premise necessarily carries with it the implication that school boards cannot act pursuant to such laws. Or, in other words, *Brown* v. *Board of Education* imposed an immediate obligation on the part of school boards not to segregate in the public schools under their authority. It would then follow logically that no suit should be necessary in order to create the duty of bringing about an end to segregated school systems.

Such decisions may be rendered in the future. But no court has yet gone this far. The Supreme Court obviously wanted the flexibility necessary to meet varying local conditions when it applied the Holmes principle to its implementation decree. But it obviously did not want the type of flexibility which has resulted—a flexibility based in large measure upon the "private and public opinion as to the desirability of desegregation in the community." It certainly did not want the type of flexibility which has left the federal district courts without factual standards.

While the application of the deliberate speed mandate has been disappointing to the proponents of desegregation, it is virtually impossible to conceive of the Supreme Court having taken any other course of action. No decision—regardless of its length or erudition—could possibly have encompassed the many and varied problems of implementation from school district to school district. Nor could a body of just nine men prepare and enforce even the simplest collection of decrees necessary to control the actions of the 10,000 school districts in the Southern and border states. As a practical matter, the responsibility had to be shifted to the lower tribunals.

Reluctance on the part of some federal district judges in the Southern states to give effective meaning to the "with all deliberate speed" mandate is only one phase of the continuing legal battle against desegregation. Still to be considered are the judicial weapons which might be brought to bear to enforce strict obedience to the dictates of *Brown* v. *Board of Education,* and still to be considered are the various legal devices which have been created to avoid, evade and delay the Supreme Court decision which has now made all racial discrimination illegal *per se.*

THE JUDICIAL ARMAMENT

As the federal district courts continue the task of enforcing the Supreme Court's implementation decree, they must necessarily continue to pursue two general courses of action. At times they will be exercising their powers to compel obedience by punishing (or threatening to punish) those who attempt to evade the orders which have been promulgated. At times they will be striking down as unconstitutional the executive, legislative and administrative measures erected by the Southern states as barriers to desegregation. At other times, of course, they will be performing both functions in a single case.

The coercive powers of the federal district courts are of two types. In one set of circumstances, these courts may sit as criminal tribunals and try cases based upon charges made by a grand jury under the federal penal law. In the other set of circumstances, the punitive authority is based upon the inherent power of the judiciary to compel compliance to its decrees.

It is a crime under Title 18, Section 241 of the United States Code [27] "if two or more persons conspire to injure, oppress, threaten, or intimidate any citizen in the free exercise or enjoyment of any right or privilege secured to him by the Constitution. . . ."

Whether or not the criminal sanctions of Section 241 can be invoked to enforce the rights declared in *Brown* v. *Board of Education* is still an open question. The Supreme Court had considered the applicability of this section to the due process and equal protection clauses of the Fourteenth Amendment as late as 1951 in the case of *United States* v. *Williams*.[28] And the Supreme Court failed to provide an answer—or, more accurately, it furnished two answers. Four justices agreed on one position; four others took the opposite view. The ninth member of the Court, Justice Black, voted with Justices Frankfurter, Vinson, Jackson and Minton on another issue in the litigation which had no bearing upon the Court's interpretation of Section 241. But his vote on that issue meant that the view expressed by Justice Frankfurter constituted the majority voice. The four justices on the dissenting side were Douglas, Reed, Clark and Burton.

The Frankfurter position as to Section 241 is based on the constitutional premise that the rights created by the Fourteenth Amendment can be enforced only against the states and persons acting pursuant to the authority of a state. Turning to the specific words of Section 241, the Justice read the phrase "two or more persons" as referring to all persons, regardless of whether they have any connection with the state. This is the common, everyday meaning of the phrase and thus its "plain meaning." And if Frankfurter analyzed Section 241 in accordance with the time-honored, plain-meaning rule, he would have to interpert the words "two or more persons" without qualification. But Congress would be without power under the Fourteenth Amendment to enact a statute which would be applicable to "all persons" without the qualification of a state connection. This is so because the Fourteenth Amendment applies only to the states; and this was the teaching of the Cruikshank case.[29] Application of the plain-meaning rule to the phrase "two or more persons" would inevitably lead to a declaration that Section 241 is unconstitutional.

This position was untenable to the judicial minds of Frankfurter, Vinson, Jackson and Minton—as it is to most judges.

It is a well-established canon of statutory construction that if legislation can be interpreted in more than one way, the courts are bound to follow the interpretation which will sustain the constitutionality of the measure under review.

As a possible alternative, Frankfurter and his colleagues might have interpreted "person" by limiting the meaning of the word to "person acting under state authority." Congress would have the power to enact the section if it applied only to persons having some connection with a state. This is the meaning of the constitutional language "acting under color of state law." Although the Fourteenth Amendment applies only to the states, and cannot be invoked unless the "grievance [is] inflicted by action of the legislative or executive or judicial department of the State . . . ," [30] still the state acts only through people. Thus when a person having some official connection with the state justifies his action by relying on state law of any kind, he acts "under color of state law." And since he is then acting for the state, he is subject to the Fourteenth Amendment. It is for this reason, of course, that the defendants in *Brown* v. *Board of Education* were the members of the school boards and not the states of Delaware, Kansas, South Carolina and Virginia.

Thus, if Frankfurter limited the meaning of "person" in Section 241 to persons acting under color of state law, there would be no question of the constitutionality of the section. And it would do little violence to the rules of statutory interpretation once again to construe an ordinary word in a particular legal sense to give it a constitutional meaning. Despite repeated judicial language that it is beyond the province of the courts to rewrite legislation, courts are seldom hesitant to read restricted meanings into the words of a statute in order to preserve their constitutionality.

Yet this alternative was likewise impossible. Another—and a more important—approach to statutory interpretation was involved. Once a court decides to by-pass the "plain meaning

rule" in the construction of a statute it is judicially obliged
to consider related enactments in its search for legislative
intent. Following this approach, Frankfurter had to analyze
the meaning of Section 241 in conjunction with the words of
Section 242. This section provides for the punishment of any
person who "under color of any law . . . willfully subjects
any inhabitant of any State . . . to the deprivation of any
rights, privileges, or immunities secured or protected by the
Constitution . . . by reason of his color, or race. . . ." This
latter section makes specific reference to persons acting
"under color" of state laws. Thus, by examining Section 242,
the Court would once again be confronted by the inescapable
conclusion that Section 241 referred only to the acts of any
"person." For by including "under color of any law" in Section 242 and by omitting the phrase from Section 241, Congress had *apparently* left no doubt as to its intentions to give
different meanings to the word "person" in the different sections.

Frankfurter did not permit himself (or his concurring
colleagues) to be impaled on the horns of an "either/or"
dilemma. The question was "how" he would avoid the
dilemma.

Employing an adroit judicial technique, Frankfurter
switched the basis of interpretation from "any person" to
"any right." He restricted the applicability of Section 241 to
"rights" which are guaranteed against the federal government. The Constitution authorizes Congress "to make all
laws which shall be necessary and proper" [31] to implement
its powers, and certainly Congress can declare it a crime for
"any person" to interfere with *federal* "rights." But Congress,
according to Frankfurter, has no power to punish "any
person" whose offense relates only to "rights" guaranteed
against the states.

The Frankfurter analysis would preclude the use of Section 241 as a method of enforcing desegregation. Since it is

obvious that the "rights" declared in *Brown* v. *Board of Education* were solely against the states, it necessarily follows that this section is inapplicable.

Douglas, Reed, Clark and Burton disagreed with Frankfurter's reasoning. They did not involve themselves in so intricate a judicial analysis. They were content to rest their position on Justice Rutledge's opinion six years earlier in a case [32] which had also considered the nature of the "rights" protected by Sections 241 and 242. Justice Douglas, quoting Rutledge, declared: "[T]here are 'no differences in the basic rights guarded. Each protects in a different way the rights and privileges secured to individuals by the Constitution.' One would indeed have to strain hard at words to find any difference of substance between 'any right or privilege secured' by the Constitution or laws of the United States [Section 241] and 'any rights, privileges, or immunities secured or protected by the Constitution and laws of the United States' [Section 242]." [33]

Under this view, Section 241 could be applied to enforce the decree in *Brown* v. *Board of Education*. But the Frankfurter interpretation, of course, would remain a bar to its use.

Since Section 242 contains the specific phrase "under color of any law," it would appear that this congressional enactment is less prone to constitutional attack than Section 241. Yet this section, too, is subject to constitutional disabilities as a judicial weapon against school segregation.

Another time-honored principle of statutory interpretation stands in the way of full judicial approval of Section 242. It is a generally stated rule that no enactment imposing a criminal penalty will be upheld unless its terms set forth ascertainable standards of guilt. A penal statute will be declared unconstitutional where it "either forbids or requires the doing of an act in terms so vague that men of common intelligence must necessarily guess at its meaning and differ as to its application." [34]

When Section 242 was subject to Supreme Court scrutiny in 1945,[35] the nine men expressed their divergent views in four separate opinions, each of which recognized the possibility of the vagueness defect.

The facts of that case are important. Screws, a Georgia sheriff, had arrested a Negro charged with the theft of a tire. And in the course of that arrest the alleged thief was brutally beaten to death. Since it was impossible to secure a murder conviction against the sheriff in the Georgia courts, the United States attorney pressed for, and secured, a federal indictment under Section 242. Screws was charged with wilfully depriving the suspect of a right protected by the Constitution—"the right not to be deprived of life without due process of law." The defendant's attorneys argued that nothing was said in the statute specifically declaring it a crime under the Fourteenth Amendment to deprive a person of his life and that therefore Section 242 was unconstitutional as being vague and indefinite. The government prosecution also recognized the problem of vagueness, but argued that the word "wilful" cured the defect.

The government position found no supporters on the Supreme Court. Every one of the nine men was disturbed by the vagueness problem. Even those who voted to uphold the statute had to admit that the legislative use of "wilful" did nothing toward achieving definiteness. But, wrote Justice Douglas for himself, Chief Justice Stone and Justices Black and Reed, the section would not be indefinite if it only applied to "rights" which were expressly set forth in the Constitution, precisely enumerated in an act of Congress or specifically declared by the Supreme Court. By thus limiting the "rights" which were guaranteed by the section against deprivation "under color of any law," the majority was able to interpret the statute in a manner which would sustain its constitutionality.

In the 1945 Screws decision, Justice Douglas reasoned:

"He who defies a decision interpreting the Constitution knows precisely what he is doing. If sane, he hardly may be heard to say that he knew not what he did. Of course, willful conduct cannot make definite that which is undefined. But willful violators of constitutional requirements, *which have been defined,* certainly are in no position to say that they had no adequate advance notice that they would be visited with punishment. When they act willfully in the sense in which we use the word, they act in open defiance or in reckless disregard of a constitutional requirement which has been made specific and definite. When they are convicted for so acting, they are not punished for violating an unknowable something." [36]

Justice Rutledge both agreed and disagreed. While he recognized the vagueness problem inherent in Section 242, he felt that Screws' action was so outrageous a violation of constitutional rights that the statute was not vague as applied to the facts in the case. Rutledge could not conceive of anyone committing so heinous a crime and not knowing that he was violating someone's constitutional rights. But Rutledge joined with Douglas and his concurring colleagues to provide the necessary fifth vote which would remand the case for a new trial—a new trial predicated upon the newly stated rule of law. Screws would now be guilty of the crime of depriving another of life without due process of law only if it could be proved that he *knew* of the right not to be deprived of life without due process of law.

The fact that Screws was found not guilty in his second trial has no bearing on the possible application of Section 242 as a method of enforcing *Brown* v. *Board of Education.* What is far more important is the Douglas analysis in the Screws case. His opinion appears to require a great deal more than the mere refusal of a school board to institute desegregation before the members of that board can be found guilty of a crime under the statute. Prior to any criminal action under Section 242, the Douglas view would require a positive judicial determination that the constitutional right declared in *Brown* v. *Board of Education* was both personal and *present*. And, since the opinion of May 31, 1955, gave school boards an opportunity to postpone implementation of the right within the limitations of "with all deliberate speed," there was no general judicial determination that the right of Negro children to attend all-white schools is present in nature. Under the law as it existed two years after Chief Justice Warren first declared the constitutional right, the right could only be enforced under Section 242 after a federal district court made it *present* by setting a specific date to desegregate a specific school. The imposition of the criminal sanction of Section 242 is thus subject to the frustrations inherent in securing lower court determinations fixing specific dates for desegregation.

Because the potential sanctions of Section 242 must await the expiration of a "deliberate speed" time limitation, it is a far less potent weapon than Section 241 as a method of enforcing desegregation through the criminal law. And Section 241 has the additional advantage of operating directly against individuals (if the Rutledge construction is accepted), while Section 242 requires that the act which provides the basis of a criminal charge be under color of state law.

These sections have not been used in the field of school segregation, even after two and one-half years of substantial noncompliance with the mandate of *Brown* v. *Board of Education.* There was, of course, a reluctance on the part of federal authorities to impose the law of the Supreme Court by coercive methods. But this was by no means the only reason why the Attorney General, representing the government, had been loath to bring proceedings under either Section 241 or 242. Despite the many recommendations that these civil rights acts be used to bring about speedy compliance, lawyers have been very much aware of the legal difficulty involved. Both statutes verge on unconstitutionality. Unless the new members of the Supreme Court adopt the Rutledge viewpoint, the Frankfurter position on Section 241 and the Douglas position on Section 242 stand as a bar to effective criminal enforcement.

Coercive measures under the federal criminal code, however, constitute but one part of the judicial armament. Of even greater importance is the authority of the courts to compel obedience by exercising their contempt power.

Unlike the traditional common-law courts, which could do no more than award or deny money damages, equity courts may impose punishment upon those who disobey their decrees.[37] This is the contempt power—and it may be exercised by the federal district courts as they sit in equity to hear the school segregation cases.

The contempt power is derived from two sources. It has been held by the Supreme Court to be inherent in the judicial function.[38] It has also been specifically authorized by Congress. Federal law gives every federal court the authority to punish by fine or imprisonment any person who disobeys or resists any "lawful writ, process, order, rule, decree or command." [39]

This contempt power is obviously a more efficient judicial remedy than the criminal sanctions of Sections 241 and 242. But even the use of the contempt power has its constitutional limitations. Where a contempt citation involves a criminal penalty, it cannot be based upon a court order which is either vague or uncertain. Unless the federal district courts clarify the terms of their desegregation orders as to the persons affected and as to the conduct prohibited, there will be a constitutional obstacle in the path of the full use of the contempt power.

Although broadly phrased desegregation orders might raise serious constitutional questions, the exercise of contempt power, when based upon narrowly drawn orders, has a number of advantages over the sanctions of Sections 241 and 242. It need not await a prior determination setting the time limits of "with all deliberate speed." It may be used at any time during a judicial proceeding, and need not be held in abeyance pending an actual interference with a right previously declared by a federal district court. It may even be used to prevent a threatened interference with a potential right as yet undeclared. It is usually exercised by the judge acting without a jury,[40] and is not subject to the necessity of having a United States attorney present charges to a grand jury and having the grand jury hand down an indictment. Further, the contempt power can be exercised against "strangers" to the judicial proceeding then before the court as well as against litigants. It can be used to enforce commands directly to those who merely indicate a desire to resist the orders of the federal district court. And it can be used to prevent any actual interference with judicial proceedings themselves. The only qualification limiting the court's power in punishing a "stranger" for disobedience is that he have some notice of a "lawful writ, process, order, rule, decree or command" issued by the court.

Despite its potential effectiveness, the contempt power has been used sparingly by the federal courts as a method of enforcing desegregation. In the first two years following the decision of May 17, 1954, the courts threatened the exercise of this power in a few instances in order to compel the court attendance of school board members. But the power was not exercised in the one case in which it was sought by Negro applicants,[41] and it has yet to be invoked where school boards have failed to make "a prompt and reasonable start toward full compliance" with the Supreme Court's mandate.

One of the most publicized examples of the use of the contempt power occurred during the height of the desegregation disturbances in Clinton, Tennessee, in 1956. Pro-segregation agitator John Kasper, of New Jersey, was "adjudged in contempt of a federal court order not to interfere with integration," [42] and was sentenced to a year in jail for his part in fomenting resistance to the admission of Negroes to Clinton High School.

In most instances, however, neither the Attorney General nor the federal district judges have sought to enforce desegregation by contempt citations. The unchecked exercise of this power would result in jailing most of the members of some Southern school boards. And it is generally recognized that implementation of *Brown* v. *Board of Education* cannot be achieved by imposition of prison terms on those responsible for bringing about desegregation.

Chapter 15

AVOIDANCE, EVASION AND DELAY

Southern opposition to desegregation has led directly to legal measures admittedly designed to circumvent the mandate of *Brown* v. *Board of Education*. But while the avowed purpose of those legal devices is to frustrate the Supreme Court determinations of May 17, 1954, and May 31, 1955, that fact alone does not necessarily make them unconstitutional. Southern lawyers have entered upon a concerted program to find doctrine and precedent which will permit the continued existence of racial segregation and still somehow survive the scrutiny of judicial review. Should they succeed in their quest, those pro-segregation measures which do survive will have met the test of constitutional "legality." Other governmental measures (meaning other governmental actions under color of law) obviously will not survive the requirements of "constitutional" or "legal."

Every legislative enactment, executive order or court decision which conforms to constitutional procedures is a "legal" measure in the sense that it is a manifestation of state action under color of law. And any measure which would be effective in avoiding desegregation would be "legal" in the sense that it had been held valid and binding.

In analyzing the legality of any measure designed to circumvent the operation of an announced rule of law, the courts make an important distinction between "avoidance" and "evasion." There are no constitutional limitations to measures of "avoidance." It is perfectly proper—at least as

240

far as the courts are concerned—for an individual or a state full of individuals to attempt to "avoid" the consequences of desegregation. "Evasion," on the other hand, is against the law. Individuals who attempt to evade the mandate of *Brown* v. *Board of Education* would be subject to punishment; and governmental measures designed to evade the Supreme Court's conclusions would be struck down as unconstitutional.

Whether an attempt to circumvent a rule of law is "illegal" because it involves "evasion," or whether an attempt at circumvention is labeled "evasion" because it is "illegal" is immaterial. Solution to this problem necessitates an excursion into the realm of legal dialectics which sheds no light on the enforcement problems involved in racial desegregation. The important fact is that circumvention measures in the field of desegregation *may* be "legal," just as they may be "illegal."

An amendment to the Constitution specifically authorizing the states to enact segregation laws would obviously be a legal method of "avoiding" the effects of *Brown* v. *Board of Education*. Legislative re-enactment of the laws which the Supreme Court declared unconstitutional on May 17, 1954, would just as obviously be struck down as an attempt to "evade" the law.

It is inconceivable that a constitutional amendment could be passed in mid-century America authorizing racial segregation, and just as incongruous to think in terms of re-enacting legislation already declared unconstitutional. What the South is really doing lies somewhere between such extremes of "avoidance" and "evasion."

The various legal attempts to avoid the consequences of desegregation fall into four categories. Many of the Southern states have reintroduced into the legal scene one or more of the multiple variations of the pre-Civil War doctrines of interposition and nullification. Other states have entered upon a course of legislative action designed to disqualify potential plaintiffs and the NAACP from bringing court actions to end segregation. Still other states have sought to retain separate school systems by changing the theoretical basis of the separation from a classification explicitly based upon race to a classification based upon such factors as "scholastic aptitude," "psychological aptitude" and "free choice." In the fourth category are the various ways and means which have been devised to separate the operation of the schools from the state.

INTERPOSITION AND NULLIFICATION

Derived from constitutional doctrines first advanced by Jefferson and Madison, the concepts of interposition and nullification have long provided the theoretical basis of the states' rights philosophy. This is the view that the central government is nothing more than a compact between and among the several sovereign states, and that each state has the right to determine the constitutionality of any act of federal authority. In declaring a federal act unconstitutional, a state would be interposing its sovereignty between the central government and the state's own citizens—hence the term interposition.

The formal statement of the interposition theory was largely developed during the course of a single evening at Jefferson's Monticello home. It was first employed in the Kentucky and Virginia Resolutions of 1798 and 1799 [1] which declared the Federal Alien and Sedition Laws of 1798 null and void. These Resolutions, however, had virtually no force and effect since the federal laws continued to be enforced by the Federalist Government. In 1800, when Jefferson was elected president, his Democratic-Republican Congress repealed the acts. All that the Resolutions really accomplished was to provide the first coherent statement of the states' rights position.

It is important to note that these Resolutions preceded Chief Justice Marshall's 1803 opinion in *Marbury* v. *Madison* [2] in which he declared that the Supreme Court had the ultimate power of determining the constitutionality of federal legislative and executive acts. This case was followed in 1809 by another Marshall opinion, in *United States* v. *Peters*, declaring the invalidity of interposition. The Chief Justice wrote: "If the legislatures of the several states may, at will, annul the judgments of the courts of the United States, and destroy the rights acquired under those judgments, the constitution itself becomes a solemn mockery; and the nation is deprived of the means of enforcing its laws by the instrumentality of its own tribunals." [3] These Marshall decisions were then supplemented by the 1816 case of *Martin* v. *Hunter's Lessee* [4] in which Justice Story asserted that a Supreme Court declaration of constitutionality overrides any declaration of unconstitutionality made by a state.

Despite these Supreme Court opinions, South Carolina's Senator John C. Calhoun in 1830 carried the interposition philosophy to its logical extreme by advancing the doctrines of nullification and, by implication, secession. Calhoun's theories were first fully expounded by the junior senator from South Carolina, Robert Young Hayne, in the famous Hayne-Webster debates. Two years later South Carolina passed the Ordinance of Nullification [5] in which the state declared the following: (1) that the federal Tariff Bill of 1828 was null and void; (2) that all state officials were prohibited from enforcing its provisions; and (3) that if any federal official attempted to enforce those provisions in South Carolina, the state would then leave the Union. The Ordinance of Nullification became meaningless when President Jackson threatened to enforce the Tariff Bill with federal troops and secured congressional enactment of the Force Bill of 1832 authorizing such action. South Carolina then withdrew its Ordinance of Nullification but, as a last-minute gesture of defiance, passed another meaningless ordinance nullifying the Force Bill.

The authority of the Constitution was again challenged on December 20, 1860, four months before the outbreak of the Civil War, when South Carolina became the first of the eleven Southern states to assert its right to leave the Union. Attempting to forestall this impending Southern reaction to Lincoln's election, President Buchanan had on December 3, 1860, delivered a message to Congress denying the constitutionality of secession. But the question of "legality" was soon lost in combat. It was not to be considered by the courts until the Supreme Court decision of *Texas* v. *White* in 1869.[6] And then it was judicially declared that secession was "illegal" and that, constitutionally, the Southern states had never left the Union at all.

Chief Justice Chase spoke for the Court: "The Constitution, in all its provisions, looks to an indestructible Union, composed of indestructible States. When, therefore, Texas became one of the United States, she entered into an indissoluble relation. All the obligations of perpetual union, and all the guaranties of republican government in the Union, attached at once to the State. The Act which consummated her admission into the Union was something more than a compact; it was the incorporation of a new member into the political body. And it was final." [7]

Since secession is the logical ultimate of the interposition-nullification-secession sequence developed by Calhoun and adopted by the South as its legal justification for leaving the Union, any judicial attack upon secession is necessarily an attack upon interposition and nullification. This is especially true in view of the fact that all three theories (or, more properly, all three aspects of the one theory) are based upon the concept that the government of the United States is nothing more than a compact made by the sovereign states. And this concept was definitely rejected by both Chief Justice Marshall's Supreme Court before the Civil War and Chief Justice Chase's Supreme Court after the Civil War.

Virtually dormant for more than eighty years, these theories have been revived as one aspect of the legal struggle to circumvent the consequences of *Brown* v. *Board of Education.* It started in Virginia. On January 11, 1956, an interposition act was introduced in the Virginia General Assembly [8] asserting the "right" of the state to maintain a segregated school system. Making obvious reference to *Brown* v. *Board of Education,* the proposed act declared that the "commonwealth is under no obligation to accept supinely an unlawful decree of the Supreme Court of the United States based upon an authority which is not found in the Constitution of the United States nor any amendment thereto." [9] Three weeks later, the General Assembly restated the compact theory in passing a joint resolution "interposing the sovereignty of Virginia against encroachment upon the reserved powers of this state." [10]

But the resolution meant little more than an expression of dissent—even in Virginia. The state attorney general delivered an opinion as to the "scope, effect, and legal efficacy" of the resolution on February 14, 1956, and admitted its lack of legal validity. While he characterized the legislative action as "far more than a 'stern protest and a memorial,' " he was forced to give negative answers to the two important legal questions submitted for his opinion:

"6. Is it within the powers of (a) the General Assembly of Virginia by resolution, or (b) the people of Virginia in convention assembled by ordinance, to legally nullify, in whole or in part, the said [*Brown* v. *Board of Education*] decision, or to thereby suspend for any period of time its enforcement in Virginia?"

The response of Virginia's attorney general was simply: "a (No), b (No)." [11]

This was followed by similar resolutions from the legislatures of other Southern states. In response to these declarations, California passed an anti-interposition resolution a month later.[12] The Assembly of the state legislature "memorialize[d] the Executive Branch and Congress of the United States to take the necessary action to support the recent decisions of the Supreme Court on civil rights. . . ." Giving reasons for its action, the Assembly criticized the South for "nefarious attempts to defy the Supreme Court of the United States and to threaten nullification of the Constitution."

The interposition declarations leave no doubt as to the continued opposition of the South to desegregation. They do no more. The Supreme Court spoke strongly on this subject both in 1809 and in 1869. And it is clear that any interposition arguments which might be raised before a judicial tribunal would be summarily rejected.

An even stronger document [13] of protest—one predicated upon legal argument though not intended as law—was proclaimed in March, 1956, by nearly all of the members of Congress from the eleven states in the deep South. Ninety-six senators and representatives joined in a "Declaration of Constitutional Principles," describing *Brown* v. *Board of Education* as "an abuse of judicial power" and pledging "all lawful means" to avoid desegregation.

Closely related to the assertions of state power under the interposition doctrine are the enactments in Louisiana [14] and a few other states ostensibly based upon the Tenth Amendment to the Constitution. That Amendment provides that "The powers not delegated to the United States by the Constitution, nor prohibited by it to the states, are reserved to the states respectively, or to the people." Within this residue of powers, according to Louisiana, is "the exercise of the State's police power" which "shall never be abridged." Specifically citing its police power as authority, Louisiana in 1954 passed additional legislation requiring the separation of whites and Negroes in the public schools. The segregation

provision was followed by a statement of "purpose," and the
purpose given was "to promote and protect public health,
morals, better education and the peace and good order in
the State *and not because of race.*" (Italics added.)

This method of circumventing the consequences of *Brown*
v. *Board of Education* has already been labeled an act of
"evasion." The special three-judge federal district court
which heard the case of *Bush* v. *Orleans Parish School
Board* [15] in early 1956 disposed of the validity of such legislation in a single sentence: "In so far as the provisions of
the Louisiana Constitution and statutes in suit require or
permit segregation of the races in public schools, they are
invalid under the ruling of the Supreme Court in Brown."

DISQUALIFYING POTENTIAL LITIGANTS

In the second broad classification of Southern legal action
are the various enactments designed to forestall judicial enforcement of the decree of May 31, 1955. The lower federal
courts, charged by the Supreme Court with the responsibility
for implementation, are powerless to act unless a desegregation suit is in litigation before them. The South is trying to
take advantage of this situation by creating legal barriers
which would preclude potential plaintiffs' seeking judicial
remedies.

Litigation is expensive. Few Southern Negroes could possibly afford to bring suit against school boards in order to
obtain admission to all-white elementary and high schools.
And, as no governmental agency had taken the initiative in
bringing legal proceedings, the task of instituting litigation
fell by default to the National Association for the Advancement of Colored People. Where proceedings have been begun
in the name of individual Negro school children, it is common knowledge that the NAACP has usually been behind
the suit. Consequently, an important part of the Southern

legal strategy has been to prevent the NAACP from operating in the deep South.

Three devices have been used to gain this end. The first involved court actions brought by state attorneys general seeking to enjoin the NAACP from any activities within the state. The legal theory behind these actions is that the national organization of the NAACP is a New York corporation. Thus, according to Southern legal tacticians, the NAACP groups in the South are merely branches of the national association and the NAACP is thus required to register as a foreign (out-of-state) corporation. The argument runs that since it has not so registered, it should be enjoined from conducting any operations in the Southern states.

The NAACP has studiously avoided registering as a foreign corporation in the states below the Mason-Dixon Line. It takes the legal position that the state groups are separate, unincorporated associations and thus not subject to the foreign corporation registration requirements. As a practical matter, the NAACP adheres to this position on two grounds. The organization has eschewed registration in order to encourage the type of effort which results from local autonomy. It also objects to the registration requirement of recording membership lists and the names of contributors. The NAACP is anxious to avoid the economic reprisals which would be forthcoming should those lists become a matter of public record.

The first court actions against the NAACP—decided in 1956 and 1957—were successful.[16] Several state tribunals ruled that registration was required and that, in its absence, the organization was enjoined from any activities within the states involved.

Other court injunctions against the NAACP had been begun or were being planned in the first three years following the desegregation decision of May 17, 1954, and it is certain that at least one of them will eventually reach the Supreme Court. It is impossible to predict the ultimate determination. Final decision will depend upon recognition or denial of a federal right which the NAACP might have as a nation-wide organization desiring to conduct noncommercial activities within a state.

A second method of undermining the NAACP is through its members. South Carolina has taken the lead in this area, enacting legislation [17] prohibiting the employment of any NAACP member by a state agency. The statute also provides for a fine against any person hiring a NAACP member for a public post.

Criminal sanctions, obviously directed against the NAACP, represent the third line of attack. This is the Mississippi approach.[18] And it is certain that other Southern states will enact statutes like the one in Mississippi making it a crime for an organization to institute desegregation litigation in the state courts. Punishment by imprisonment of up to one year in the state penitentiary may be adjudged against those who violate the newly created Mississippi rules governing state court actions. The legislation is ostensibly designed "to prohibit the solicitation, receipt or donation of funds for the purpose of filing or prosecuting law suits, etc." But a careful reading of the exceptions noted in the statute makes it clear that the only litigation which would be prohibited would be that in the field of desegregation. Obviously, the legislation does not and could not affect suits brought in the federal courts.

In addition to their campaign against the NAACP, the Southern states have taken legislative action to harass others who would assist potential plaintiffs—as well as the potential plaintiffs themselves. One of the many Virginia plans [19] to circumvent the Supreme Court's determination requires each plaintiff in a state court desegregation proceeding to prepare a long and complicated statement, listing the organizations and individuals who have provided advice or contributed funds in the suit. Failure to reveal the names of those assisting in the litigation—and even failure to comply completely with the vaguely worded statutory requirements—may subject the would-be plaintiffs to judicial punishment. Even where a potential plaintiff is able to comply with the rules, he may be reluctant to do so. Once the names of his advisors and contributors become matters of public record, those listed become prone to community reprisals—usually in the form of economic sanctions. The threat of such reprisals, coupled with the additional paper-work burden, acts as a deterrent to bringing desegregation proceedings.

North Carolina has set up a lengthy, time-consuming procedure to handle—and discourage—desegregation litigation. All public school children in that state are subject to a pupil assignment plan [20] which authorizes the school boards to designate those who are to attend each elementary and high school. As might be expected, the education authorities execute this plan by assigning white and Negro children to different schools. If any pupil—meaning any Negro pupil—objects to his assignment, he may then take an appeal.

The procedure which has been set up for such appeals creates a series of remedies for the dissatisfied plaintiff desiring a different decision. The appeal must first be heard by the school board which made the original assignment. If the school authorities refuse to override their prior action, the appeal must then be taken to the state superior court. The next court in the judicial hierarchy which would then hear the case is the state supreme court. The North Carolina plan is designed to take advantage of the fact that no proceedings can be begun in the federal courts until a plaintiff has exhausted all the possible remedies which might be available through the action of the state courts. This is known as the "exhaustion of remedies" doctrine.

Time-consuming (and expensive) as these procedures may be, they are certainly not unusual. The North Carolina rules are ostensibly in accord with accepted judicial practices. But the way in which the state courts have interpreted these rules has compounded delay to such an extent that there is grave doubt as to the constitutionality of the prescribed method of taking appeals.

In late 1955, the United States Court of Appeals for the Fourth Circuit had before it an action [21] begun in the federal district court in North Carolina, seeking to enjoin a school board from denying admission to Negro children. On the basis of the North Carolina enactment setting up appeals procedures, the Court of Appeals ruled that the statutory remedies had not as yet been exhausted. The district court was ordered to dismiss the proceedings without prejudice as having been prematurely brought. The plaintiffs were required to prosecute their action in the state courts first.

Attempting to exhaust their judicial remedies in the state tribunals, these same Negro plaintiffs finally came before the North Carolina Supreme Court in May, 1956.[22] And the state supreme court refused to consider their case. Suit had been begun by the named plaintiffs as a class action in their own behalf and on behalf of all other Negro children in that same school district "similarly situated." The action was dismissed on the theory that the North Carolina School Placement Act required proceedings on an *individual* basis, and that class suits had now been outlawed by statute. Under this interpretation, each of the Negro children in the school district would have to commence a separate suit in order to be admitted to what had formerly been an all-white school. This would make it virtually impossible for individual plaintiffs to obtain the sums necessary to commence judicial proceedings. Nor could any individual litigant wait out the interminable delays which would inevitably accompany this multiplicity of litigation.

It is this decision of the North Carolina Supreme Court which may well have rendered the entire delaying scheme invalid. For there is a well-recognized exception to the exhaustion of remedies rule which will probably come into play in this situation. As repeated again and again by the Supreme Court, "the doctrine of exhaustion of state remedies, to which this Court has required the scrupulous adherence of all federal courts . . . presupposes that some adequate state remedy exists." [23] Phrased in another way: "Strict local rules of pleading cannot be used to impose unnecessary burdens upon rights of recovery authorized by federal laws. 'Whatever springes the State may set for those who are endeavoring to assert rights that the State confers, the assertion of Federal rights, when plainly and reasonably made, is not to be defeated under the name of local practice.' . . . Should this Court fail to protect federally created rights from dismissal because of over-exacting local requirements for meticulous pleadings, desirable uniformity in adjudication of federally created rights could not be achieved." [24]

North Carolina's delaying action, which was so adroitly conceived to forestall desegregation litigation, may have become *too* effective. And if the Supreme Court equates North Carolina's "exhaustion of remedies" scheme with "no remedies at all," the entire plan will be doomed to failure.

Separation—But Not by Race

The third general approach to avoiding the consequences of *Brown* v. *Board of Education* is an attempt to find some method of classification ostensibly devoid of racial overtones —which will still result in the continued separation of the races in the Southern school systems. Many of the Southern states believe that they have found the desired classification factor.

One of the reasons given for the decision of May 17, 1954,

was that separate schools "deprive the children of the minority group of equal educational opportunities." Segregated education is more than a century old, and in the absence of equal educational opportunities, most Negro pupils are considerably less advanced than white children of the same age and school grade. By setting up a classification factor based upon scholastic achievement, the Southern states would be creating a dividing line which would separate white and Negro school children in by far the majority of cases.

This method of classification has been supplemented by the amorphous test of "aptitude." Proposed legislation in Arkansas, for example, sets forth these factors as the principal bases of its pupil assignment plan: Before any child can be assigned to any particular school, the boards must consider "the effect of the admission of new pupils upon established or proposed academic programs; the suitability of established curricula for particular pupils; the adequacy of the pupil's academic preparation for admission to a particular school and curriculum; the scholastic aptitude and relative intelligence or mental energy or ability of the pupil; the psychological qualification of the pupil for the type of teaching and associations involved; the effect of admission of the pupil upon the academic program of other students in a particular school or facility thereof; [and] the effect of admission upon prevailing academic standards at a particular school. . . ." [25]

Florida's Pupil Assignment Law uses this language: ". . . the rules and regulations to be prescribed by the Board may include, but be not limited to provisions for the conduct of such uniform tests as may be deemed necessary or advisable in classifying the pupils according to intellectual ability and scholastic proficiency to the end that there will be established in each school within the county an environment of equality among pupils of like qualifications and academic attainments. In the preparation and conduct of such tests and in classifying the pupils for assignment to the schools which they will attend, the board shall take into account such sociological, psychological, and like intangible social scientific factors as will prevent, as nearly as practicable, any condition of socio-economic class consciousness among the pupils attending any given school in order that each pupil may be afforded an opportunity for a normal adjustment to his environment and receive the highest standard of instruction within his ability to understand and assimilate. In designating the school to which pupils may be assigned there shall be taken into consideration the available facilities and teaching capacity of the several schools within the county, the effect of the admission of new students upon established academic programs, the suitability of established curriculum to the students enrolled or to be enrolled in a given school. The scholastic aptitude, intelligence, mental energy or ability of the pupil applying for admission and the psychological, moral, ethical and cultural background and qualifications of the pupil applying for admission as compared with other pupils previously assigned to the school in which admission is sought." [26]

Mississippi and Virginia have also enacted legislation setting up classification tests which appear to be nonracial in character.

While the Mississippi statute makes reference to "the educational needs and welfare of the child involved," it puts primary emphasis on "health and moral factors." [27] In order to provide a moral basis which would justify racial segregation, the Mississippi legislature passed another statute which takes advantage of the prevalent disregard for marriage licenses in large parts of the state. Deeply religious, many of the people of rural Mississippi are married by a duly ordained minister of the gospel, but few ever register such marriages with the office of the county clerk. In the eyes of governmental authority, such marriages are deemed common law marriages—both recognized and respected until 1956. Now the State of Mississippi has abolished common law marriages and has declared "any children born as a result thereof illegitimate." [28] This statute applies to the whites as well as to the Negroes of the "Bible Belt," but it is unlikely that it will result in any investigation of the marriage contract of the parents of the white children who apply for admission to the schools.

The test of "aptitude" also appears in the legislation proposed in 1955 by the Gray Commission in Virginia. Giving local school boards all pupil assignment responsibilities, the statute authorizes these boards "to take into consideration such factors as availability of facilities, health, aptitude of the child and the availability of transportation." [29]

All these plans are constitutionally valid—if they are literally enforced without regard to race or color. And whether or not any of these statutes will be held constitutional must depend upon a factual determination. The key is not whether race is omitted as a classification factor, but whether race is truly disregarded in the process of enforcement.

Virginia's Federal District Judge Walter E. Hoffman understood this when he was called upon to interpret the pupil assignment aspects of the Virginia statute in February, 1957.[30] He reiterated the fact that "there is no inherent right of any particular child to attend any particular school," [31] and that local authorities are fully authorized to assign pupils as they will, so long as racial factors are not the criterion. Yet, because the actual pupil assignments had been made on a racial basis, the plan had to be declared unconstitutional.

The approach which the federal courts will probably take in deciding the constitutionality of such plans is indicated in an analogous case [32] involving the Fifteenth Amendment. This is the Amendment which denied the states the power to deprive Negroes of the right to vote. In an attempt to circumvent this Amendment, Oklahoma amended its state constitution in 1910, setting up a literacy test as a prerequisite to voting. There was certainly nothing invalid about such a qualification. But the Oklahoma law made a significant exception to the list of potential voters required to take its examination. No person "who was on January 1, 1866, or at any time prior thereto, entitled to vote under any form of government . . . and no *lineal descendant of such person,* [was to be] denied the right to register and vote because of his inability to so read and write . . ." (italics added). In other words, the only persons who would be required to pass a difficult literacy test in order to vote were those whose grandfathers had been slaves.

Such provision could not meet the test of constitutionality. Its enforcement would deny Negroes—and only Negroes—the right to vote. It was an obvious attempt to "evade" the Fifteenth Amendment, and the Supreme Court had no difficulty in declaring its invalidity.

Thwarted in its attempt to deprive Negroes of the franchise by means of a "Grandfather Clause," Oklahoma then passed a statute in 1916 requiring that all persons who had previously been denied the right to vote must register within a twelve-day period. Since this obviously applied only to Negroes and since the "practical difficulties in the administration of such a strict registration provision" would undoubtedly keep most Negroes from the polls, this statute was likewise struck down as unconstitutional. The Fifteenth Amendment, wrote the Court, "nullifies sophisticated as well as simple-minded modes of discrimination. It hits onerous procedural requirements which effectively handicap exercise of the franchise by the colored race although the abstract right to vote may remain unrestricted as to race." [33]

This same principle would undoubtedly be applied in any case in which the classification factor would result in the continued separation of the races.

THE NEW "PRIVATE-PUBLIC" SCHOOLS

Recognizing the constitutional infirmities of these classification schemes, Virginia's Gray Commission recommended a final statutory provision, "that no child be required to attend an integrated school." [34] Virginia seeks to implement this policy by either of two methods.

Under one aspect of the Virginia plan, any child who objects to his assignment to a nonsegregated school has a "free choice" to attend a segregated school. Theoretically, this would result in the maintenance of three separate school systems: white, Negro and mixed. As a practical matter, however, since adherence to the Virginia "way of life" would result in objections by substantially all the white children assigned to integrated schools, the state would continue to run the same sort of segregated school organization as it operated prior to *Brown* v. *Board of Education*. The fact that the Virginia plan really provides for the continuation of the traditional Negro-white school separation is further evidenced by resolutions passed by various county school boards in 1956. These boards have provided that no public revenue will be used for the support of "public schools in said count[ies] wherein white and colored children are taught together under any plan or arrangement whatsoever." [35]

As a second means of effectuating the Virginia policy, provision has been made for the payment of tuition grants to those children who object to attending an integrated school and who are unable to find a segregated public school in the local area. This would have the effect of creating a state-wide system of new "private-public" schools such as has been proposed by many of the Southern states as a means of avoiding desegregation.

The decision of May 17, 1954, was directed only against state action which required or permitted racial discrimination. Nothing was said—or could be said—about all-white or all-Negro private schools. Southern lawyers thus hope to avoid desegregation through the device of separating the schools from the states. It is their view that constitutionally they can do indirectly what they cannot do directly: that is, give Southern children segregated education by appropriating state funds to be given to the pupils for tuition rather than appropriating those same funds to maintain the public schools.

There are several different ways which have been adopted or proposed to accomplish this method of circumvention. Virginia would abolish all public schools threatened with integration and provide tuition grants which would in effect subsidize the existence of private schools. The Georgia plan calls for the closing of all public schools and the leasing of all present public school facilities to private persons who would be expected to carry on segregated education.[36] The South Carolina scheme merely provides that once a court order requires the admission of a Negro child to a particular all-white school that particular school will be closed.[37] No alternative has been proposed as a method of maintaining elementary and secondary education in that state. More accurately, since any alternative which would result in racial segregation would be unconstitutional state action, South Carolina has purposely refused to provide such alternative.

Whether or not any of these plans—or any other plans to circumvent *Brown* v. *Board of Education* by separating the schools from the state—meets the test of constitutionality depends upon the expanding concept of "state action."

In citing precedent for its decision of May 17, 1954, the Supreme Court reaffirmed the legal principles established in the first cases construing the Fourteenth Amendment. And what these cases held was that the restrictions of the Fourteenth Amendment were restrictions against the states and not against individuals. Thus before the protections of the

Amendment can be invoked, it must be shown that there was some action on the part of the state.

There was never any question about what constituted a "state." The Constitution recognizes only two sovereign entities, the states and the federal government. All forty-eight of the political subdivisions which run the alphabetical gamut from Alabama to Wyoming are, of course, states. And there is state action when any creature of the state—be it the governor, the legislature, a city, a county, or a district school board—passes a law or promulgates a regulation.

Since the Eleventh Amendment prohibits any suit against the state without its consent, the only way in which a litigant can secure the rights guaranteed by the Fourteenth Amendment is to bring suit against an individual who has acted for or on behalf of the state.[38] This is something quite different from a suit against an individual who has discriminated against a member of another race in his individual capacity.

A system of state-operated public schools is, of course, a manifestation of state action. And the Supreme Court has held that state action which results in racial discrimination is unconstitutional *per se*. But the Supreme Court has no power to interfere with racial discrimination as practiced by private schools. What South Carolina, Georgia and Virginia have done is to enact and propose legislation which would remove the "state action" from the operation of the schools within those states.

If South Carolina *completely* abandons its public school system and makes no provision for any alternate system of education, it will have effectively avoided the consequences of *Brown* v. *Board of Education*. If, on the other hand, South Carolina pursues its present plan of closing a public school whenever a court orders the admission of a Negro to a particular school, the whole scheme will probably be held unconstitutional. At such time as the state would have closed down some schools and would still be operating others, it

obviously would be denying some of its school children—
both white and colored—the equal protection of the laws.

The Georgia plan would almost certainly be declared unconstitutional in its present form. By providing for the leasing of existing public school facilities to private individuals,
Georgia is apparently acting under the presumed authority
of *Berea College* v. *Kentucky*,[39] decided by the Supreme
Court in 1908. That was the case which sanctioned the action
of the Kentucky legislature requiring segregation in private
schools. The Supreme Court reasoned that a state had the
power to regulate the activities of any corporation—including
college corporations—within its border.

But that was 1908. In 1948, the Supreme Court handed
down the landmark decision of *Shelley* v. *Kraemer*.[40] Before
the nine men was a restrictive covenant preventing the sale
of a piece of real property to a Negro. No action could be
taken by the Supreme Court declaring the invalidity of the
privately drawn restrictive covenant. But what the nine men
did was to prohibit the state, through its courts, from enforcing that covenant. Where state action would result in racial
discrimination, such action immediately becomes unconstitutional. And certainly, under the rule of *Shelley* v. *Kraemer*,
the Georgia legislature would not be permitted to enact any
law requiring the newly established private schools to maintain racial segregation. Under the Georgia plan, the schools
which would come under private control would be those formerly owned by the state—and the process of "giving away"
a state function would certainly be frowned upon by the
courts under the *Shelley* v. *Kraemer* doctrine.

While it might appear possible to circumvent *Shelley* v.
Kraemer by leasing the school facilities to known pro-segregationists and thus avoiding the necessity of enacting pro-
segregation statutes, such a plan would likewise be doomed
to unconstitutionality. In a long series of voting cases, cul-
minating in the Texas Jaybird decision [41] in 1952, the Su-

preme Court held that a private organization which in reality controlled nominations for primary elections was engaged in state action.

This is what happened in the Texas voting cases: Up until 1932, the State of Texas was the agency which prohibited Negroes from voting in party primaries. Foreseeing constitutional difficulties, Texas repealed its anti-Negro statutes at that time and enacted other laws allowing the political parties to prescribe the qualifications for voting. When the regulation of the state Democratic Party proscribing Negro voting was declared unconstitutional,[42] Texas repealed all of its statutes dealing with membership in political parties. But the Democratic Party still excluded Negroes and again the issue came before the Supreme Court. The nine men then declared that the action of the Democratic Party was the action of the state and was invalid despite the absence of a statute authorizing discrimination.[43] Still trying to avoid the state action label, the Texas Democratic Party then attempted to divest itself of primary nominations by transferring this responsibility to the privately operated Jaybird Clubs whose membership was restricted to whites. And in its 1952 determination the Supreme Court again struck down the racial classification; the action of the Jaybird Clubs was— for the purposes of the Fourteenth Amendment—still the action of the State of Texas.

The Texas attempt to find a nongovernmental agency which might constitutionally preclude Negro voting had failed. Several of the Supreme Court judges felt that since voting is a responsibility of the state, any agency which directs this function is automatically engaged in state action. And Chief Justice Warren in *Brown* v. *Board of Education* specifically described education as "perhaps the most important function of state and local governments." Interpreting the Jaybird and Brown decisions together gives new meaning to state action: it not only includes action directly on behalf of the state, but also the performance of those functions which are normally the responsibility of the state. Following this line of reasoning, any racial discrimination in any school would be held unconstitutional. And this would be the rule regardless of the public or private character of the agency operating the school.

There is a very strong analogy between Texas's attempt to divest itself of the voting function through a privately operated agency and Georgia's attempt to divest itself of its educational responsibilities. And a similar type of Supreme Court determination can be safely predicted.

Under the Virginia plan, on the other hand, the schools which would educate the children who had received state tuition grants would be schools which had always been private in character. And whether or not racial segregation would be constitutionally valid in those private schools would depend upon whether the Supreme Court held that the receipt of the tuition grants from the states by those institutions transformed them into state agencies for the purposes of the Fourteenth Amendment.

Virginia believed that it had precedent to sustain the validity of this aspect of its tuition grant program. But despite the cases which appeared to support the Virginia action, this plan was also subject to constitutional disabilities. While there was no Supreme Court case precisely in point, there was one state court decision and two by the lower federal courts which had direct bearing on the subject. Then, after the promulgation of the Virginia plan, came a Supreme Court order which clearly indicated that any system of "private-public" schools would fall within the state action definition and would be invalidated if racial segregation was maintained.

Analogous to the Virginia position was a 4 to 3 decision by New York's highest court, the Court of Appeals, in 1949.[44] This was the case which upheld the refusal of the Stuyvesant

Town Corp. to rent an apartment in its $90 million housing development to a Negro. While the corporation was owned by a private insurance company, plaintiff argued that since Stuyvesant Town had been granted a state tax exemption and since the property had been acquired through the city's eminent domain power, state action was involved. And the plaintiff further argued state action on the theory that Stuyvesant Town was "a large community" within the city and should be treated in the same manner as a political subdivision of the State. The Court of Appeals, however, denied both contentions, and the Supreme Court refused to review the New York determination.

In another pro-segregation case, *Norris* v. *Mayor and City Council of Baltimore*,[45] Negroes who had been denied admission to a Baltimore art school in 1948 claimed that state action was involved because the city had paid for the tuition of outstanding students. This time it was a federal district court which denied that the discrimination practiced was state action.

A contrary position was taken by the lower federal courts in the 1945 decision of *Kerr* v. *Enoch Pratt Free Library*.[46] This case involved a will which had provided funds for the establishment of a private school—and a school policy which denied the admission of Negro students. Since the terms of the will were silent on the subject of racial discrimination, it was successfully argued that it must have been the State of Maryland itself which had imposed segregation. It was also shown that the state owned and contributed the use of the land on which the school stood and gave considerable financial support to the school's operations. The federal court of appeals ruled that the facts fell within the state action definition and ordered the admission of qualified Negro students.

These were the leading cases on the subject when the Southern states first advanced their private-public school plans in the months immediately following *Brown* v. *Board of Education.* And these were the leading cases on the subject until the Pennsylvania Supreme Court [47] and the United States Supreme Court [48] spoke in the hotly contested Girard College case.

In his will, probated in 1831, Stephen Girard left a fund in trust for the erection, maintenance and operation of a "college." Further, the will provided that the college was to admit "as many poor, white male orphans between the ages of 6 and 10 years as the said income should be adequate to maintain." The City of Philadelphia was named as trustees. Since 1869, under a statute of the Pennsylvania legislature, the trust has been administered and the college operated by the "Board of Directors of City Trusts of the City of Philadelphia."

Lawyers for the Negro plaintiffs (who had been denied admission solely because of race) argued that state action was involved. The defendants countered with the argument that the testator's wishes were clear, and that an individual has the right to will his property as he sees fit.

While there is a general rule of law that a man may dispose of his estate as he wishes, no will or trust can be judicially enforced if its provisions are contrary to existing law. Certainly no court would enforce the terms of a will setting up a school for thieves, for example. And the provision of the Girard will restricting college admission to white students would be illegal if the discrimination being enforced by the managers of the school—the City of Philadelphia—constituted state action. That was precisely the question before the Pennsylvania Supreme Court in November, 1956. By a divided vote, the court ruled that the extent of control exercised by the city was insufficient to meet the state action requirement.

The United States Supreme Court disagreed. In a *per curiam* order issued April 29, 1957, the Court specifically stated that, "The Board which operates Girard College is an agency of the State of Pennsylvania." [49] The judgment of the state tri-

bunal was reversed and the case "remanded for further proceedings not inconsistent with the opinion." As a result of
this decision, there is little possibility that the Virginia plan
or any of the other private-public school devices will be able
to meet the test of constitutionality.

It is probable that the Supreme Court will go even further
in extending the application of the present meaning of state
action. Language indicating this trend was used by Chief Justice Warren and Justices Black and Douglas in a dissenting
opinion during the summer of 1956. "[T]he courts may not
be implicated in . . . a discriminatory scheme," wrote the
dissenters. "Once the courts put their imprimatur on such a
contract, government, speaking through the judicial branch,
acts. . . . And it is governmental action that the Constitution controls." [50] This represents an extremely broad reading
of the restrictive covenant case of *Shelley* v. *Kraemer* where
the Supreme Court declared that the state could not enforce
private discriminations. For in the Warren-Black-Douglas
view, any slight participation by any state instrumentality
in a discriminatory scheme—no matter how limited that
"participation"—is unconstitutional state action.

The rule of law that state-imposed racial discrimination is
unconstitutional may well result in decisions of future Supreme Courts declaring the invalidity of the racial discrimination now practiced legally by privately operated schools,
privately operated businesses and privately operated clubs.
This can be done in one of two ways: either by applying the
existing law to new factual situations, or by changing the
present legal meaning of state action.

The Warren-Black-Douglas position on *Shelley* v. *Kraemer,*
strengthened by the decision in the Girard College case, represents the first of these approaches. They would declare unconstitutional any racial discrimination where its existence
could *possibly* be connected with the state. Racial classifications might be outlawed in the operation of a private school

on the theory that its educational standards are prescribed by the state; racial classifications might be struck down in the employment policies of a private corporation on the theory that the existence of the corporation depended upon a state charter; racial classifications might be invalidated in the membership requirements of a fraternal order on the theory that it had received a state-authorized tax exemption.

The second way in which the Fourteenth Amendment can be extended to preclude *all* racial discrimination is by changing the actual meaning of state action. This can be accomplished by developing the thinking of the Supreme Court in the Jaybird decision. In that case, the discrimination practiced by a private group in election primaries was invalidated on the theory that voting was a state function—and that any agency performing a state function would have to meet the requirements of the Fourteenth Amendment. Following this line of reasoning, any task which historically has been a function of the state (like voting and jury service) will always be judicially considered a function of the state. Accordingly, such function would have to be performed on a racially non-discriminatory basis, regardless of the absence of specific state action.

A change in the meaning of state action can also be accomplished by reintroducing into this area of constitutional thinking some basic common law principles. Some future Supreme Court might well hold that any activity which affects large numbers of the general public automatically becomes a matter of governmental concern, and thus falls within the state action concept. Under such an analysis the services of hotels, restaurants and theaters would have to be made available to the general public without regard to race. This was the old English common law rule governing inns and common carriers, since those facilities are inherently public in character. And while housing was not of public concern at common law, present-day, large-scale housing developments could be declared a matter of governmental interest within the context of the Fourteenth Amendment. This approach would preclude racial discrimination in these private activities regardless of any specific action on the part of the state and regardless of whether the state had ever undertaken such activities in the past.

COURSE OF IMPLEMENTATION

It was not until the Supreme Court issued its implementation decree of May 31, 1955, that even the most astute of lawyers became aware of the far-reaching implications of the *School Segregation Cases.* It was only by studying the 1955 determination that the 1954 decision could be understood. And it was not until 1956 that it became obvious that all state-imposed racial discrimination had been declared unconstitutional *per se.*

But a real understanding of what the nine men said and did on May 17, 1954, goes far beyond the issue of school segregation and far beyond its attendant legal implications. Regardless of personal feelings about racial segregation and regardless of social attitudes toward the Supreme Court's approach and conclusion, *Brown* v. *Board of Education* must be acknowledged as an important, existing fact. While no attempt has been made within these pages to arrive at sociological judgments as to the rights and wrongs of segregation, there is no discounting the fact that the Supreme Court has spoken and that the law has been determined. Whatever may be done in the future to advance or delay the course of desegregation must be accomplished within the legal framework of this decision. *Brown* v. *Board of Education* must stand as the most significant civil rights decision ever rendered by an American court and as the symbol of the social revolution which marks mid-twentieth-century America.

What *Brown* v. *Board of Education* will come to mean in

later years—and there are undoubtedly implications as yet undiscovered—will depend in large measure upon the developing definition of "with all deliberate speed" and the expanding concept of state action. But such definition and expansion will be confined to the ever-growing significance of *Brown* v. *Board of Education* as the key decision in the field of racial discrimination. To the lawyer, the action taken by the nine men on May 17, 1954, means even more.

A revolutionary judicial technique—one which will govern the course of decision in many fields of the law—was evolved for the first time in Chief Justice Warren's unanimous opinion. It was a technique giving increased importance to the utilization of nonlegal data and developing a new use for such materials as a means of informing and guiding the judicial mind.

Of even greater legal significance was the precedent-making manifestation of judicial flexibility evidenced in the manner in which the decision was implemented. Virtually no judicial decisions are handed down in two parts, first setting forth the nature of the right and then providing the remedy which would effectuate that right. Never before had the lower courts been given so much discretion in carrying out the enforcement mandate of the high tribunal. New light was shed on what a judicial decision could accomplish and the ways in which a judicial dictate could be adapted to a complex problem.

But there are deficiencies as well as advantages in the Supreme Court's newly developed method of implementation. This was not a case in which the rewards of a favorable judicial determination came quickly to the victorious litigant. Inherent in the mode of enforcement was a factor of delay—and it was a delay which could easily be multiplied manyfold by judges reluctant to give co-operation. And the delay was further augmented by a legal tug-of-war in which the leading lawyers of the South sought new approaches to legal doctrine in order to avoid desegregation.

What has delayed desegregation perhaps even more is the fact that judicial enforcement is dependent upon someone initiating litigation. And this task has fallen by default to those who are in a disadvantageous position for instituting legal proceedings—the Southern Negroes. Subject to economic pressures which can be brought to bear by members of the dominant white majority, the Southern Negro has been discouraged from asserting his constitutional rights. More, he is fearful of losing the position he has achieved in the South since slavery days. He is fearful of the influence of the White Citizens' Councils, which might result in the loss of his job or the inability to obtain credit. He is fearful of such laws as the Georgia statute of 1956 which requires all state employees to enforce segregation laws or lose their positions and the privileges pertaining to those positions.[51] This is an important law to the most educated Negro group in Georgia and the Negro group most anxious to advance the cause of Negro education—the thousands of Negroes who are employed by the state as school teachers.

Since implementation necessitates court proceedings and since the Negro is at a disadvantage in bringing such proceedings, another "plaintiff" must be found. Most desegregation proponents believe that the ideal party to institute enforcement litigation is the Attorney General of the United States.

The advantages are obvious. Under the Attorney General's Department of Justice command is a network of United States attorneys throughout the country possessing the necessary facilities to handle desegregation litigation. The Attorney General has at his disposal the legal talent to undertake the task, sufficient funds for investigation and the resources of the Federal Bureau of Investigation—all safe from the economic pressures which might be brought to bear by the pro-segregation forces.

There is some precedent for such action. The law books are filled with decisions in which the Department of Justice has taken the lead in investigating and prosecuting vote fraud cases involving Negroes who had been deprived of their right of franchise.[52] All of these cases, however, were criminal actions.

As far as civil actions are concerned, there is no law to be found in the federal statutes [53] or in the decisions of the Supreme Court [54] which would enable the Attorney General to sue either for damages or for an injunction as a means of enforcing desegregation. Although the Civil Rights Acts [55] do grant some noncriminal remedies, the statutory language limits suits based on such remedies to those who are actually deprived of their constitutional rights. Thus, in the absence of additional legislation augmenting the authority of the Attorney General, it appears that his powers are confined to criminal prosecutions.

Indications that the Attorney General might assume the leadership in bringing about desegregation through these criminal proceedings appeared at the end of 1956. It was then that Attorney General Herbert Brownell called a December conference of all United States attorneys representing the Southern states to see what steps might be taken to end racial segregation in intrastate bus travel. The year 1957 might well be the year of governmental initiative. And such initiative might well be supplemented by government intervention in pending litigation and by government action to enforce district court decrees through contempt procedures.

To the lawyer—and to the historian and political scientist—*Brown* v. *Board of Education* has yet another meaning. It is a case which clearly reveals the role of the Supreme Court as the ultimate guardian of American civil liberties. It is a case which keynotes the Court's decided preference for those controversies which afford the opportunity to proclaim constitutional principles. The approach of the Supreme Court toward racial discrimination is indicative of its approach toward all civil liberties. Despite any and all of the rules which ostensibly govern questions of constitutionality, there is no doubt of the intention of the high tribunal to put the protection of civil rights in a preferred position.

Justice Black presaged present-day Supreme Court thinking in an opinion rendered in 1940: "Under our Constitutional system," he wrote, "courts stand against any winds that blow as havens of refuge for those who might otherwise suffer because they are helpless, weak, outnumbered, or because they are non-conforming victims of prejudice and public excitement. . . . No higher duty, no more solemn responsibility rests upon this Court, than that of translating into living law and maintaining this constitutional shield deliberately planned and inscribed for the benefit of every human being subject to our Constitution—of whatever race, creed or persuasion." [56]

THE SCHOOL SEGREGATION CASES

UNITED STATES SUPREME COURT
BROWN et al. v. BOARD OF EDUCATION
OF TOPEKA et al.

NO. 1. APPEAL FROM THE UNITED STATES DISTRICT COURT
FOR THE DISTRICT OF KANSAS.*

Argued December 9, 1952.—Reargued December 8, 1953.—
Decided May 17, 1954.

MR. CHIEF JUSTICE WARREN delivered the opinion of the
Court.

These cases come to us from the States of Kansas, South
Carolina, Virginia, and Delaware. They are premised on different facts and different local conditions, but a common legal
question justifies their consideration together in this consolidated opinion.[1]

---

* Together with No. 2, *Briggs et al.* v. *Elliott et al.*, on appeal from the
United States District Court for the Eastern District of South Carolina, argued
December 9-10, 1952, reargued December 7-8, 1953; No. 4, *Davis et al.* v.
County School Board of Prince Edward County, Virginia, et al., on appeal
from the United States District Court for the Eastern District of Virginia,
argued December 10, 1952, reargued December 7-8, 1953; and No. 10, *Gebhart
et al.* v. *Belton et al.*, on certiorari to the Supreme Court of Delaware, argued
December 11, 1952, reargued December 9, 1953.

1. In the Kansas case, Brown v. Board of Education, the plaintiffs are Negro
children of elementary school age residing in Topeka. They brought this action in the United States District Court for the District of Kansas to enjoin
enforcement of a Kansas statute which permits, but does not require, cities of
more than 15,000 population to maintain separate school facilities for Negro
and white students. Kan.Gen.Stat.1949, § 72-1724. Pursuant to that authority,
the Topeka Board of Education elected to establish segregated elementary
schools. Other public schools in the community, however, are operated on a
nonsegregated basis. The three-judge District Court, convened under 28 U.S.C.
§§ 2281 and 2284, 28 U.S.C.A. §§ 2281, 2284, found that segregation in public
education has a detrimental effect upon Negro children, but denied relief on
the ground that the Negro and white schools were substantially equal with
respect to buildings, transportation, curricula, and educational qualifications

273

of teachers. 98 F.Supp. 797. The case is here on direct appeal under 28 U.S.C. § 1253, 28 U.S.C.A. § 1253.

In the South Carolina case, Briggs v. Elliott, the plaintiffs are Negro children of both elementary and high school age residing in Clarendon County. They brought this action in the United States District Court for the Eastern District of South Carolina to enjoin enforcement of provisions in the state constitution and statutory code which require the segregation of Negroes and whites in public schools. S.C.Const. Art. XI, § 7; S.C. Code 1942, § 5377. The three-judge District Court, convened under 28 U.S.C. §§ 2281 and 2284, 28 U.S.C.A. §§ 2281, 2284, denied the requested relief. The court found that the Negro schools were inferior to the white schools and ordered the defendants to begin immediately to equalize the facilities. But the court sustained the validity of the contested provisions and denied the plaintiffs admission to the white schools during the equalization program. 98 F.Supp. 529. This Court vacated the District Court's judgment and remanded the case for the purpose of obtaining the court's views on a report filed by the defendants concerning the progress made in the equalization program. 342 U.S. 350, 72 S.Ct. 327, 96 L.Ed. 392. On remand, the District Court found that substantial equality had been achieved except for buildings and that the defendants were proceeding to rectify this inequality as well. 103 F.Supp. 920. The case is again here on direct appeal under 28 U.S.C. § 1253, 28 U.S.C.A. § 1253.

In the Virginia case, Davis v. County School Board, the plaintiffs are Negro children of high school age residing in Prince Edward County. They brought this action in the United States District Court for the Eastern District of Virginia to enjoin enforcement of provisions in the state constitution and statutory code which require the segregation of Negroes and whites in public schools. Va.Const. § 140; Va.Code 1950, § 22-221. The three-judge District Court, convened under 28 U.S.C. §§ 2281 and 2284, 28 U.S.C.A. §§ 2281, 2284, denied the requested relief. The court found the Negro school inferior in physical plant, curricula, and transportation, and ordered the defendants forthwith to provide substantially equal curricula and transportation and to "proceed with all reasonable diligence and dispatch to remove" the inequality in physical plant. But, as in the South Carolina case, the court sustained the validity of the contested provisions and denied the plaintiffs admission to the white schools during the equalization program. 103 F.Supp. 337. The case is here on direct appeal under 28 U.S.C. § 1253, 28 U.S.C.A. § 1253.

In the Delaware case, Gebhart v. Belton, the plaintiffs are Negro children of both elementary and high school age residing in New Castle County. They brought this action in the Delaware Court of Chancery to enjoin enforcement of provisions in the state constitution and statutory code which require the segregation of Negroes and whites in public schools. Del-Const. Art. X, § 2; Del-Rev. Code, 1935, § 2631, 14 Del.C. § 141. The Chancellor gave judgment for the plaintiffs and ordered their immediate admission to schools previously attended only by white children, on the ground that the Negro schools were inferior with respect to teacher training, pupil-teacher ratio, extracurricular activities, physical plant, and time and distance involved in travel. Del.Ch., 87 A.2d 862. The Chancellor also found that segregation itself results in an inferior education for Negro children (see note 10, *infra*), but did not rest his decision on that ground. 87 A.2d at page 865. The Chancellor's decree was affirmed by the Supreme Court of Delaware, which intimated, however, that the defendants might be able to obtain a modification of the decree after equalization of the Negro and white schools had been accomplished. 91 A.2d 137, 152. The defendants, contending only that the Delaware courts had erred in ordering the immediate admission of the Negro plaintiffs to the white schools, applied to this Court for certiorari. The writ was granted, 344 U.S. 891, 73 S.Ct. 213, 97 L.Ed. 689. The plaintiffs, who were successful below, did not submit a cross-petition.

In each of the cases, minors of the Negro race, through their legal representatives, seek the aid of the courts in obtaining admission to the public schools of their community on a nonsegregated basis. In each instance, they have been denied admission to schools attended by white children under laws requiring or permitting segregation according to race. This segregation was alleged to deprive the plaintiffs of the equal protection of the laws under the Fourteenth Amendment. In each of the cases other than the Delaware case, a three-judge federal district court denied relief to the plaintiffs on the so-called "separate but equal" doctrine announced by this Court in Plessy v. Ferguson, 163 U.S. 537, 16 S.Ct. 1138, 41 L.Ed. 256. Under that doctrine, equality of treatment is accorded when the races are provided substantially equal facilities, even though these facilities be separate. In the Delaware case, the Supreme Court of Delaware adhered to that doctrine, but ordered that the plaintiffs be admitted to the white schools because of their superiority to the Negro schools.

The plaintiffs contend that segregated public schools are not "equal" and cannot be made "equal," and that hence they are deprived of the equal protection of the laws. Because of the obvious importance of the question presented, the Court took jurisdiction.[2] Argument was heard in the 1952 Term, and reargument was heard this Term on certain questions propounded by the Court.[3]

Reargument was largely devoted to the circumstances surrounding the adoption of the Fourteenth Amendment in 1868. It covered exhaustively consideration of the Amendment in Congress, ratification by the states, then existing practices in racial segregation, and the views of proponents and opponents of the Amendment. This discussion and our

2. 344 U.S. 1, 73 S.Ct. 1, 97 L.Ed. 3, Id., 344 U.S. 131, 73 S.Ct. 124, 97 L.Ed. 152; Gebhart v. Belton, 344 U.S. 891, 73 S.Ct. 213, 97 L.Ed. 689.
3. 345 U.S. 972, 73 S.Ct. 1118, 97 L.Ed. 1388. The Attorney General of the United States participated both Terms as *amicus curiae*.

own investigation convince us that, although these sources cast some light, it is not enough to resolve the problem with which we are faced. At best, they are inconclusive. The most avid proponents of the post-War Amendments undoubtedly intended them to remove all legal distinctions among "all persons born or naturalized in the United States." Their opponents, just as certainly, were antagonistic to both the letter and the spirit of the Amendments and wished them to have the most limited effect. What others in Congress and the state legislatures had in mind cannot be determined with any degree of certainty.

An additional reason for the inconclusive nature of the Amendment's history, with respect to segregated schools, is the status of public education at that time.[4] In the South, the movement toward free common schools, supported by general taxation, had not yet taken hold. Education of white children was largely in the hands of private groups. Education of Negroes was almost nonexistent, and practically all of the race were illiterate. In fact, any education of Negroes was forbidden by law in some states. Today, in contrast, many Negroes have achieved outstanding success in the arts and sciences as well as in the business and professional world. It

4. For a general study of the development of public education prior to the Amendment, see Butts and Cremin, A History of Education in American Culture (1953), Pts. I, II; Cubberley, Public Education in the United States (1934 ed.), cc. II-XII. School practices current at the time of the adoption of the Fourteenth Amendment are described in Butts and Cremin, supra, at 269-275; Cubberley, supra, at 288-339, 408-431; Knight, Public Education in the South (1922), cc. VIII, IX. See also H. Ex. Doc. No. 315, 41st Cong., 2d Sess. (1871). Although the demand for free public schools followed substantially the same pattern in both the North and the South, the development in the South did not begin to gain momentum until about 1850, some twenty years after that in the North. The reasons for the somewhat slower development in the South (e.g., the rural character of the South and the different regional attitudes toward state assistance) are well explained in Cubberley, supra, at 408-423. In the country as a whole, but particularly in the South, the War virtually stopped all progress in public education. Id., at 427-428. The low status of Negro education in all sections of the country, both before and immediately after the War, is described in Beale, A History of Freedom of Teaching in American Schools (1941), 112-132, 175-195. Compulsory school attendance laws were not generally adopted until after the ratification of the Fourteenth Amendment, and it was not until 1918 that such laws were in force in all the states. Cubberley, supra, at 563-565.

is true that public school education at the time of the Amendment had advanced further in the North, but the effect of the Amendment on Northern States was generally ignored in the congressional debates. Even in the North, the conditions of public education did not approximate those existing today. The curriculum was usually rudimentary; ungraded schools were common in rural areas; the school term was but three months a year in many states; and compulsory school attendance was virtually unknown. As a consequence, it is not surprising that there should be so little in the history of the Fourteenth Amendment relating to its intended effect on public education.

In the first cases in this Court construing the Fourteenth Amendment, decided shortly after its adoption, the Court interpreted it as proscribing all state-imposed discriminations against the Negro race.[5] The doctrine of "separate but equal" did not make its appearance in this Court until 1896 in the case of Plessy v. Ferguson, supra, involving not education but transportation.[6] American courts have since labored with

5. In re Slaughter-House Cases, 1873, 16 Wall. 36, 67-72, 21 L.Ed. 394; Strauder v. West Virginia, 1880, 100 U.S. 303, 307-308, 25 L.Ed. 664:
"It ordains that no State shall deprive any person of life, liberty, or property, without due process of law, or deny to any person within its jurisdiction the equal protection of the laws. What is this but declaring that the law in the States shall be the same for the black as for the white; that all persons, whether colored or white, shall stand equal before the laws of the States, and, in regard to the colored race, for whose protection the amendment was primarily designed, that no discrimination shall be made against them by law because of their color? The words of the amendment, it is true, are prohibitory, but they contain a necessary implication of a positive immunity, or right, most valuable to the colored race,—the right to exemption from unfriendly legislation against them distinctively as colored,—exemption from legal discriminations, implying inferiority in civil society, lessening the security of their enjoyment of the rights which others enjoy, and discriminations which are steps towards reducing them to the condition of a subject race."
See also State of Virginia v. Rives, 1879, 100 U.S. 313, 318, 25 L.Ed. 667; Ex parte Virginia, 1879, 100 U.S. 339, 344-345, 25 L.Ed. 676.
6. The doctrine apparently originated in Roberts v. City of Boston, 1850, 5 Cush. 198, 59 Mass. 198, 206, upholding school segregation against attack as being violative of a state constitutional guarantee of equality. Segregation in Boston public schools was eliminated in 1855. Mass. Acts 1855, c. 256. But elsewhere in the North segregation in public education has persisted in some communities until recent years. It is apparent that such segregation has long been a nationwide problem, not merely one of sectional concern.

the doctrine for over half a century. In this Court, there have been six cases involving the "separate but equal" doctrine in the field of public education.[7] In Cumming v. Board of Education of Richmond County, 175 U.S. 528, 20 S.Ct. 197, 44 L.Ed. 262, and Gong Lum v. Rice, 275 U.S. 78, 48 S.Ct. 91, 72 L.Ed. 172, the validity of the doctrine itself was not challenged.[8] In more recent cases, all on the graduate school level, inequality was found in that specific benefits enjoyed by white students were denied to Negro students of the same educational qualifications. State of Missouri ex rel. Gaines v. Canada, 305 U.S. 337, 59 S.Ct. 232, 83 L.Ed. 208; Sipuel v. Board of Regents of University of Oklahoma, 332 U.S. 631, 68 S.Ct. 299, 92 L.Ed. 247; Sweatt v. Painter, 339 U.S. 629, 70 S.Ct. 848, 94 L.Ed. 1114; McLaurin v. Oklahoma State Regents, 339 U.S. 637, 70 S.Ct. 851, 94 L.Ed. 1149. In none of these cases was it necessary to re-examine the doctrine to grant relief to the Negro plaintiff. And in Sweatt v. Painter, supra, the Court expressly reserved decision on the question whether Plessy v. Ferguson should be held inapplicable to public education.

In the instant cases, that question is directly presented. Here, unlike Sweatt v. Painter, there are findings below that the Negro and white schools involved have been equalized, or are being equalized, with respect to buildings, curricula, qualifications and salaries of teachers, and other "tangible" factors.[9] Our decision, therefore, cannot turn on merely a

7. See also Berea College v. Kentucky, 1908, 211 U.S. 45, 29 S.Ct. 33, 53 L.Ed. 81.

8. In the Cumming case, Negro taxpayers sought an injunction requiring the defendant school board to discontinue the operation of a high school for white children until the board resumed operation of a high school for Negro children. Similarly, in the Gong Lum case, the plaintiff, a child of Chinese descent, contended only that state authorities had misapplied the doctrine by classifying him with Negro children and requiring him to attend a Negro school.

9. In the Kansas case, the court below found substantial equality as to all such factors. 98 F.Supp. 797, 798. In the South Carolina case, the court below found that the defendants were proceeding "promptly and in good faith to comply with the court's decree." 103 F.Supp. 920, 921. In the Virginia case, the court below noted that the equalization program was already "afoot and pro-

comparison of these tangible factors in the Negro and white schools involved in each of the cases. We must look instead to the effect of segregation itself on public education.

In approaching this problem, we cannot turn the clock back to 1868 when the Amendment was adopted, or even to 1896 when Plessy v. Ferguson was written. We must consider public education in the light of its full development and its present place in American life throughout the Nation. Only in this way can it be determined if segregation in public schools deprives these plaintiffs of the equal protection of the laws.

Today, education is perhaps the most important function of state and local governments. Compulsory school attendance laws and the great expenditures for education both demonstrate our recognition of the importance of education to our democratic society. It is required in the performance of our most basic public responsibilities, even service in the armed forces. It is the very foundation of good citizenship. Today it is a principal instrument in awakening the child to cultural values, in preparing him for later professional training, and in helping him to adjust normally to his environment. In these days, it is doubtful that any child may reasonably be expected to succeed in life if he is denied the opportunity of an education. Such an opportunity, where the state has undertaken to provide it, is a right which must be made available to all on equal terms.

We come then to the question presented: Does segregation of children in public schools solely on the basis of race, even though the physical facilities and other "tangible" factors may be equal, deprive the children of the minority group of equal educational opportunities? We believe that it does.

gressing," 103 F.Supp. 337, 341; since then, we have been advised, in the Virginia Attorney General's brief on reargument, that the program has now been completed. In the Delaware case, the court below similarly noted that the state's equalization program was well under way. 91 A.2d 137, 139.

In Sweatt v. Painter, supra [339 U.S. 629, 70 S.Ct. 850], in finding that a segregated law school for Negroes could not provide them equal educational opportunities, this Court relied in large part on "those qualities which are incapable of objective measurement but which make for greatness in a law school." In McLaurin v. Oklahoma State Regents, supra [339 U.S. 637, 70 S.Ct. 853], the Court, in requiring that a Negro admitted to a white graduate school be treated like all other students, again resorted to intangible considerations: "* * * his ability to study, to engage in discussions and exchange views with other students, and, in general, to learn his profession." Such considerations apply with added force to children in grade and high schools. To separate them from others of similar age and qualifications solely because of their race generates a feeling of inferiority as to their status in the community that may affect their hearts and minds in a way unlikely ever to be undone. The effect of this separation on their educational opportunities was well stated by a finding in the Kansas case by a court which nevertheless felt compelled to rule against the Negro plaintiffs:

"Segregation of white and colored children in public schools has a detrimental effect upon the colored children. The impact is greater when it has the sanction of the law; for the policy of separating the races is usually interpreted as denoting the inferiority of the negro group. A sense of inferiority affects the motivation of the child to learn. Segregation with the sanction of law, therefore, has a tendency to [retard] the educational and mental development of Negro children and to deprive them of some of the benefits they would receive in a racial[ly] integrated school system." [10]

10. A similar finding was made in the Delaware case: "I conclude from the testimony that in our Delaware society, State-imposed segregation in education itself results in the Negro children, as a class, receiving educational opportunities which are substantially inferior to those available to white children otherwise similarly situated." 87 A.2d 862, 865.

Whatever may have been the extent of psychological knowledge at the time of Plessy v. Ferguson, this finding is amply supported by modern authority.[11] Any language in Plessy v. Ferguson contrary to this finding is rejected.

We conclude that in the field of public education the doctrine of "separate but equal" has no place. Separate educational facilities are inherently unequal. Therefore, we hold that the plaintiffs and others similarly situated for whom the actions have been brought are, by reason of the segregation complained of, deprived of the equal protection of the laws guaranteed by the Fourteenth Amendment. This disposition makes unnecessary any discussion whether such segregation also violates the Due Process Clause of the Fourteenth Amendment.[12]

Because these are class actions, because of the wide applicability of this decision, and because of the great variety of local conditions, the formulation of decrees in these cases presents problems of considerable complexity. On reargument, the consideration of appropriate relief was necessarily subordinated to the primary question—the constitutionality of segregation in public education. We have now announced that such segregation is a denial of the equal protection of the laws. In order that we may have the full assistance of the parties in formulating decrees, the cases will be restored to the docket, and the parties are requested to present further argument on Questions 4 and 5 previously propounded by

11. K. B. Clark, Effect of Prejudice and Discrimination on Personality Development (Midcentury White House Conference on Children and Youth, 1950); Witmer and Kotinsky, Personality in the Making (1952), c. VI; Deutscher and Chein, The Psychological Effects of Enforced Segregation: A Survey of Social Science Opinion, 26 J.Psychol. 259 (1948); Chein, What are the Psychological Effects of Segregation Under Conditions of Equal Facilities?, 3 Int. J. Opinion and Attitude Res. 229 (1949); Brameld, Educational Costs, in Discrimination and National Welfare (MacIver, ed., 1949), 44-48; Frazier, The Negro in the United States (1949), 674-681. And see generally Myrdal, An American Dilemma (1944).

12. See Bolling v. Sharpe, 347 U.S. 497, 74 S.Ct. 693, concerning the Due Process Clause of the Fifth Amendment.

the Court for the reargument this Term.[13] The Attorney General of the United States is again invited to participate. The Attorneys General of the states requiring or permitting segregation in public education will also be permitted to appear as *amici curiae* upon request to do so by September 15, 1954, and submission of briefs by October 1, 1954.[14]

It is so ordered.

BOLLING et al. v. SHARPE et al.

CERTIORARI TO THE UNITED STATES COURT OF APPEALS
FOR THE DISTRICT OF COLUMBIA CIRCUIT.

No. 8. Argued December 10-11, 1952.—Reargued December 8-9, 1953.—Decided May 17, 1954.

Mr. Chief Justice Warren delivered the opinion of the Court.

This case challenges the validity of segregation in the public schools of the District of Columbia. The petitioners,

13. "4. Assuming it is decided that segregation in public schools violates the Fourteenth Amendment
"(a) would a decree necessarily follow providing that, within the limits set by normal geographic school districting, Negro children should forthwith be admitted to schools of their choice, or
"(b) may this Court, in the exercise of its equity powers, permit an effective gradual adjustment to be brought about from existing segregated systems to a system not based on color distinctions?
"5. On the assumption on which questions 4(a) and (b) are based, and assuming further that this Court will exercise its equity powers to the end described in question 4(b),
"(a) should this Court formulate detailed decrees in these cases;
"(b) if so, what specific issues should the decree reach;
"(c) should this Court appoint a special master to hear evidence with a view to recommending specific terms for such decrees;
"(d) should this Court remand to the courts of first instance with directions to frame decrees in these cases, and if so what general directions should the decrees of this Court include and what procedures should the courts of first instance follow in arriving at the specific terms of more detailed decrees?"
14. See Rule 42, Revised Rules of this Court, effective July 1, 1954, 28 U.S.C.A.

minors of the Negro race, allege that such segregation deprives them of due process of law under the Fifth Amendment. They were refused admission to a public school attended by white children solely because of their race. They sought the aid of the District Court for the District of Columbia in obtaining admission. That court dismissed their complaint. The Court granted a writ of certiorari before judgment in the Court of Appeals because of the importance of the constitutional question presented. 344 U.S. 873, 73 S.Ct. 173, 97 L.Ed. 676.

We have this day held that the Equal Protection Clause of the Fourteenth Amendment prohibits the states from maintaining racially segregated public schools.[1] The legal problem in the District of Columbia is somewhat different, however. The Fifth Amendment, which is applicable in the District of Columbia, does not contain an equal protection clause as does the Fourteenth Amendment which applies only to the states. But the concepts of equal protection and due process, both stemming from our American ideal of fairness, are not mutually exclusive. The "equal protection of the laws" is a more explicit safeguard of prohibited unfairness than "due process of law," and, therefore, we do not imply that the two are always interchangeable phrases. But, as this Court has recognized, discrimination may be so unjustifiable as to be violative of due process.[2]

Classifications based solely upon race must be scrutinized with particular care, since they are contrary to our traditions and hence constitutionally suspect.[3] As long ago as 1896, this Court declared the principle "that the constitution of the

1. Brown v. Board of Education, 347 U.S. 483, 74 S.Ct. 686.
2. Detroit Bank v. United States, 317 U.S. 329, 63 S.Ct. 297, 87 L.Ed. 304; Currin v. Wallace, 306 U.S. 1, 13-14, 59 S.Ct. 379, 386, 83 L.Ed. 441; Steward Machine Co. v. Davis, 301 U.S. 548, 585, 57 S.Ct. 883, 890, 81 L.Ed. 1279.
3. Korematsu v. United States, 323 U.S. 214, 216, 65 S.Ct. 193, 194, 89 L.Ed. 194; Hirabayashi v. United States, 320 U.S. 81, 100, 63 S.Ct. 1375, 1385, 87 L.Ed. 1774.

United States, in its present form, forbids, so far as civil and political rights are concerned, discrimination by the general government, or by the states, against any citizen because of his race." [4] And in Buchanan v. Warley, 245 U.S. 60, 38 S.Ct. 16, 62 L.Ed. 149, the Court held that a statute which limited the right of a property owner to convey his property to a person of another race was, as an unreasonable discrimination, a denial of due process of law.

Although the Court has not assumed to define "liberty" with any great precision, that term is not confined to mere freedom from bodily restraint. Liberty under law extends to the full range of conduct which the individual is free to pursue, and it cannot be restricted except for a proper governmental objective. Segregation in public education is not reasonably related to any proper governmental objective, and thus it imposes on Negro children of the District of Columbia a burden that constitutes an arbitrary deprivation of their liberty in violation of the Due Process Clause.

In view of our decision that the Constitution prohibits the states from maintaining racially segregated public schools, it would be unthinkable that the same Constitution would impose a lesser duty on the Federal Government.[5] We hold that racial segregation in the public schools of the District of Columbia is a denial of the due process of law guaranteed by the Fifth Amendment to the Constitution.

For the reasons set out in Brown v. Board of Education, this case will be restored to the docket for reargument on Questions 4 and 5 previously propounded by the Court. 345 U.S. 972, 73 S.Ct. 1114, 97 L.Ed. 1388.

It is so ordered.

4. Gibson v. Mississippi, 162 U.S. 565, 591, 16 S.Ct. 904, 910, 40 L.Ed. 1075. Cf. Steele v. Louisville & Nashville R. Co., 323 U.S. 192, 198-199, 65 S.Ct. 226, 230, 89 L.Ed. 173.
5. Cf. Hurd v. Hodge, 334 U.S. 24, 68 S.Ct. 847, 92 L.Ed. 1187.

BROWN ET AL. v. BOARD OF EDUCATION OF TOPEKA ET AL.

NO. 1. APPEAL FROM THE UNITED STATES DISTRICT COURT FOR THE DISTRICT OF KANSAS.*

Reargued on the question of relief April 11-14, 1955.—
Opinion and judgments announced May 31, 1955.

MR. CHIEF JUSTICE WARREN delivered the opinion of the Court.

These cases were decided on May 17, 1954. The opinions of that date [1] declaring the fundamental principle that racial discrimination in public education is unconstitutional, are incorporated herein by reference. All provisions of federal, state, or local law requiring or permitting such discrimination must yield to this principle. There remains for consideration the manner in which relief is to be accorded.

Because these cases arose under different local conditions and their disposition will involve a variety of local problems, we requested further argument on the question of relief.[2] In

* Together with No. 2, *Briggs et al.* v. *Elliott et al.,* on appeal from the United States District Court for the Eastern District of South Carolina; No. 3, *Davis et al.* v. *County School Board of Prince Edward County, Virginia, et al.,* on appeal from the United States District Court for the Eastern District of Virginia; No. 4, *Bolling et al.* v. *Sharpe et al.,* on certiorari to the United States Court of Appeals for the District of Columbia Circuit; and No. 5, *Gebhart et al.* v. *Belton et al.,* on certiorari to the Supreme Court of Delaware.

1. 347 U.S. 483, 74 S.Ct. 686, 98 L.Ed. 873; 347 U.S. 497, 74 S.Ct. 693, 98 L.Ed. 884.

2. Further argument was requested on the following questions, 347 U.S. 483, 495-496, note 13, 74 S.Ct. 686, 692, 98 L.Ed. 873, previously propounded by the Court:

"4. Assuming it is decided that segregation in public schools violates the Fourteenth Amendment

"(a) would a decree necessarily follow providing that, within the limits set by normal geographic school districting, Negro children should forthwith be admitted to schools of their choice, or

"(b) may this Court, in the exercise of its equity powers, permit an effective gradual adjustment to be brought about from existing segregated systems to a system not based on color distinctions?

"5. On the assumption on which questions 4(a) and (b) are based, and as-view of the nationwide importance of the decision, we invited the Attorney General of the United States and the Attorneys General of all states requiring or permitting racial discrimination in public education to present their views on that question. The parties, the United States, and the States of Florida, North Carolina, Arkansas, Oklahoma, Maryland, and Texas filed briefs and participated in the oral argument.

These presentations were informative and helpful to the Court in its consideration of the complexities arising from the transition to a system of public education freed of racial discrimination. The presentations also demonstrated that substantial steps to eliminate racial discrimination in public schools have already been taken, not only in some of the communities in which these cases arose, but in some of the states appearing as *amici curiae,* and in other states as well. Substantial progress has been made in the District of Columbia and in the communities in Kansas and Delaware involved in this litigation. The defendants in the cases coming to us from South Carolina and Virginia are awaiting the decision of this Court concerning relief.

Full implementation of these constitutional principles may require solution of varied local school problems. School authorities have the primary responsibility for elucidating, assessing, and solving these problems; courts will have to consider whether the action of school authorities constitutes good faith implementation of the governing constitutional principles. Because of their proximity to local conditions and the possible need for further hearings, the courts which origi-

suming further that this Court will exercise its equity powers to the end described in question 4(*b*),

   "(*a*) should this Court formulate detailed decrees in these cases;

   "(*b*) if so, what specific issues should the decrees reach;

   "(*c*) should this Court appoint a special master to hear evidence with a view to recommending specific terms for such decrees;

   "(*d*) should this Court remand to the courts of first instance with directions to frame decrees in these cases, and if so what general directions should the decrees of this Court include and what procedures should the courts of first instance follow in arriving at the specific terms of more detailed decrees?"

nally heard these cases can best perform this judicial appraisal. Accordingly, we believe it appropriate to remand the cases to those courts.[3]

In fashioning and effectuating the decrees, the courts will be guided by equitable principles. Traditionally, equity has been characterized by a practical flexibility in shaping its remedies [4] and by a facility for adjusting and reconciling public and private needs.[5] These cases call for the exercise of these traditional attributes of equity power. At stake is the personal interest of the plaintiffs in admission to public schools as soon as practicable on a nondiscriminatory basis. To effectuate this interest may call for elimination of a variety of obstacles in making the transition to school systems operated in accordance with the constitutional principles set forth in our May 17, 1954, decision. Courts of equity may properly take into account the public interest in the elimination of such obstacles in a systematic and effective manner. But it should go without saying that the vitality of these constitutional principles cannot be allowed to yield simply because of disagreement with them.

While giving weight to these public and private considerations, the courts will require that the defendants make a prompt and reasonable start toward full compliance with our May 17, 1954, ruling. Once such a start has been made, the courts may find that additional time is necessary to carry out the ruling in an effective manner. The burden rests upon the defendants to establish that such time is necessary in the public interest and is consistent with good faith compliance at the earliest practicable date. To that end, the courts may

3. The cases coming to us from Kansas, South Carolina, and Virginia were originally heard by three-judge District Courts convened under 28 U.S.C. §§ 2281 and 2284, 28 U.S.C.A. §§ 2281, 2284. These cases will accordingly be remanded to those three-judge courts. See Briggs v. Elliott, 342 U.S. 350, 72 S.Ct. 327, 96 L.Ed. 392.

4. See Alexander v. Hillman, 296 U.S. 222, 239, 56 S.Ct. 204, 209, 80 L.Ed. 192.

5. See Hecht Co. v. Bowles, 321 U.S. 321, 329-330, 64 S.Ct. 587, 591, 592, 88 L.Ed. 754.

consider problems related to administration, arising from the physical condition of the school plant, the school transportation system, personnel, revision of school districts and attendance areas into compact units to achieve a system of determining admission to the public schools on a nonracial basis, and revision of local laws and regulations which may be necessary in solving the foregoing problems. They will also consider the adequacy of any plans the defendants may propose to meet these problems and to effectuate a transition to a racially nondiscriminatory school system. During this period of transition, the courts will retain jurisdiction of these cases.

The judgments below, except that in the Delaware case, are accordingly reversed and the cases are remanded to the District Courts to take such proceedings and enter such orders and decrees consistent with this opinion as are necessary and proper to admit to public schools on a racially nondiscriminatory basis with all deliberate speed the parties to these cases. The judgment in the Delaware case—ordering the immediate admission of the plaintiffs to schools previously attended only by white children—is affirmed on the basis of the principles stated in our May 17, 1954, opinion, but the case is remanded to the Supreme Court of Delaware for such further proceedings as that Court may deem necessary in light of this opinion.

It is so ordered.

TABLE OF AUTHORITIES

PREFACE

1. Life, Aug. 27, 1956, p. 114.
2. John N. Popham, *Integration: A Balance Sheet,* New York Times, Sept. 30, 1956, p. 6E. (Italics added.)

CHAPTER 1

THE SUPREME COURT SPEAKS . . .

1. Schechter Corp. v. United States, 295 U.S. 495, 55 Sup. Ct. 837, 79 L. Ed. 1570 (1935).
2. Youngstown Sheet and Tube Co. v. Sawyer, 343 U.S. 579, 72 Sup. Ct. 863, 96 L. Ed. 1153 (1952).
3. Brown v. Board of Education, 347 U.S. 483, 74 Sup. Ct. 686, 98 L. Ed. 873 (1954).
4. See Time, May 24, 1954, p. 21.
5. *Racial Segregation in the Public Schools,* 5 CATHOLIC U. L. REV. 141 (1955).
6. Thomas R. Waring, *The Southern Case Against Desegregation,* Harper's Magazine, Jan. 1956, p. 39. (Mr. Waring is editor of the Charleston, South Carolina, News and Courier.)
7. New York Times, May 18, 1954, pp. 1, 18.
8. Washington Evening Star, May 17, 1954, p. 1.
9. Eighteen jurisdictions made segregated public schools mandatory—Alabama: ALA. CONST. Art. XIV, § 256; ALA. CODE tit. 52, §§ 93, 167 (1940); Arkansas: ARK. STAT. ANN. § 80-509(c) (1947); Delaware: DEL. CONST. Art. X, § 2; DEL. CODE ANN. tit. 14, § 141(b) (1953); District of Columbia: D. C. CODE ANN. §§ 31-1110-13 (1951); Florida: FLA. CONST. Art. 12,

§ 12; FLA. STAT. §§ 228.09, 230.23 (6) (a) (1951); Georgia: GA. CONST. Art. VIII, § 1; GA. CODE ANN. §§ 32-909, 32-937 (1952); Kentucky: KY. CONST. § 187; KY. REV. STAT. §§ 158.-020, 158.021 (1953); Louisiana: LA. CONST. Art. XII, § 1; Maryland: MD. ANN. CODE GEN. LAWS Art. 77, §§ 84, 124, 207 (1951); Mississippi: MISS. CONST. Art. 8, § 207; MISS. CODE ANN. §§ 6276, 6276.5, 6453.01 (1952); Missouri: MO. CONST. Art. IX, § 1(a); MO. REV. STAT. § 163.130 (1949); North Carolina: N. C. CONST. Art. IX, § 2; N. C. GEN. STAT. § 115-2 (1952); Oklahoma: OKLA. CONST. Art. XIII, § 3; OKLA. STAT. tit. 70, §§ 5-1 *et seq.* (1951); South Carolina: S. C. CONST. Art. XI, § 7; S. C. CODE § 21-751 (1952); Tennessee: TENN. CONST. Art. XI, § 12; TENN. CODE ANN. §§ 2377, 2393.9, 11395-97 (Williams 1934); Texas: TEX. CONST. Art. VII, § 7; TEX. STAT., REV. CIV. Arts. 2719, 2755 (1948); Virginia: VA. CONST. Art. IX, § 140; VA. CODE § 22-221 (1950); West Virginia: W. VA. CONST. Art. XII, § 8; W. VA. CODE ANN. §§ 1775, 1777 (1949).

10. Four jurisdictions in varying degrees permit but do not require segregation—Arizona: ARIZ. CODE ANN. §§ 54-430 (1939), 54-416 (2) (Supp. 1952); Kansas: KAN. GEN. STAT. § 72-1724 (1949); New Mexico: N. M. CONST. Art. XII, §§ 1, 10; N. M. STAT. ANN. § 55-1201 (1941); Wyoming: WYO. COMP. STAT. ANN. § 67-624 (1945).

11. Gebhart v. Belton, 32 Del. Ch. 343, 87 A.2d 862, *aff'd,* 33 Del. Ch. 144, 91 A.2d 137 (1952).

12. Bolling v. Sharpe, 347 U.S. 497, 74 Sup. Ct. 693, 98 L. Ed. 884 (1954).

13. Desegregation: Can Washington Be the Showcase?, Newsweek, Sept. 13, 1954, p. 39.

14. *Supra,* note 7.

15. Tom P. Brady, A Review of "Black Monday," address delivered before the Indianola, Miss. Citizens' Council, Oct. 28, 1954. Tract published by the Association of Citizens' Councils of Mississippi, Winona, Miss., p. 14.

16. James O. Eastland, address at Columbia, S. C., Jan. 26, 1956. Reported in Look, April 3, 1956, p. 24.

17. James O. Eastland, The Supreme Court's "Modern Scientific Authorities" in the Segregation Cases, speech before the U.S. Senate, May 26, 1955, 101 CONG. REC. 7119, 7122 (1955).

18. *Ibid.* (Italics added.)

19. Sam J. Ervin, Jr., *The Case for Segregation,* Look, April 3, 1956, p. 32.

20. James F. Byrnes, *The Supreme Court Must Be Curbed,* U.S. News and World Report, May 18, 1956, pp. 50, 56, 58.

21. Hugh V. Wall, A Lawyer Challenges the U.S. Supreme Court, address before the Mississippi State Bar Association at Edgewater Park, Miss., June 23, 1955. See also in this connection, Herman E. Talmadge, YOU AND SEGREGATION (Birmingham, Ala., 1955). The following report on the book appears in Harper's Magazine, Jan. 1956, p. 22: Talmadge "argues that 'God advocates segregation' . . . that integration of the schools is a Soviet plot to debauch the white race and undermine the Constitution . . . that the Supreme Court's decision against segregation resulted from 'pro-Communist influence.' "

22. Life, Feb. 27, 1956, p. 14.

23. Title of a law course given at Yale Law School.

24. Plessy v. Ferguson, 163 U.S. 537, 16 Sup. Ct. 1138, 41 L. Ed. 256 (1896).

25. *Supra,* note 3.

26. Oliver Wendell Holmes, Jr., THE COMMON LAW (Boston, 1881), p. 1.

27. Paul A. Freund, ON UNDERSTANDING THE SUPREME COURT (Boston, 1951), p. 36.

28. Brief for appellants in cases 1, 2 and 4 and for respondents in case number 10, Supreme Court of the United States, Oct. Term, 1953, p. 194.

29. Brief for the United States as *Amicus Curiae* in cases 8, 101, 191, 413, 448, Supreme Court of the United States, Oct. Term, 1952, p. 6. (Note that the numbers assigned by the Court to the several school segregation cases varied in the different court terms.)

30. *Supra,* note 4.

31. Life, May 31, 1954, p. 11.

32. Newsweek, May 24, 1954, p. 26.

33. Herbert Hill and Jack Greenberg, CITIZEN'S GUIDE TO DE-SEGREGATION (Boston, 1955), p. 117.

34. Ebony, Nov., 1955, p. 135.

35. Finley Peter Dunne ("Mr. Dooley"), The Supreme Court's Decisions, MR. DOOLEY'S OPINIONS (New York, 1900).

36. *Supra,* note 20, p. 52.

37. *Supra,* note 6, p. 40.

38. "Segregation in the Nation's Capitol Must Be Abolished." From Dwight D. Eisenhower's campaign speech in Wheeling, West Virginia, Sept. 24, 1952.

39. Felix Frankfurter, *"Moral Grandeur"* of *Justice Brandeis,* New York Times Magazine, Nov. 11, 1956, pp. 26, 65.

40. Robert H. Jackson, THE SUPREME COURT IN THE AMERICAN SYSTEM OF GOVERNMENT (Cambridge, Mass., 1955), p. 53.

CHAPTER 2

NINE MEN

1. These words were written by John Adams into the Declaration of Rights of the 1780 Constitution of Massachusetts, Art. 30.

2. William Blackstone, I COMMENTARIES 69.

3. See, Fischer's Blend Station v. State Tax Commission, 297 U.S. 650, 56 Sup. Ct. 608, 80 L. Ed. 956 (1935).

4. Jerome N. Frank, LAW AND THE MODERN MIND, (New York, 1930), especially pp. 127-128.

5. Paul A. Freund, ON UNDERSTANDING THE SUPREME COURT (Boston, 1951), p. 3.

6. *Ibid.*

7. Charles Evans Hughes, speech at Elmira, New York, May 3, 1907.

8. Jerome N. Frank, *What Courts Do in Fact,* 26 ILL. L. REV. 645 (1932).

9. Joseph C. Hutcheson, *The Judgment Intuitive: The Function of the "Hunch" in Judicial Decision,* 14 CORNELL L. Q. 274 (1929).

10. Charles Grove Haines, *General Observations on the Effects of Personal, Political, and Economic Influences in the Decision of Judges,* 17 ILL. L. REV. 96 (1922).

11. Benjamin N. Cardozo, *Jurisprudence* (address before New York State Bar Association, Jan. 22, 1932), 55 N. Y. STATE BAR ASSN. REP. 263, 288 (1932).

12. *Id.,* at p. 273.

13. See generally in this connection, Edwin W. Patterson, JURISPRUDENCE, MEN AND IDEAS OF THE LAW (Brooklyn, 1953), pp. 537, 571, 573.

14. *Id.,* at p. 573.

15. David J. Brewer, 1898. Quoted in Drew Pearson and Rob-

ert S. Allen, THE NINE OLD MEN (Garden City, New York, 1937), Table of Contents.

16. Attributed to Andrew Jackson by Horace Greeley, THE AMERICAN CONFLICT (Hartford, Conn., 1866), Vol. I, p. 106. Discussed in Marquis James, ANDREW JACKSON, PORTRAIT OF A PRESIDENT (Indianapolis, 1937), pp. 304, 305. Compare, Arthur M. Schlesinger, Jr., THE AGE OF JACKSON (Boston, 1947), p. 350.

17. Worcester v. Georgia, 6 Pet. (31 U.S.) 515, 8 L. Ed. 483 (1832).

18. Scott v. Sandford, 19 How. (60 U.S.) 393, 15 L. Ed. 691 (1857).

19. Charles Evans Hughes, THE SUPREME COURT OF THE UNITED STATES (New York, 1947), pp. 50, 51.

20. "The most gratifying thing, in addition to the fact it was in favor of our side, is the unanimous decision and the language used." Thurgood Marshall, Counsel, NAACP. Quoted in Time, May 24, 1954, p. 22.

21. Hammer v. Dagenhart, 247 U.S. 251, 38 Sup. Ct. 529, 62 L. Ed. 1101 (1918).

22. National Labor Relations Board v. Jones & Laughlin Steel Corp., 301 U.S. 1, 57 Sup. Ct. 615, 81 L. Ed. 893 (1937).

23. United States v. Butler, 297 U.S. 1, 56 Sup. Ct. 312, 80 L. Ed. 477 (1936).

24. *Supra,* note 13, p. 589.

25. *Supra,* note 5, p. 4.

26. Robert H. Jackson, THE SUPREME COURT IN THE AMERICAN SYSTEM OF GOVERNMENT (Cambridge, Mass., 1955), p. 16.

27. Rochin v. California, 342 U.S. 165, 175, 177, 72 Sup. Ct. 205, 211, 212, 96 L. Ed. 183, 191, 192 (1952).

28. William O. Douglas, *The Dissent: A Safeguard of Democracy,* 32 J. AM. JUD. SOC. 104, 105 (1948).

29. *Id.,* at p. 106.

30. William O. Douglas, *"Stare Decisis,"* 49 COLUM. L. REV. 735, 736 (1949).

31. William O. Douglas, WE THE JUDGES (Garden City, 1956), p. 431.

32. *Ibid.*

33. Briggs v. Elliott, 342 U.S. 350, 72 Sup. Ct. 327, 96 L. Ed. 392 (1952).

34. Brown v. Board of Education, 344 U.S. 1, 73 Sup. Ct. 1, 97 L. Ed. 3 (1952).

35. Nominated to the Supreme Court by President Eisenhower on October 5, 1953, Chief Justice Warren served under a recess appointment until March 2, 1954. The Senate confirmed his nomination on March 1, 1954, and a new commission was issued on the following day.

36. Pennsylvania v. Nelson, 350 U.S. 491, 76 Sup. Ct. 477, 100 L. Ed. Adv. 415 (1956).

37. Slochower v. Board of Higher Education, 350 U.S. 551, 76 Sup. Ct. 637, 100 L. Ed. Adv. 449 (1956).

38. UAW-CIO v. Wisconsin Employment Relations Board, 251 U.S. 266, 76 Sup. Ct. 794, 100 L. Ed. Adv. 666 (1956).

39. Black v. Cutter Laboratories, 351 U.S. 292, 76 Sup. Ct. 824, 100 L. Ed. Adv. 681 (1956).

40. C. Herman Pritchett, THE ROOSEVELT COURT; A STUDY IN JUDICIAL POLITICS AND VALUES 1937-1947 (New York, 1948), p. xii.

41. See, Beverly Smith, *Earl Warren's Greatest Moment,* Saturday Evening Post, July 24, 1954, p. 17.

42. Brown v. Board of Education, 345 U.S. 972, 73 Sup. Ct. 1115, 97 L. Ed. 1388 (1953).

43. Brown v. Board of Education, 349 U.S. 294, 75 Sup. Ct. 753, 99 L. Ed. 1083 (1955).

44. The steps leading to the 1954 decision are detailed in Chapter 3. The relationships between and among the decisions of 1953, 1954 and 1955 are discussed throughout the remainder of the volume.

45. The three school segregation cases decided by the Vinson Court and their influence on the 1954 decision in Brown v. Board of Education are discussed in Chapters 7, 8 and 9.

46. *Supra,* note 41, p. 19.

47. Edward McWhinney, *An End to Racial Discrimination in the United States?,* 32 CAN. B. REV. 545, 549 (1954).

48. Fred Rodell, NINE MEN (New York, 1955), p. 271.

49. The Supreme Court Ends a Busy Term, Draws a Heavy Fire, Time, June 25, 1956, p. 14.

50. Philip Elman, ed., OF LAW AND MEN: PAPERS AND ADDRESSES OF FELIX FRANKFURTER, 1939-1956 (New York, 1956).

51. Edmond Cahn, Review of Elman, OF LAW AND MEN, New York Times Book Review, May 27, 1956, pp. 3, 18.

52. West Virginia State Board of Education v. Barnette, 319 U.S. 624, 648, 63 Sup. Ct. 1178, 1190, 87 L. Ed. 1628, 1642 (1943).

53. Uveges v. Pennsylvania, 335 U.S. 437, 449, 69 Sup. Ct. 184, 190, 93 L. Ed. 127, 135 (1948).

54. James F. Byrnes, *The Supreme Court Must Be Curbed,* U.S. News and World Report, May 18, 1956, p. 53.

55. James O. Eastland, The Supreme Court's "Modern Scientific Authorities" in the Segregation Cases, speech before the U.S. Senate, May 26, 1955, 101 CONG. REC. 7119, 7120 (1955).

56. Eugene Cook and William I. Potter, *The School Segregation Cases: Opposing the Opinion of the Supreme Court,* 42 A.B.A.J. 313, 315 (1956).

57. Beauharnais v. Illinois, 343 U.S. 250, 263, 72 Sup. Ct. 725, 733, 734, 96 L. Ed. 919, 930 (1952).

58. *Supra,* note 52.

59. *Id.,* at 319 U.S. 624, 646, 63 Sup. Ct. 1178, 1189, 87 L. Ed. 1628, 1642.

60. Concurring in Griffin v. Illinois, 351 U.S. 12, 26, 76 Sup. Ct. 585, 593, 100 L. Ed. Adv. 483, 494 (1956).

61. On Frankfurter generally, see, Samuel J. Konefsky, THE CONSTITUTIONAL WORLD OF MR. JUSTICE FRANKFURTER (New York, 1949), and Louis L. Jaffee, *The Judicial Universe of Mr. Justice Frankfurter,* 62 HARV. L. REV. 357 (1949).

62. Charles Fairman, Associate Justice of the Supreme Court, part of a Symposium on Justice Jackson, 55 COLUM. L. REV. 445, 487 (1955).

63. Concurring in Railway Express v. New York, 336 U.S. 106, 111, 69 Sup. Ct. 463, 466, 93 L. Ed. 533, 539 (1949).

64. Edwards v. California, 314 U.S. 160, 185, 62 Sup. Ct. 164, 172, 86 L. Ed. 119, 131 (1941).

65. *Supra,* note 26, p. 68.

66. *Supra,* note 49.

67. C. B. Dutton, *Mr. Justice Tom C. Clark,* 26 IND. L.J. 169, 171 (1950).

68. Confirmation Hearings of Tom C. Clark, pp. 55, 87, 93, 104, 113, 115 (1949).

69. CURRENT BIOGRAPHY, 1945, p. 107.

70. Cassell v. Texas, 339 U.S. 282, 296, 70 Sup. Ct. 629, 636, 94 L. Ed. 839, 852 (1950).

71. Smith v. Allwright, 321 U.S. 649, 64 Sup. Ct. 757, 88 L. Ed. 987 (1944).

72. *Id.,* at 321 U.S. 649, 662, 664, 64 Sup. Ct. 757, 764, 765, 88 L. Ed. 987, 996, 997.

73. Plessy v. Ferguson, 163 U.S. 537, 559, 560, 16 Sup. Ct. 1138, 1146, 1147, 41 L. Ed. 256, 263, 264 (1895).

CHAPTER 3

OLIVER BROWN GOES TO COURT

1. Concurring in Coleman v. Miller, 307 U.S. 433, 462, 59 Sup. Ct. 972, 986, 83 L. Ed. 1385 (1939).

2. Youngstown Sheet & Tube Co. v. Sawyer, 343 U.S. 579, 72 Sup. Ct. 863, 96 L. Ed. 1153 (1952).

3. Norman v. Baltimore & Ohio R.R., 294 U.S. 240, 55 Sup. Ct. 407, 79 L. Ed. 885 (1935). See Paul A. Freund, ON UNDERSTANDING THE SUPREME COURT (Boston, 1951), pp. 82-83.

4. See Kelly v. Roetzel, 64 Okla. 36, —, 165 Pac. 1150, 1153 (1917). See also BLACK'S LAW DICTIONARY, 4th ed. (St. Paul, 1951), p. 271.

5. John M. Kernochan, *Origin of Doctrine of Judicial Review*, in Noel T. Dowling, CASES ON CONSTITUTIONAL LAW, 5th ed. (Brooklyn, 1954), p. 20. Professor Kernochan's excellent article treats of the meaning of judicial review in its historical context.

6. James Bryce, THE AMERICAN COMMONWEALTH, 2d ed., rev. (London, 1891), Vol. I, p. 264.

7. Alexis de Tocqueville, DEMOCRACY IN AMERICA (1835), rev. ed. (New York, 1945), Vol. I, p. 101. Judicial review is currently practiced in Australia, Colombia, India, and Venezuela and is the subject of bitter dispute in South Africa. It is practiced in a modified form in Canada.

8. *Supra,* note 5, p. 2.

9. 1 STAT. 73 (1789).

10. Marbury v. Madison, 1 Cranch (5 U.S.) 137, 2 L. Ed. 60 (1803).

11. Crowell v. Benson, 285 U.S. 22, 62, 52 Sup. Ct. 285, 296, 76 L. Ed. 598, 619 (1931).

12. Ashwander v. Tennessee Valley Authority, 297 U.S. 288, 347, 56 Sup. Ct. 466, 483, 80 L. Ed. 688, 711 (1936).

13. Burton v. United States, 196 U.S. 283, 295, 25 Sup. Ct. 243, 245, 49 L. Ed. 482, 485 (1905).

14. *Supra,* note 12, 297 U.S. 345, 56 Sup. Ct. 482, 80 L. Ed. 710.

15. Muskrat v. United States, 219 U.S. 346, 356, 31 Sup. Ct. 250, 254, 55 L. Ed. 246, 250 (1911).

16. Liverpool, N. Y. & P. S. S. Co. v. Emigration Commissioners, 113 U.S. 33, 39, 5 Sup. Ct. 352, 28 L. Ed. 899, 901 (1885).

17. Chicago & Grand Trunk Ry. v. Wellman, 143 U.S. 339, 12 Sup. Ct. 400, 36 L. Ed. 176 (1892).

18. Great Falls Mfg. Co. v. Attorney General, 124 U.S. 581, 8 Sup. Ct. 631, 31 L.Ed. 527 (1887).

19. Tyler v. The Judges, 179 U.S. 405, 21 Sup. Ct. 206, 45 L. Ed. 252 (1900). See generally, Massachusetts v. Mellon, 262 U.S. 447, 43 Sup. Ct. 597, 67 L. Ed. 1078 (1923).

20. See Robert H. Jackson, THE SUPREME COURT IN THE AMERICAN SYSTEM OF GOVERNMENT (Cambridge, 1955), pp. 11-12.

21. *Supra,* note 16.

22. *Supra,* note 20, p. 13.

23. Brief for appellees in case 4, Supreme Court of the United States, Oct. Term, 1953, p. 1.

24. Brown v. Board of Education of Topeka, 98 F. Supp. 797 (Kan. 1951).

25. 62 STAT. 968 (1948), 28 U.S.C. §§ 2281, 2284 (1952).

26. Plessy v. Ferguson, 163 U.S. 537, 16 Sup. Ct. 1138, 41 L. Ed. 256 (1896).

27. Briggs v. Elliott, 98 F. Supp. 529 (E.D.S.C. 1951).

28. Briggs v. Elliott, 342 U.S. 350, 72 Sup. Ct. 327, 96 L. Ed. 392 (1952).

29. Davis v. County School Board, 103 F. Supp. 337 (E.D. Va. 1952).

30. Briggs v. Elliott, 103 F. Supp. 920 (E.D.S.C. 1952).

31. Belton v. Gebhart, 32 Del. Ch. 343, 87 A.2d 862 (1952).

32. Gebhart v. Belton, 33 Del. Ch. 144, 91 A.2d 137 (1952).

33. Bolling v. Sharpe, 347 U.S. 497, 74 Sup. Ct. 693, 98 L. Ed. 884 (1954).

34. Brown v. Board of Education, 344 U.S. 1, 73 Sup. Ct. 1, 97 L. Ed. 3 (1952).

35. Bolling v. Sharpe, 344 U.S. 873, 73 Sup. Ct. 173, 97 L. Ed. 676 (1952).

36. Gebhart v. Belton, 344 U.S. 891, 73 Sup. Ct. 213, 97 L. Ed. 689 (1952).

37. Brown v. Board of Education, 344 U.S. 141, 73 Sup. Ct. 124, 97 L. Ed. 152 (1952).

38. Brown v. Board of Education, 345 U.S. 972, 73 Sup. Ct. 1115, 97 L. Ed. 1388 (1953).

39. The cases were actually argued Dec. 7-9, 1953.

40. Brown v. Board of Education, 347 U.S. 483, 74 Sup. Ct. 686, 98 L. Ed. 873 (1954).

41. Bolling v. Sharpe, 347 U.S. 497, 74 Sup. Ct. 693, 98 L. Ed. 884 (1954).
42. Brown v. Board of Education, 349 U.S. 294, 75 Sup. Ct. 753, 99 L. Ed. 1083 (1955).

CHAPTER 4

INTERPRETING THE CONSTITUTION

1. Marbury v. Madison, 1 Cranch (5 U.S.) 137, 177, 2 L. Ed. 73 (1803).
2. 26 STAT. 209 (1890).
3. United States v. Interstate Circuit, 304 U.S. 55, 58 Sup. Ct. 768, 82 L. Ed. 1146 (1937), compare United States v. Paramount Pictures, 334 U.S. 131, 68 Sup. Ct. 915, 92 L. Ed. 1260 (1948).
4. Olmstead v. United States, 277 U.S. 438, 48 Sup. Ct. 564, 72 L. Ed. 944 (1928).
5. U.S. CONSTITUTION, Fourth Amendment.
6. Benjamin N. Cardozo, NATURE OF THE JUDICIAL PROCESS (New Haven, 1921), p. 14.
7. McBoyle v. United States, 283 U.S. 25, 51 Sup. Ct. 340, 75 L. Ed. 816 (1931).
8. United States v. Butler, 283 U.S. 1, 62, 56 Sup. Ct. 312, 318, 80 L. Ed. 477, 486 (1936).
9. Panama Refining Co. v. Ryan, 293 U.S. 388, 55 Sup. Ct. 241, 79 L. Ed. 446 (1935).
10. Railroad Retirement Board v. Alton Railroad Company, 295 U.S. 330, 55 Sup. Ct. 758, 79 L. Ed. 1468 (1935).
11. Schechter Corp. v. United States, 295 U.S. 495, 55 Sup. Ct. 837, 79 L. Ed. 1570 (1935).
12. Gompers v. United States, 233 U.S. 604, 610, 34 Sup. Ct. 693, 695, 58 L. Ed. 1115, 1120 (1913).
13. Quoted in Alexander M. Bickel, *The Original Understanding and the Segregation Decision,* 69 HARV. L. REV. 1, 34 (1955).
14. *Id.,* footnote 67 at p. 35.
15. *Id.,* at pp. 43-45.
16. *Id.,* at p. 53.
17. See U. S. CONSTITUTION, Article V.
18. 14 STAT. 428 (1867).
19. Texas v. White, 7 Wall. (74 U.S.) 700, 19 L. Ed. 227 (1869).
20. *Supra,* note 18.

21. Brief for appellees in case 2, Supreme Court of the United States, Oct. Term, 1953, p. 39.

22. Governor's Message of January 11, 1867, INDIANA GENERAL Ass. Doc., Part I, 1867, p. 21.

23. NEVADA STAT., C. LIII, § 21 (1867).

24. See, Report, Superintendent of Public Instruction, State of Illinois, 1865-1866, p. 28.

25. Kansas, Laws, c. 46, Art. IV, §§ 3, 18 (1862).

26. New York: Laws, title X, c. 555, § 1 (1864). New Jersey: See, Annual Report, State Superintendent of Schools, 1868, pp. 41-42. Pennsylvania: Laws of 1854, Act 610, § 24.

27. See, II PENNSYLVANIA LEGISLATIVE RECORDS, Appendix (1867).

28. People *ex rel.* Workman v. Board of Education, 18 Mich. 400 (1869).

29. John P. Frank and Robert F. Munro, *The Original Understanding of "Equal Protection of the Laws,"* 50 COLUM. L. REV. 131, 133 (1950).

30. Brief for appellants, cases 1, 2 and 4, and for respondent in case 10, Supreme Court of the United States, Oct. Term, 1953, p. 139.

31. *Supra,* note 21, p. 3.

32. Full question appears in Chapter 3, pp. 52-53.

33. Slaughter-House Cases, 16 Wall. 36, 81, 21 L. Ed. 394, 410 (1873).

34. *Supra,* note 13, p. 55.

35. James F. Byrnes, *The Supreme Court Must Be Curbed,* U.S. News and World Report, May 18, 1956, p. 52.

36. *Supra,* note 13, p. 64.

37. *Supra,* note 35.

38. *Supra,* note 13, p. 65.

CHAPTER 5

INTERPRETATION OR AMENDMENT

1. James F. Byrnes, *The Supreme Court Must Be Curbed,* U.S. News and World Report, May 18, 1956, p. 52.

2. See, Thomas Cooley, CONSTITUTIONAL LIMITATIONS (Boston, 1927), Vol. I, p. 124.

3. Sam Ervin, Jr., *The Case for Segregation,* Look, April 3, 1956, pp. 32, 33.

4. Dissenting in Home Building and Loan Ass'n v. Blaisdell, 290 U.S. 398, 453, 54 Sup. Ct. 245, 78 L. Ed. 413, 437 (1934).

5. Dred Scott v. Sandford, 19 How. (60 U.S.) 393, 426, 15 L. Ed. 691, 709 (1857).

6. *Supra,* note 3, p. 33.

7. People *ex rel.* Workman v. Board of Education, 18 Mich. 400 (1869).

8. Carl Brent Swisher, ROGER B. TANEY (New York, 1936), pp. 511-523.

9. *Supra,* note 4, Opinion of the Court, 290 U.S. 398, 442, 54 Sup. Ct. 231, 242, 78 L. Ed. 413, 431 (1934). Chief Justice Marshall's statement appears in M'Culloch v. Maryland, 4 Wheat. (17 U.S.) 316, 407, 4 L. Ed. 579, 601 (1817).

10. See, John P. Foley, ed., THE JEFFERSONIAN CYCLOPEDIA (New York, 1900), p. 1733.

11. Earl Warren, *The Law and the Future,* Fortune, Nov. 1955, pp. 106, 107.

12. Justice Frankfurter, concurring in Griffin v. People, 351 U.S. 12, 26, 76 Sup. Ct. 585, 593, 100 L. Ed. 483, 493 (1956).

13. Eugene Cook and William I. Potter, *The School Segregation Cases: Opposing the Opinion of the Supreme Court,* 42 A.B.A.J. 313, 317 (1956).

14. Marbury v. Madison, 1 Cranch (5 U.S.) 137, 180, 2 L. Ed. 60, 74 (1803).

15. U.S. CONSTITUTION, Article I, § 8, cl. 18, and Fourteenth Amendment, § 5.

16. Luther v. Borden, 7 How. (48 U.S.) 1, 48 L. Ed. 581 (1849), see also, Pacific States Telephone and Telegraph Co. v. Oregon, 223 U.S. 118, 32 Sup. Ct. 224, 56 L. Ed. 377 (1912).

17. Colsgrove v. Green, 328 U.S. 549, 66 Sup. Ct. 1189, 90 L. Ed. 1432 (1946).

18. *Supra,* note 13, p. 317.

CHAPTER 6

TURNING BACK THE CLOCK

1. Cloyd LaPorte, Introduction to William O. Douglas, STARE DECISIS (New York, 1949), p. 3.

2. Karl N. Llewellyn, *Case Law,* ENCYCLOPEDIA OF THE SOCIAL SCIENCES (New York, 1937), Vol. III, p. 249.

3. Oliver Wendell Holmes, Jr., *The Path of the Law,* 10 HARV. L. REV. 457, 469 (1897).

4. See, Lon L. Fuller, PROBLEMS OF JURISPRUDENCE (Brooklyn, 1949), p. 708 (Temporary Edition).

5. William O. Douglas, STARE DECISIS (New York, 1949), p. 7.

6. James F. Byrnes, *The Supreme Court Must Be Curbed,* U.S. News and World Report, May 18, 1956, p. 52.

7. Mayer v. Hellman, 91 U.S. 496, 23 L. Ed. 377 (1876); Boese v. King, 108 U.S. 379, 2 Sup. Ct. 765, 27 L. Ed. 760 (1883).

8. See, Pobreslo v. Boyd, 287 U.S. 518, 53 Sup. Ct. 262, 77 L. Ed. 318 (1933); International Shoe Co. v. Pinkus, 278 U.S. 261, 49 Sup. Ct. 108, 73 L. Ed. 318 (1929).

9. See, Security Trust Co. v. Dodd, Mead & Co., 173 U.S. 624, 19 Sup. Ct. 545 (1899).

10. Clark v. Williard, 294 U.S. 211, 55 Sup. Ct. 356, 79 L. Ed. 865 (1935).

11. *Supra,* note 5, p. 9.

12. Robert H. Jackson, *The Task of Maintaining Our Liberties,* 39 A.B.A.J. 961, 962 (1953).

13. Dred Scott v. Sandford, 19 How. (60 U.S.) 393, 15 L. Ed. 691 (1857).

14. U.S. CONSTITUTION, Article III.

15. *Supra,* note 13.

16. *Id.,* at 19 How. (60 U.S.) 407, 15 L.Ed. 701.

17. Charles Warren, THE SUPREME COURT IN UNITED STATES HISTORY (Boston, 1928), Vol. II, p. 285.

18. *Supra,* note 16.

19. *Ibid.*

20. On February 1, 1865, John S. Rock, a Negro lawyer of Massachusetts, was admitted to the Bar of the Supreme Court on motion of Charles Sumner. Rock's admission was construed as a disavowal by the Court of its decision in *Dred Scott.* See, *supra,* note 17, pp. 411-412.

21. *Ex parte* Merryman, Fed. Cas. No. 9487 (1861), opinion by Taney, C. J., as Circuit Judge; *Ex parte* Milligan, 4 Wall. (71 U.S.) 2, 18 L. Ed. 281 (1866).

22. 15 STAT. 44 (1868). See, *Ex parte* McCardle, 7 Wall. (74 U.S.) 506, 19 L. Ed. 264 (1869).

23. *Supra,* note 17, quoted at p. 370.

24. See, Chapter 4.

25. 16 STAT. 140 (1870).

26. *Id.,* and 16 STAT. 433 (1871).

27. 17 STAT. 13 (1871).

28. 18 STAT. 335 (1875).

29. See, 14 STAT. 428, 485 (1867); 15 STAT. 2 (1867); 15 STAT. 14 (1867).

30. United States v. Williams, 341 U.S. 70, 74, 71 Sup. Ct. 581, 583, 95 L. Ed. 758, 763 (1951).

31. Mississippi v. Johnson, 4 Wall. (71 U.S.) 475, 18 L. Ed. 437 (1867); Georgia v. Stanton, 6 Wall. (73 U.S.) 50, 18 L. Ed. 721 (1868); *Ex parte* McCardle, 7 Wall. (74 U.S.) 506, 19 L. Ed. 264 (1869).

32. Slaughter-House Cases, 16 Wall. (83 U.S.) 36, 21 L. Ed. 394 (1873).

33. *Id.,* at 16 Wall. (83 U.S.) 44-45, 21 L. Ed. 395-399.

34. *Id.,* at 16 Wall. (83 U.S.) 81, 21 L. Ed. 410.

35. Colgate v. Harvey, 296 U.S. 404, 56 Sup. Ct. 252, 80 L. Ed. 299 (1935).

36. *Id.,* dissenting opinion of Stone, J., at 296 U.S. 436, 445, 56 Sup. Ct. 262, 266, 80 L. Ed. 314, 319.

37. Madden v. Kentucky, 309 U.S. 83, 60 Sup. Ct. 406, 84 L. Ed. 590 (1940).

38. United States v. Cruikshank, 2 Otto (92 U.S.) 542, 23 L. Ed. 588 (1876).

39. *Supra,* note 17, quoted at p. 608.

40. See, Eugene Gressman, *The Unhappy History of Civil Rights Legislation,* 50 MICH. L. REV. 1323, 1336 (1952).

41. *Supra,* note 38, 2 Otto (92 U.S.) 542, 554, 23 L. Ed. 588, 592.

42. Civil Rights Cases, 109 U.S. 3, 3 Sup. Ct. 18, 27 L. Ed. 835 (1883).

43. *Supra,* note 28.

44. *Supra,* note 42, 109 U.S. 26, 3 Sup. Ct. 33, 27 L. Ed. 844.

45. *Id.,* at 109 U.S. 24, 3 Sup. Ct. 31, 27 L. Ed. 844.

46. *Supra,* note 17, p. 608.

47. *Id.,* at pp. 622-662.

CHAPTER 7

SEPARATE BUT EQUAL

1. Plessy v. Ferguson, 163 U.S. 537, 16 Sup. Ct. 1138, 41 L. Ed. 256 (1896).

2. *Ibid.*

3. *Id.,* at 163 U.S. 543, 16 Sup. Ct. 1140, 41 L. Ed. 258.

4. *Id.,* at 163 U.S. 550, 16 Sup. Ct. 1143, 41 L. Ed. 260.

5. Roberts v. City of Boston, 5 Cush. (59 Mass.) 198 (1849).

6. Ferguson v. Gies, 82 Mich. 358, 364, 46 N.W. 718, 720 (1890).

7. *Supra,* note 1, 163 U.S. 559, 16 Sup. Ct. 1146, 41 L. Ed. 263.

8. *Id.,* at 163 U.S. 552, 16 Sup. Ct. 1143, 41 L. Ed. 261.

9. Cummings v. Board of Education, 175 U.S. 528, 20 Sup. Ct. 197, 44 L. Ed. 262 (1899).

10. *Id.,* at 175 U.S. 543, 20 Sup. Ct. 200, 44 L. Ed. 266.

11. James F. Byrnes, *The Supreme Court Must Be Curbed,* U.S. News and World Report, May 18, 1956, p. 52.

12. Berea College v. Kentucky, 211 U.S. 45, 29 Sup. Ct. 33, 53 L. Ed. 81 (1908).

13. Gong Lum v. Rice, 275 U.S. 78, 48 Sup. Ct. 91, 72 L. Ed. 172 (1927).

14. *Id.,* at 275 U.S. 85, 48 Sup. Ct. 93, 72 L. Ed. 177.

15. *Ibid.*

16. See, Herbert Hill and Jack Greenberg, CITIZEN'S GUIDE TO DE-SEGREGATION (Boston, 1955), p. 45.

17. See, Butler v. Wilemon, 86 F. Supp. 397 (Tex. 1949); Moore v. Porterfield, 113 Okla. 234, 241 Pac. 346 (1925); Lowery v. School Trustees, 140 N.C. 33, 52 S.E. 267 (1905).

18. See, Reynold v. Board of Education, 66 Kan. 672, 72 Pac. 274 (1903); Williams v. Zimmerman, 172 Md. 563, 192 Atl. 353 (1937); Carter v. School Board, 182 F.2d 531 (4th Cir. 1950).

19. *E.g.,* Davenport v. Cloverport, 72 Fed. 689 (Ky. 1896); Lowery v. School Trustees, *supra,* note 17.

20. See, Miller v. Board of Education, 106 F. Supp. 988 (D.C. 1952); Williams v. Board of Education, 79 Kan. 202, 99 Pac. 216 (1908); *cf.* Wrighten v. Board of Trustees, 72 F. Supp. 948 (S.C. 1947).

21. Robert A. Leflar and Wylie H. Davis, *Public School Segregation,* 67 HARV. L. REV. 377, 392 (1954).

22. John W. Davis, Oral argument in Brown v. Board of Education (private printing), p. 18.

23. Santa Clara County v. Southern Pacific Ry. Co., 118 U.S. 294, 30 L.Ed. 118 (1886); Minneapolis Ry. Co. v. Beckwith, 129 U.S. 26, 9 Sup. Ct. 207, 32 L. Ed. 586 (1889).

24. Connecticut General Co. v. Johnson, 303 U.S. 77, 85, 58 Sup. Ct. 436, 439, 82 L. Ed. 673, 678 (1938).

25. *Supra,* note 22.

Iver, ed., 1949), 44-48; Frazier, The Negro in the United States (1949), 674-681. And see generally Myrdal, An American Dilemma (1944)."

6. U.S. CONSTITUTION, Seventh Amendment.

7. Lindsley v. Natural Carbonic Gas Co., 220 U.S. 61, 78, 31 Sup. Ct. 337, 340, 55 L. Ed. 369, 377 (1911).

8. Jack Greenberg, *Social Scientists Take the Stand: A Review and Appraisal of Their Testimony in Litigation,* 54 MICH. L. REV. 953, 954 (1956).

9. *Id.,* at pp. 954-966.

10. James O. Eastland, THE SUPREME COURT'S "MODERN SCIENTIFIC AUTHORITIES" IN THE SEGREGATION CASES (Washington, 1955), p. 4.

11. Kenneth B. Clark, *Desegregation: An Appraisal of the Evidence,* 9 J. SOCIAL ISSUES, No. 4 (1953), p. 3.

12. Edmond Cahn, *Jurisprudence,* 30 N.Y.U. L. REV. 150, 159 (1955).

13. *Id.,* at p. 157.

14. *Id.,* at p. 167.

CHAPTER 10

THE COLOR-BLIND CONSTITUTION

1. William S. Jenkins, PRO-SLAVERY THOUGHT IN THE OLD SOUTH (Chapel Hill, 1935), p. 243.

2. Quaker City Cab Co. v. Pennsylvania, 277 U.S. 389, 406, 48 Sup. Ct. 553, 556, 72 L. Ed. 927, 932 (1928).

3. Tom P. Brady, A Review of "Black Monday," address delivered before Indianola, Mississippi Citizens Council, Oct. 28, 1954. Tract published by Association of Citizens Councils of Mississippi, Winona, Mississippi, p. 16.

4. Herman Lewis, BIOLOGY OF THE NEGRO (Chicago, 1942), pp. 139, 227, 249.

5. William O. Douglas, WE THE JUDGES (Garden City, 1956), pp. 398-399.

6. United States v. Holliday, 3 Wall. (70 U.S.) 407, 18 L. Ed. 182 (1865).

7. State v. Rorvick, 76 Idaho 58, 277 P.2d 566, 576 (1954).

8. Slaughter-House Cases, 16 Wall. (83 U.S.) 36, 71, 21 L. Ed. 394, 407 (1873).

9. Strauder v. West Virginia, 100 U.S. 303, 307, 25 L. Ed. 664, 665 (1880).

10. Virginia v. Rives, 100 U.S. 313, 318, 25 L. Ed. 667, 669 (1880); *Ex parte* Virginia, 100 U.S. 339, 344, 25 L. Ed. 677, 678 (1880).

11. See Gibson v. Mississippi, 162 U.S. 565, 591, 16 Sup. Ct. 904, 910, 40 L. Ed. 1075, 1082 (1896).

12. Nixon v. Herndon, 273 U.S. 536, 541, 47 Sup. Ct. 446, 447, 71 L. Ed. 759, 761 (1927).

13. Edwards v. California, 314 U.S. 160, 185, 62 Sup. Ct. 164, 172, 86 L. Ed. 119, 131 (1941).

14. Kotch v. Board of River Boat Pilot Commissioners, 330 U.S. 552, 565, 566, 67 Sup. Ct. 910, 917, 91 L. Ed. 1093, 1101 (1947).

15. Korematsu v. United States, 323 U.S. 214, 216, 65 Sup. Ct. 193, 194, 89 L. Ed. 194, 199 (1944).

16. *Ibid.*

17. Yick Wo v. Hopkins, 118 U.S. 356, 6 Sup. Ct. 1064, 30 L. Ed. 220 (1886).

18. *Id.*, at 118 U.S. 369, 6 Sup. Ct. 1070, 30 L. Ed. 226.

19. *Id.*, at 118 U.S. 374, 6 Sup. Ct. 1073, 30 L. Ed. 228.

20. *Supra,* note 14, 330 U.S. 556, 67 Sup. Ct. 912, 91 L. Ed. 1097.

21. *Supra,* note 15, 323 U.S. 216, 65 Sup. Ct. 194, 89 L. Ed. 199.

22. Joseph Tussman and Jacobus Ten Broek, *The Equal Protection of the Laws,* 37 CALIF. L. REV. 341, 358 (1949).

23. Takahashi v. Fish Commission, 334 U.S. 410, 68 Sup. Ct. 1138, 92 L. Ed. 1478 (1948).

24. *Id.*, at 334 U.S. 418, 68 Sup. Ct. 1142, 92 L. Ed. 1486.

25. *Id.*, at 334 U.S. 422, 68 Sup. Ct. 1144, 92 L. Ed. 1489.

26. Robert B. McKay, *Segregation and Public Recreation,* 40 VA. L. REV. 697, 717 (1954).

27. Gunnar Myrdal, AN AMERICAN DILEMMA (New York, 1944), Vol. I, pp. 608, 610.

28. Mayor and City Council of Baltimore City v. Dawson, 220 F.2d 386 (4th Cir. 1955), *aff'd per curiam,* 350 U.S. 877, 76 Sup. Ct. 133, 100 L. Ed. 75 (1955).

29. Dawson v. Baltimore, Lonesome v. Maxwell, and Isaacs v. Baltimore, 123 F. Supp. 193 (Md. 1954).

30. *Id.*, at p. 195.

31. *Id.*, at p. 198.

32. *Supra,* note 28, 220 F.2d 386, 387.

33. DeAngelis v. Board of Liquor License Commissioners of Baltimore, 135 Daily Record, Balto., No. 21, p. 3 (Balto. City Ct., July 26, 1955), 1 RACE REL. L. REP. 370 (1956).

34. *Supra,* note 32, at p. 387.

35. Plessy v. Ferguson, 163 U.S. 537, 559, 16 Sup. Ct. 1138, 1146, 41 L. Ed. 256, 263 (1896).

CHAPTER 11

IMPACT OF DECISION

1. Brown v. Board of Education, 347 U.S. 483, 496, 74 Sup. Ct. 686, 692, 98 L. Ed. 873, 881 (1954).

2. Norton v. Shelby County, 118 U.S. 425, 442, 6 Sup. Ct. 1121, 1125, 30 L. Ed. 178, 186 (1886).

3. Ernst Borinski, *A Legal and Sociological Analysis of the Segregation Decision of May 17, 1954,* 15 U. OF PITT. L. REV. 622, 627 (1954). Dr. Borinski is head of the Social Science Division at Tougaloo College in Mississippi.

4. This argument is discussed in Chapter 5.

5. 62 STAT. 696 (1948), 18 U.S.C. § 242 (1950).

6. Brown v. Board of Education, 349 U.S. 294, 75 Sup. Ct. 753, 99 L. Ed. 653 (1955); Brown v. Board of Education, 345 U.S. 972, 73 Sup. Ct. 1115, 97 L. Ed. 1388 (1953); Brown v. Board of Education, 347 U.S. 483, 495-496, note 13, 74 Sup. Ct. 686, 692, 98 L. Ed. 873, 881 (1954).

7. John W. Davis, Argument on behalf of appellees in Briggs v. Elliott, delivered before the Supreme Court on Dec. 7, 1953 (private printing), p. 20.

8. Supplemental Brief Supreme Court of the United States, for the United States on Reargument, cases 1, 2, 4, 8 and 10, Oct. Term, 1953, p. 154. Brief for the United States on the Further Argument of the Questions of Relief, cases 1, 2, 3, 4 and 5, Supreme Court of the United States, Oct. Term, 1954, p. 4.

9. *Id.,* 1953 Brief, at p. 167; 1954 Brief, at p. 3.

10. Standard Oil Co. v. United States, 221 U.S. 1, 81, 31 Sup. Ct. 502, 524, 55 L. Ed. 619, 653-654 (1910).

11. Georgia v. Tennessee Copper Co., 206 U.S. 230, 239, 27 Sup. Ct. 618, 620, 51 L. Ed. 1038, 1045 (1907). This particular litigation remained before the Court for nine years. See 237 U.S. 474, 35 Sup. Ct. 631, 59 L. Ed. 1054 (1915); 237 U.S. 678, 35 Sup.

Ct. 752, 59 L. Ed. 1173 (1915); 240 U.S. 650, 36 Sup. Ct. 465, 60 L. Ed. 846 (1916).

12. United States v. American Tobacco Co., 221 U.S. 106, 187, 31 Sup. Ct. 632, 651, 55 L. Ed. 663, 697 (1911).

13. Brief of Harry McMullan, Attorney General of North Carolina, *Amicus Curiae,* cases 1, 2, 3 and 4, Supreme Court of the United States, Oct. Term, 1954, p. 13.

14. *Id.,* at p. 14.

15. *Id.,* at p. 12.

16. Brief for appellants in cases 1, 2 and 4, and for respondents in case 10, Supreme Court of the United States, Oct. Term, 1953, pp. 190, 191.

17. 62 STAT. 963 (1948), 28 U.S.C. § 2106 (1950).

18. 2 STAT. 244 (1803), REV. STAT. § 698 (1875), 28 U.S.C. § 863 (1946).

19. 62 STAT. 992 (1948).

20. *Supra,* note 16, p. 195.

21. *Id.,* at p. 193.

22. Sweatt v. Painter, 339 U.S. 629, 635, 70 Sup. Ct. 848, 851, 94 L. Ed. 1114, 1120 (1950).

23. *Supra,* note 16, p. 190.

24. *Supra,* note 8, 1953 Brief, p. 165.

25. *Id.,* at p. 166.

26. *Amicus Curiae* Brief of the Attorney General of Florida, cases 1, 2, 3 and 4, Supreme Court of the United States, Oct. Term, 1954, p. 3.

27. *Amicus Curiae* Brief of the Attorney General of Arkansas, cases 1, 2, 3 and 4, Supreme Court of the United States, Oct. Term, 1954, p. 13.

28. *Supra,* note 7.

29. Hugh V. Wall, A Lawyer Challenges the U.S. Supreme Court, address before the Mississippi State Bar Association at Edgewater Park, Mississippi, June 23, 1955.

30. *Supra,* note 13, p. 19. See, William F. Winter, *Mississippi's Legislative Approach to the School Segregation Problem,* 26 MISS. L.J. 165 (1955).

31. Bolling v. Sharpe, 347 U.S. 497, 500, 74 Sup. Ct. 693, 695, 98 L. Ed. 884, 887 (1954).

32. Sabine v. Sharpe, Civ. No. 3694-54 (D.C. 1955). Unreported. See 1 RACE REL. L. REP. 305 (1956).

33. Steiner v. Simmons,— Del. Ch.—, 111 A.2d 574 (1955).

34. *Id.*, at — Del. Ch.—, —, 111 A.2d 574, 575, 576.
35. Brown v. Board of Education, 139 F. Supp. 468, 470 (Kan. 1955).
36. Davis v. County School Board of Prince Edward County, Civ. No. 1333 (E.D. Va. 1955). Unreported. See 1 RACE REL. L. REP. 82 (1956).
37. Briggs v. Elliott, 132 F. Supp. 776, 777 (E.D.S.C. 1955).

CHAPTER 12

BROWN BECOMES A PRECEDENT

1. Shepard v. Wheeling, 30 W. Va. 479, 482, 4 S.E. 635, 637 (1887).
2. The authority to institute a class action is conferred by Rule 23 (a) in the following terms:

". . . If persons constituting a class are so numerous as to make it impracticable to bring them all before the court, such of them, one or more, as will fairly insure the adequate representation of all may, on behalf of all, sue or be sued, when the character of the right sought to be enforced for or against the class is

"(1) joint, or common, or secondary in the sense that the owner of a primary right refuses to enforce that right and a member of the class thereby becomes entitled to enforce it;

"(2) several, and the object of the action is the adjudication of claims which do or may affect specific property involved in the action; or

"(3) several, and there is a common question of law or fact affecting the several rights and a common relief is sought."

The class actions instituted in the school segregation cases were brought under subsection (3).

3. Original complaint in Brown v. Board of Education, par. 3c.
4. James William Moore, FEDERAL PRACTICE, 2d ed. (New York, 1948), pp. 3443, 3465.
5. Supplemental Memorandum for the United States on the Further Argument of the Questions of Relief, cases 1, 2, 3, 4 and 5, Supreme Court of the United States, Oct. Term, 1954, p. 9.

Table of Authorities 311

6. Mendez v. Westminster School District, 64 F. Supp. 544, 551 (S.D. Cal. 1946), aff'd, 161 F.2d 744 (C.A. 9, 1947).

7. Wilson v. City of Paducah, 100 F. Supp. 116 (W.D. Ky. 1951).

8. See supra, note 4, pp. 3474-3476.

9. Davis v. County School Board of Prince Edward County, Civ. No. 1333 (E.D. Va. 1955). Unreported. See 1 RACE REL. L. REP. 82 (1956); Briggs v. Elliott, 132 F. Supp. 776, 777 (E.D.S.C. 1955).

10. Willis v. Walker, 136 F. Supp. 177 (W.D. Ky. 1955).

11. Dunn v. Board of Education, Civ. No. 1693 (S.D. W. Va. 1956). Unreported. See 1 RACE REL. L. REP. 319 (1956). Taylor v. Board of Education, Civ. No. 159 (S.D. W. Va. 1956). Unreported. See 1 RACE REL. L. REP. 321 (1956).

12. McSwain v. County Board of Education, 138 F. Supp. 570 (1956).

13. Hoxie School District v. Brewer, No. J-918 (E.D. Ark. 1955). Unreported. See 1 RACE REL. L. REP. 43 (1956).

14. Hoxie School District v. Brewer, 137 F. Supp. 364 (E.D. Ark. 1956).

15. Burr v. Sondheim, Civ. No. 35526 (Super. Ct., Balto., 1954). Unreported. See 1 RACE REL. L. REP. 309 (1956).

16. Bush v. Orleans Parish School Board, Civ. No. 3630 (E.D. La. 1956). Unreported. See 1 RACE REL. L. REP. 305 (1956).

17. Id., at 1 RACE REL. L. REP. 306-308.

18. McKinney v. Blankenship, 154 Tex. 632, 282 S.W.2d 691 (1955).

19. Two of the nine justices concurred in a separate opinion, disagreeing with the majority only on the question of the constitutionality of one of the statutes allocating state funds to the schools.

20. The opinion should read "Article VI."

21. Supra, note 18, 154 Tex. —, 282 S.W.2d 691, 694.

22. Bell v. Rippy, Civ. No. 6165 (N.D. Tex. 1955). Unreported. See 1 RACE REL. L. REP. 318 (1956).

23. Jackson v. Rawdon, 135 F. Supp. 936 (N.D. Tex. 1955).

24. Id., at p. 937.

25. Brown v. Reppy, 223 F.2d 796 (4th Cir. 1956).

26. Jackson v. Rawdon, 235 F.2d 93 (5th Cir. 1956).

27. This case has had a long litigation history: Florida ex rel. Hawkins v. Board of Control, 47 So.2d 608 (1950); 53 So.2d 116

(1951), *cert. denied,* 342 U.S. 877, 72 Sup. Ct. 166, 96 L. Ed. 659 (1951), 60 So.2d 162 (1952).

28. *Ibid., cert. granted,* 347 U.S. 971, 74 Sup. Ct. 783, 98 L. Ed. 1112 (1954).

29. Florida *ex rel.* Hawkins v. Board of Control, 83 So.2d 20, 21 (1955).

30. *Id.,* at p. 23.

31. *Id.,* at pp. 20 *et seq.,* 31, 32.

32. Florida *ex rel.* Hawkins v. Board of Control, 350 U.S. 413, 76 Sup. Ct. 464, 100 L. Ed. Adv. 348 (1956).

CHAPTER 13

TREND OF DECISION

1. James F. Byrnes, *The Supreme Court Must Be Curbed,* U.S. News and World Report, May 18, 1956, p. 56.

2. Florida *ex rel.* Hawkins v. Board of Control, 347 U.S. 971, 74 Sup. Ct. 784, 98 L. Ed. 1112 (1954) (discussed at length in the preceding chapter), and Tureaud v. Board of Supervisors, 347 U.S. 971, 74 Sup. Ct. 784, 98 L. Ed. 1112 (1954). Other relevant citations in the Tureaud case are 116 F. Supp. 248 (E.D. La. 1953) and 225 F.2d 434 (5th Cir. 1955). No attempt has been made to cover all of the segregation cases which have been handed down, and the Florida dispute was selected as a better example of the "impact of decision" than the Louisiana litigation.

3. Muir v. Louisville Park Theatrical Association, 347 U.S. 971, 74 Sup. Ct. 783, 98 L. Ed. 1112 (1954).

4. Mayor and City Council of Baltimore City v. Dawson, 350 U.S. 877, 76 Sup. Ct. 133, 100 L. Ed. Adv. 75 (1955). The Supreme Court opinion affirmed Dawson v. Mayor and City Council of Baltimore City, 220 F.2d 386 (4th Cir. 1955).

5. Robert B. McKay, *Segregation and Public Recreation,* 40 VA. L. REV. 697, 710-711 (1954).

6. Mayor and City Council of Baltimore City v. Dawson, 220 F.2d 386, 387 (4th Cir. 1955).

7. Tate v. Dept. of Conservation and Development, 133 F. Supp. 53, 58 (E.D. Va. 1955).

8. Rice v. Arnold, 340 U.S. 848, 71 Sup. Ct. 77, 95 L. Ed. 621 (1950).

9. Fayson v. Beard, 134 F. Supp. 379, 381 (E.D. Tex. 1955).

10. Moorman v. Morgan, — Ky. —, 285 S.W.2d 146 (1955).

11. Hayes v. Crutcher, 137 F. Supp. 853 (M.D. Tenn. 1956).
12. Holmes v. City of Atlanta, 124 F. Supp. 290 (N.D. Ga. 1954).
13. *Id.,* at 223 F.2d 93 (5th Cir. 1955).
14. *Id.,* at 350 U.S. 879, 76 Sup. Ct. 141, 100 L. Ed. Adv. 76 (1955).
15. *Id.,* at case no. 4621 (N.D. Ga. 1955). Unreported. See 1 RACE REL. L. REP. 150 (1956).
16. Heyward v. Public Housing Administration, 135 F. Supp. 217 (S.D. Ga. 1955).
17. *Id.,* at 220.
18. Davis v. St. Louis Housing Authority, Civ. No. 8637 (E.D. Mo. 1955). Unreported. See 1 RACE REL. L. REP. 353 (1956).
19. Detroit Housing Commission v. Lewis, 226 F.2d 180 (6th Cir. 1955).
20. Flemming v. South Carolina Electric and Gas Co., 128 F. Supp. 469 (E.D.S.C. 1955).
21. *Id.,* at 224 F.2d 752 (4th Cir. 1955).
22. *Id., appeal dismissed,* at 351 U.S. 901, 76 Sup. Ct. 692, 100 L. Ed. Adv. 533 (1956).
23. Browder v. Gayle, 142 F. Supp. 707 (M.D. Ala. 1956).
24. Flemming v. South Carolina Electric and Gas Co., Civ. No. 4386 (E.D.S.C. 1956). Unreported. See 1 RACE REL. L. REP. 679 (1956).
25. *Id.,* at p. 680.
26. *Ibid.*
27. Gayle v. Browder, 352 U.S. 903, 77 Sup. Ct. 145, 1 L. Ed.2d Adv. 114 (1956).
28. New York Times, Nov. 14, 1956, p. 1.

CHAPTER 14

PATTERNS OF COMPLIANCE

1. Jackson v. Rawdon, 235 F.2d 93, 96 (5th Cir. 1956).
2. Report of an unpublished survey by Harold C. Fleming, Assistant Director of the Southern Regional Council, Atlanta. The Southern Regional Council is an interracial group devoted "to equal opportunity for all." Its membership is confined to Southerners. Ben Price, Associated Press staff writer, prepared a special news story on the Fleming report on Sept. 15, 1956. The story appeared throughout the United States on the follow-

ing day. See, for example, Southern Racial Barriers Eased in 1,100 Instances, Philadelphia Bulletin, Sept. 16, 1956, p. 5.

3. *Ibid.*

4. William Attwood, *Is This the Pattern of the Future?*, Look, April 3, 1956, p. 46.

5. Report of the Southern Education Reporting Service, Sept. 1956. This organization is a nonpartisan, fund-supported, fact-finding agency operated by Southern editors. Reported by John N. Popham, *Integration: A Balance Sheet,* The New York Times, Sept. 30, 1956, p. 6E.

6. Desegregation: Can Washington Be the Showcase?, Newsweek, Sept. 13, 1954, p. 39.

7. Popham, *supra,* note 5.

8. *Supra,* note 6, p. 40.

9. District of Columbia v. Thompson Co., 346 U.S. 100, 73 Sup Ct. 1007, 97 L. Ed. 1480 (1952).

10. Act of the Legislative Assembly of the District of Columbia, June 26, 1873, Dist. Col. Laws 1871-1873, pp. 65, 116.

11. Negro Progress in 1953, Ebony, Jan., 1954, p. 18.

12. *Supra,* note 2.

13. *Supra,* note 4.

14. Quoted in The Voices of the White South, Divergent Views of Public Men, Life, Sept. 17, 1956, pp. 104, 120.

15. *Ibid.*

16. Minton Sure Bias Will End, Newark Sunday News, Oct. 7, 1956, p. 5.

17. Virginia v. West Virginia, 222 U.S. 17, 32 Sup. Ct. 4, 56 L. Ed. 71 (1911).

18. *Id.,* at 222 U.S. 19, 32 Sup. Ct. 6, 56 L. Ed. 72.

19. Matthews v. Launius, 134 F. Supp. 684, 686 (W.D. Ark. 1955).

20. *Id.,* at 687.

21. Dunn v. Board of Education of the County of Greenbrier, Civ. No. 1693 (S.D. W. Va. 1956). Unreported. See 1 RACE REL. L. REP. 319 (1956); Taylor v. Board of Education of the County of Raleigh, Civ. No. 159 (S.D. W. Va. 1956). Unreported. See 1 RACE REL. L. REP. 321 (1956).

22. Bell v. Rippy, Civ. No. 6165 (N.D. Tex. 1955). Unreported. See 1 RACE REL. L. REP. 318 (1956).

23. Clemons v. Board of Education of Hillsboro, 228 F.2d 853 (6th Cir. 1956).

24. *Id.,* at 859.

25. A decision of this type will, of course, necessitate intricate legal analysis and purposive interpretation. Lines of legal authorities upon which such a decision could be based include the following: (1) the establishment of *general* rights arising out of multi-party litigation, *see, e.g.,* John Norton Pomeroy, EQUITY JURISPRUDENCE, 5th ed. (San Francisco, 1941), §§ 247, 249; (2) the underlying principles of the traditional equity class suit, *see, e.g.,* Zechariah Chafee, Jr., *Bills of Peace with Multiple Parties,* 45 HARV. L. REV. 1297 (1932); and (3) the binding effect of a class suit upon parties who were in the same position as defendants but who were not technically involved in the litigation, *see, e.g.,* Supreme Tribe of Ben-Hur v. Cauble, 255 U.S. 356, 41 Sup. Ct. 338, 65 L. Ed. 673 (1921). Compare: James William Moore, MOORE'S FEDERAL PRACTICE, 2d ed. (New York, 1948), §§ 23.07, 23.10. (3) The effect of the proposed development would manifest itself in increased attention to the binding force of "remedies holdings."

26. Covington v. Montgomery County School Officials, 139 F. Supp. 161, 163 (M.D.N.C. 1956).

27. 18 U.S.C. § 241 (1952). Derived from Act of May 31, 1870, § 6, 16 STAT. 141.

28. United States v. Williams, 341 U.S. 70, 71 Sup. Ct. 581, 95 L. Ed. 758 (1951).

29. United States v. Cruikshank, 2 Otto (92 U.S.) 542, 23 L. Ed. 588 (1876).

30. Barney v. City of New York, 193 U.S. 430, 438, 248 Sup. Ct. 502, 503, 48 L. Ed. 737, 740 (1904).

31. U.S. CONSTITUTION, Article I, § 8.

32. Rutledge, J., in Screws v. United States, 325 U.S. 91, 65 Sup. Ct. 1031, 89 L. Ed. 1495 (1945).

33. *Supra,* note 28, at 341 U.S. 88, 71 Sup. Ct. 591, 95 L. Ed. 770.

34. Connally v. General Construction Co., 269 U.S. 385, 391, 46 Sup. Ct. 126, 127, 70 L. Ed. 322, 328 (1926).

35. Screws v. United States, 325 U.S. 91, 65 Sup. Ct. 1031, 89 L. Ed. 1495 (1945).

36. *Id.,* at 325 U.S. 104, 105, 65 Sup. Ct. 1037, 89 L. Ed. 1504.

37. While the contempt power was (and is) exercised in the common-law courts, it was used as a means of punishing misconduct in the course of litigation and not as a means of enforcing

judgments. *See, e.g.,* Fisher v. Pace, 336 U.S. 155, 69 Sup. Ct. 425, 93 L. Ed. 569 (1949).

38. U.S. v. Hudson, 7 Cranch (11 U.S.) 32, 3 L. Ed. 259 (1812). See also, *In re* Terry, 128 U.S. 289, 9 Sup. Ct. 77, 32 L. Ed. 405 (1888).

39. 18 U.S.C. § 401 (1952).

40. No attempt has been made in this brief discussion to distinguish between the law governing civil contempts and the law governing criminal contempts. In a considerable number of criminal contempts, the United States attorney may prosecute the action on behalf of the government asking for the exercise of the contempt power, although it is possible for a private party to prosecute such proceedings. There are also many procedural differences of substantial importance between these two types of contempt actions. And, on the basis of these "differences," there is no question but that civil contempt proceedings would afford the more efficient and effective means of enforcing desegregation. One of the most authoritative discussions of the relationship between the civil and criminal contempt powers is Chief Justice Vinson's majority opinion in United States v. United Mine Workers of America, 330 U.S. 258, 67 Sup. Ct. 677, 91 L. Ed. 884 (1947). See also FEDERAL RULES OF CRIMINAL PROCEDURE, Rule 48.

41. Lucy v. Adams, Civ. No. 652 (N.D. Ala. 1956). Unreported. See 1 RACE REL. L. REP. 323 (1956).

42. New York Times, Sept. 1, 1956, p. 1.

CHAPTER 15

AVOIDANCE, EVASION AND DELAY

1. The Kentucky and Virginia Resolutions of 1798 and 1799. See Henry Steele Commager, DOCUMENTS OF AMERICAN HISTORY, 4th ed. (New York, 1948), pp. 178-184.

2. Marbury v. Madison, 1 Cranch (5 U.S.) 137, 2 L. Ed. 73 (1803).

3. United States v. Peters, 5 Cranch (9 U.S.) 115, 136, 3 L. Ed. 53, 59 (1809).

4. Martin v. Hunter's Lessee, 1 Wheat. (14 U.S.) 304, 4 L. Ed. 97 (1816).

5. South Carolina Ordinance of Nullification of 1832. See Commager, *supra,* note 1, p. 261.

6. Texas v. White, 7 Wall. (74 U.S.) 700, 19 L. Ed. 227 (1869).

7. *Id.*, at 7 Wall. (74 U.S.) 725-726, 19 L. Ed. 237.

8. See 1 RACE REL. L. REP. 252 (1956).

9. *Id.*, at 253.

10. Senate Joint Resolution No. 3, General Assembly of Virginia, Feb. 1, 1956. See 1 RACE REL. L. REP. 445 (1956).

11. Opinion of the Attorney General, State of Virginia, Feb. 14, 1956. See 1 RACE REL. L. REP. 462, 464 (1956).

12. House Resolution No. 16, California Legislature, March 15, 1956. See 1 RACE REL. L. REP. 756 (1956).

13. New York Times, March 12, 1956, pp. 1, 21.

14. Act 555 of 1954. 17 LA. REV. STAT. §§ 331-334. See 1 RACE REL. L. REP. 239 (1956).

15. Bush v. Orleans Parish School Board, 138 F. Supp. 336 (E.D. La. 1956).

16. Alabama *ex rel.* Patterson v. NAACP (15th Cir. Ct., Ala., 1956). Unreported. See 1 RACE REL. L. REP. 707 (1956); Louisiana *ex rel.* Le Blanc v. Lewis, No. 55, 899 (19th Jud. Dist. Ct., La., 1956). Unreported. See 1 RACE REL. L. REP. 571 (1956).

17. Act No. 920, General Assembly of South Carolina, 1956. See 1 RACE REL. L. REP. 600 (1956); Act No. 741, General Assembly of South Carolina, 1956. See 1 RACE REL. L. REP. 751 (1956).

18. House Bill No. 33, 1956 Regular Session, State of Mississippi. (Concurred in by the Senate and signed by the Governor on Feb. 20, 1956.) See 1 RACE REL. L. REP. 451 (1956).

19. Act 670 of 1956. 22 VA. CODE § 22-10.1.

20. Chap. 366, General Assembly of North Carolina, 1955. See 1 RACE REL. L. REP. 240 (1956).

21. Carson v. Board of Education, 227 F.2d 789 (4th Cir. Ct. 1955).

22. Joyner v. McDowell County Board of Education, — N.C. —, 92 S.E.2d 795 (1956).

23. Young v. Ragen, 337 U.S. 235, 238, 239, 69 Sup. Ct. 1073, 1074, 93 L. Ed. 1333, 1336 (1949).

24. Brown v. Western Railway of Alabama, 338 U.S. 294, 298, 299, 70 Sup. Ct. 105, 108, 94 L. Ed. 100, 104 (1949).

25. School Pupil Assignment Law, Initiative Petition, Arkansas. See 1 RACE REL. L. REP. 579, 580 (1956).

26. Pupil Assignment Law, Florida, Ch. 31380, Senate Bill No. 11-XX, Approved July 26, 1956. See 1 RACE REL. L. REP. 924, 925 (1956).

27. Sec. 6334-02, MISSISSIPPI CODE ANN. (1942).

28. House Bill No. 13, Mississippi Legislature, Regular Session, 1956. See 1 RACE REL. L. REP. 434 (1956).

29. Report of Commission on Public Education (Gray Commission), Virginia, Aug. 30, 1954. See 1 RACE REL. L. REP. 241, 242 (1956).

30. Adkins v. The School Board of the City of Newport News, Civ. No. 489 (E.D. Va. 1957). Unreported. See 2 RACE REL. L. REP. 334 (1957).

31. Adkins v. The School Board of the City of Newport News, Beckett v. The School Board of the City of Norfolk, Civ. No. 489 (Newport News Div.), Civ. No. 2214 (Norfolk Div.), (E.D. Va. 1957). Unreported. See 2 RACE REL. L. REP. 46, 58 (1957).

32. Guinn v. United States, 238 U.S. 347, 35 Sup. Ct. 926, 59 L. Ed. 1340 (1915).

33. Lane v. Wilson, 307 U.S. 268, 275, 59 Sup. Ct. 872, 876, 83 L. Ed. 1281, 1287 (1939).

34. *Supra,* note 29, 1 RACE REL. L. REP. 241, 243.

35. Resolution of Board of Supervisors, Prince Edward County, Virginia, May 3, 1956. See 1 RACE REL. L. REP. 780 (1956). Resolution of Board of Supervisors, Loudoun County, Virginia, Aug. 6, 1956. See 1 RACE REL. L. REP. 940 (1956).

36. Act No. 13, General Assembly of Georgia, 1956 Session, Feb. 6, 1956. See 1 RACE REL. L. REP. 420 (1956).

37. Acts of 1955 (49), 329, South Carolina Legislature, § 21-2, CODE OF S.C. See 1 RACE REL. L. REP. 241 (1956).

38. Home Telephone & Telegraph Co. v. City of Los Angeles, 227 U.S. 278, 33 Sup. Ct. 312, 57 L. Ed. 510 (1913).

39. Berea College v. Kentucky, 211 U.S. 45, 29 Sup. Ct. 33, 53 L. Ed. 81 (1908).

40. Shelley v. Kramer, 334 U.S. 1, 68 Sup. Ct. 836, 92 L. Ed. 1161 (1948).

41. Terry v. Adams, 345 U.S. 461, 73 Sup. Ct. 809, 97 L. Ed. 1152 (1952).

42. Nixon v. Condon, 286 U.S. 73, 52 Sup. Ct. 484, 76 L. Ed. 984 (1932).

43. Smith v. Allwright, 321 U.S. 649, 64 Sup. Ct. 757, 88 L. Ed. 987 (1944).

44. Dorsey v. Stuyvesant Town Corp., 299 N.Y. 519, 87 N.E.2d 541 (1949), *cert. denied,* 339 U.S. 981, 70 Sup. Ct. 1019, 94 L. Ed. 1385 (1950).

45. Norris v. Mayor and City Council of Baltimore, 78 F. Supp. 451 (Md. 1948).

46. Kerr v. Enoch Pratt Free Library, 149 F.2d 212 (4th Cir. Ct. 1945).

47. *In re* Estate of Stephen Girard, 386 Pa. 548, 127 A.2d 287 (1956).

48. Pennsylvania v. Board of Directors of City Trusts of City of Philadelphia,— U.S.—, Sup. Ct.—, —L. Ed.2d— (1956). [25 L.W. 3316, April 30, 1957.]

49. *Ibid.*

50. Black v. Cutter Laboratories, 351 U.S. 292, 302, 76 Sup. Ct. 824, 829, 100 L. Ed. 681, 688 Adv. (1956).

51. Act No. 197, General Assembly of Georgia, Feb. 27, 1956. See 1 RACE REL. L. REP. 450 (1956).

52. *See, e.g.,* United States v. Classic, 313 U.S. 299, 61 Sup. Ct. 1031, 85 L. Ed. 1368 (1941).

53. 5 U.S.C. §§ 291-339 (1952).

54. United States v. San Jacinto Tin Co., 125 U.S. 273, 8 Sup. Ct. 850, 31 L. Ed. 747 (1888). Compare, *In re* Confiscation Cases, 7 Wall. (74 U.S.) 454, 19 L. Ed. 196 (1868).

55. 42 U.S.C. § 1983 (1952).

56. Chambers v. Florida, 309 U.S. 227, 241, 60 Sup. Ct. 472, 479, 84 L. Ed. 716, 724 (1940).

TABLE OF CASES

Adkins v. School Board of the City of Newport News, 2 Race
   Rel. L. Rep. 334 (1957), 255
Alabama *ex rel* Patterson v. NAACP, 1 Race Rel. L. Rep. 707
   (1956), 248-49
Ashwander v. Tennessee Valley Authority, 297 U.S. 288 (1936),
   42-43
Barney v. City of New York, 193 U.S. 430 (1904), 231
Beauharnais v. Illinois, 343 U.S. 250 (1952), 31
Beckett v. School Board of the City of Norfolk, 2 Race Rel. L.
   Rep. 46 (1957), 256
Bell v. Rippy, 1 Race Rel. L. Rep. 318 (1956), 190-91, 222
Belton v. Gebhart, 32 Del. Ch. 343, 87 A. 2d 862 (1952), 48
Berea College v. Kentucky, 211 U.S. 45 (1908), 100-2, 260
Black v. Cutter Laboratories, 351 U.S. 816 (1956), 27, 265
Boese v. King, 108 U.S. 379 (1883), 81
Bolling v. Sharpe, 344 U.S. 873 (1952), 51
Bolling v. Sharpe, 347 U.S. 497 (1954), 7, 49, 52, 173-74
Breedlove v. Suttles, 302 U.S. 277 (1937), 116
Briggs v. Elliott, 98 F. Supp. 529 (1951) 46, 124
Briggs v. Elliott, 103 F. Supp. 920 (1952), 48
Briggs v. Elliott, 342 U.S. 350 (1952), 25, 47
Briggs v. Elliott, 132 F. Supp. 776 (1955), 177-79, 184-85
Browder v. Gayle, 142 F. Supp. 707 (1956), 208
Brown v. Board of Education, 98 F. Supp. 797 (1951), 46
Brown v. Board of Education, 344 U.S. 1 (1952), 25, 51
Brown v. Board of Education, 344 U.S. 141 (1952), 51
Brown v. Board of Education, 345 U.S. 972 (1953), 28, 51-53, 162
Brown v. Board of Education, 347 U.S. 483 (1954) *
Brown v. Board of Education, 349 U.S. 294 (1955), 28, 52, 150-51,
   158-79

Brown v. Board of Education, 139 F. Supp. 468 (1955), 176
Brown v. Rippy, 233 F. 2d 796 (1956), 193
Brown v. Western Ry. of Alabama, 338 U.S. 294 (1949), 252-53
Burr v. Sondheim, 1 Race Rel. L. Rep. 309 (1956), 187
Burton v. U.S., 196 U.S. 283 (1905), 43
Bush v. Orleans Parish School Board, 1 Race Rel. L. Rep. 305 (1956), 188
Bush v. Orleans Parish School Board, 138 F. Supp. 336 (1956), 247
Butler v. Wilemon, 86 F. Supp. 397 (1949), 103
Carson v. Board of Education, 227 F. 2d 789 (1955), 251
Carter v. School Board, 182 F. 2d 531 (1950), 104
Cassell v. Texas, 339 U.S. 282 (1950), 35
Chambers v. Florida, 309 U.S. 227 (1940), 271
Chicago & Grand Trunk Ry. v. Wellman, 143 U.S. 339 (1892), 43
Clark v. Williard, 294 U.S. 211 (1935), 81
Clemons v. Board of Education of Hillsboro, 228 F. 2d 853 (1956), 222-23
Civil Rights Cases, 109 U.S. 3 (1883), 92-94
Coleman v. Miller, 307 U.S. 433 (1939), 39
Colgate v. Harvey, 296 U.S. 404 (1935), 91
Colsgrove v. Green, 328 U.S. 549 (1946), 73
In re Confiscation Cases, 7 Wall. (74 U.S.) 454 (1868), 270
Connally v. General Construction Co., 269 U.S. 385 (1926), 233
Connecticut General Co. v. Johnson, 303 U.S. 77 (1938), 105
Covington v. Montgomery County School Officials, 139 F. Supp. 161 (1956), 227
Crowell v. Benson, 285 U.S. 22 (1931), 42
Cummings v. Board of Education, 175 U.S. 528 (1899), 100
Davenport v. Cloverport, 72 Fed. 689 (1896), 104
Davis v. County School Board of Prince Edward County, 103 F. Supp. 337 (1952), 47, 123
Davis v. County School Board of Prince Edward County, 1 Race Rel. L. Rep. 82 (1956), 176-77, 184-85
Davis v. St. Louis Housing Authority, 1 Race Rel. L. Rep. 353 (1956), 204
Dawson v. Baltimore, 123 F. Supp. 193 (1954), 154
DeAngelis v. Board of Liquor License Commissioners of Baltimore, 1 Race Rel. L. Rep. 370 (1956), 155-56
Detroit Housing Commission v. Lewis, 226 F. 2d 180 (1955), 204
District of Columbia v. Thompson Co., 346 U.S. 100 (1952), 214
Dominion Hotel v. Arizona, 249 U.S. 265 (1919), 116

Table of Cases

323

Dorsey v. Stuyvesant Town Corp., 299 N.Y. 519, 87 N.E. 2d 541 (1949), cert. den., 339 U.S. 981 (1950), 262-63
Dred Scott v. Sandford, 19 How. (60 U.S.) 393 (1857), 81-88 *
Dunn v. Board of Education, 1 Race Rel. L. Rep. 319 (1956), 186, 222
Edwards v. California, 314 U.S. 160 (1941), 34, 148
Fayson v. Beard, 134 F. Supp. 379 (1955), 203
Ferguson v. Gies, 82 Mich. 358, 46 N.W. 718 (1890), 98
Fischer's Blend Station v. State Tax Commission, 297 U.S. 650 (1935), 16
Fisher v. Hurst, 333 U.S. 147 (1950), 110
Fisher v. Pace, 336 U.S. 155 (1949), 237
Fleming v. South Carolina Electric and Gas Co., 128 F. Supp. 469 (1955), 224 F. 2d 752 (1955), appeal dismissed, 351 U.S. 901 (1956), 205-8
Florida ex rel Hawkins v. Board of Control, 47 So. 2d 608 (1950), 53 So. 2d 116 (1951), cert. den., 342 U.S. 877 (1951), cert. granted, 347 U.S. 971 (1954), 350 U.S. 413 (1956), 193-96, 199
Gayle v. Browder, 352 U.S. 903 (1956), 208
Gebhart v. Belton, 32 Del. Ch. 343, 87 A. 2d 862 (1952), 7
Gebhart v. Belton, 33 Del. Ch. 144, 91 A. 2d 137 (1952), 49
Gebhart v. Belton, 344 U.S. 891 (1952), 51
Georgia v. Stanton, 6 Wall. (73 U.S.) 50 (1868), 89
Georgia v. Tennessee Copper Co., 206 U.S. 230 (1907), 164
Gibson v. Mississippi, 162 U.S. 565 (1896), 147
In re Estate of Stephen Girard, 386 Pa. 548, 127 A. 2d 287 (1956), 353 U.S. 230 (1957), 264-66
Goesart v. Cleary, 335 U.S. 464 (1948), 122
Gompers v. United States, 233 U.S. 604 (1913), 58
Gong Lum v. Rice, 275 U.S. 78 (1927), 101-2
Great Falls Mfg. Co. v. Attorney General, 124 U.S. 581 (1887), 43
Griffin v. Illinois, 351 U.S. 12 (1956), 32, 71
Guinn v. United States, 238 U.S. 347 (1915), 256
Hammer v. Dagenhart, 247 U.S. 251 (1918), 20
Hayes v. Crutcher, 137 F. Supp. 853 (1956), 203
Heyward v. Public Housing Administration, 135 F. Supp. 217 (1955), 204
Holmes v. City of Atlanta, 124 F. Supp. 290 (1954), 223 F. 2d 93 (1955), 350 U.S. 879 (1955), 1 Race Rel. L. Rep. 150 (1956), 203-4
Home Building and Loan Association v. Blaisdell, 290 U.S. 398 (1934), 69, 70

Home Telephone & Telegraph Co. v. City of Los Angeles, 227 U.S. 278 (1913), 259
Hoxie School District v. Brewer, 137 F. Supp. 364 (1956), 1 Race Rel. L. Rep. 43 (1956), 186-87
International Shoe Co. v. Pinkus, 278 U.S. 261 (1929), 81
Isaacs v. Baltimore, 123 F. Supp. 193 (1954), 154
Jackson v. Rawdon, 135 F. Supp. 936 (1955), 191
Jackson v. Rawdon, 235 F. 2d 93 (1956), 193, 210
Joyner v. McDowell County Board of Education, 92 S.E. 2d 795 (1956), 251-52
Kelly v. Roetzel, 64 Okla. 36, 165 Pac. 1150 (1917), 40
Kerr v. Enoch Pratt Free Library, 149 F. 2d 212 (1945), 263
Korematsu v. United States, 323 U.S. 214 (1944), 149-52
Kotch v. Board of River Boat Pilot Commissioners, 330 U.S. 552 (1947), 122, 148
Lane v. Wilson, 307 U.S. 268 (1939), 256
Leroy Fibre Co. v. Chicago, M. & St. Paul Ry. Co., 232 U.S. 340 (1914), 115
Lindsley v. Natural Carbonic Gas Co., 220 U.S. 61 (1911), 132
Liverpool, N.Y. & P.S.S. Co. v. Emigration Commissioners, 113 U.S. 33 (1885), 43, 111
Lonesome v. Maxwell, 123 F. Supp. 193 (1954), 154
Louisiana *ex rel* LeBlanc v. Lewis, 1 Race Rel. L. Rep. 571 (1956), 248-49
Lowery v. School Trustees, 140 N.C. 33, 52 S.E. 267 (1905), 103-4
Lucy v. Adams, 1 Race Rel. L. Rep. 323 (1956), 238
Luther v. Borden, 7 How. (48 U.S.) 1 (1849), 73
McBoyle v. United States, 283 U.S. 25 (1931), 57
Ex parte McCardle, 7 Wall. (74 U.S.) 506 (1869), 87, 89
McCulloch v. Maryland, 4 Wheat. (17 U.S.) 316 (1817), 70
McKinney v. Blankenship, 154 Tex. 632, 282 S.W. 691 (1955), 188-90
McLaurin v. Board of Regents, 339 U.S. 641 (1950), 110-11
McSwain v. County Board of Education, 138 F. Supp. 570 (1956), 186
Madden v. Kentucky, 309 U.S. 83 (1940), 91
Marbury v. Madison, 1 Cranch (5 U.S.) 137 (1803), 41, 56, 72, 243
Martin v. Hunter's Lessee, 1 Wheat. (14 U.S.) 304 (1816), 243
Massachusetts v. Mellon, 262 U.S. 447 (1923), 43
Matthews v. Launius, 134 F. Supp. 684 (1955), 221
Mayer v. Hellman, 91 U.S. 496 (1876), 81

Mayor and City Council of Baltimore City v. Dawson, 220 F. 2d 386 (1955), 154, 201

Mayor and City Council of Baltimore City v. Dawson, 350 U.S. 877 (1955), 154, 200

Mendez v. Westminster School District, 64 F. Supp. 544 (1946), *affirmed,* 161 F. 2d 744 (1947), 183

Ex parte Merryman, Fed. Cas. No. 9487 (1861), 86

Miller v. Board of Education, 106 F. Supp. 988 (1952), 104

Ex parte Milligan, 4 Wall. (71 U.S.) 2 (1866), 86

Minneapolis Ry. Co. v. Beckwith, 129 U.S. 26 (1889), 105

Mississippi v. Johnson, 4 Wall. (71 U.S.) 475 (1867), 89

Missouri *ex rel* Gaines v. Canada, 305 U.S. 337 (1938), 107-8

Moore v. Porterfield, 113 Okla. 234, 241 Pac. 346 (1925), 103

Moorman v. Morgan, 285 S.W. 2d 146 (1955), 203

Muir v. Louisville Park Theatrical Association, 347 U.S. 971 (1954), 199

Muller v. Oregon, 208 U.S. 412 (1908), 121, 129

Muskrat v. United States, 219 U.S. 346 (1911) 43

N.L.R.B. v. Jones & Laughlin Steel Corp., 301 U.S. 1 (1937), 20

Nixon v. Condon, 286 U.S. 73 (1932), 261

Nixon v. Herndon, 273 U.S. 536 (1927), 147

Norman v. Baltimore & Ohio R.R., 294 U.S. 240 (1935), 39

Norris v. Mayor and City Council of Baltimore, 78 F. Supp. 451 (1948), 263

Norton v. Shelby County, 118 U.S. 425 (1886), 160

Olmstead v. United States, 277 U.S. 438 (1928), 57

Pacific States T. & T. Co. v. Oregon, 223 U.S. 118 (1912), 73

Panama Refining Co. v. Ryan, 293 U.S. 388 (1935), 58

Pearson v. Murray, 169 Md. 478, 182 Atl. 590 (1936), 106-7

People *ex rel* Workman v. Board of Education, 18 Mich. 400 (1869), 64, 70

Pennsylvania v. Nelson, 350 U.S. 491 (1956), 26

Plessy v. Ferguson, 163 U.S. 537 (1896), 94-100 *

Pobreslo v. Boyd, 287 U.S. 518 (1933), 81

Quaker City Cab Co. v. Pennsylvania, 277 U.S. 389 (1928), 141

Quong Wing v. Kirkendall, 223 U.S. 59 (1912), 116

Railway Express v. New York, 336 U.S. 106 (1949), 33

Railroad Retirement Board v. Alton Railroad Co., 295 U.S. 330 (1935), 58

Reynold v. Board of Education, 66 Kan. 672, 72 Pac. 274 (1903), 104

Rice v. Arnold, 340 U.S. 848 (1950), 202-3
Roberts v. City of Boston, 5 Cush. (59 Mass.) 198 (1849), 97
Rochin v. California, 342 U.S. 165 (1952), 24
Sabine v. Sharpe, 1 Race Rel. L. Rep. 305 (1956), 174
Santa Clara County v. So. Pac. Ry. Co., 118 U.S. 294 (1886), 105
Schecter Corp. v. United States, 295 U.S. 495 (1935), 3, 58
Screws v. United States, 325 U.S. 91 (1945), 233-35
Security Trust Co. v. Dodd, Mead & Co., 173 U.S. 624 (1899), 81
Sipuel v. Board of Education, 332 U.S. 631 (1948), 109-10
Shelley v. Kraemer, 334 U.S. 1 (1948), 260, 265
Shepard v. Wheeling, 30 W. Va. 479, 4 S.E. 635 (1887), 181
Slaughter-House Cases, 16 Wall. (83 U.S.) 36 (1873), 65-66, 89-90, 146
Slochower v. Board of Higher Education, 350 U.S. 551 (1956), 27
Smith v. Allwright, 321 U.S. 649 (1944), 36, 261
Standard Oil Co. v. Tennessee *ex rel* Cates, 217 U.S. 413 (1910), 116
Standard Oil Co. v. U.S., 221 U.S. 1 (1910), 164
State v. Rorvick, 76 Ida. 58, 277 P. 2d 566 (1954), 144
Steiner v. Simmons, 111 A. 2d 574 (1955), 175-76
Strauder v. West Virginia, 100 U.S. 303 (1880), 146-47
Supreme Tribe of Ben-Hur v. Cauble, 255 U.S. 356 (1921), 227
Sweatt v. Painter, 339 U.S. 629 (1950), 108-9, 111, 169
Takahashi v. Fish and Game Commission, 334 U.S. 410 (1948), 152
Tate v. Department of Conservation and Development, 133 F. Supp. 53 (1955), 202
Taylor v. Board of Education, 1 Race Rel. L. Rep. 321 (1956), 186, 222
In re Terry, 128 U.S. 289 (1888), 237
Terry v. Adams, 345 U.S. 461 (1952), 260-61
Texas v. White, 7 Wall. (74 U.S.) 700 (1869), 62, 244
Tureaud v. Board of Supervisors, 116 F. Supp. 248 (1953), 347 U.S. 971 (1954), 225 F. 2d 434 (1955), 199
Tyler v. The Judges, 179 U.S. 405 (1900), 43
U.A.W.-C.I.O. v. Wisconsin Employment Relations Board, 351 U.S. 266 (1956), 27
U.S. v. American Tobacco Co., 221 U.S. 106 (1911), 164-65
U.S. v. Butler, 297 U.S. 1 (1936), 20, 57
U.S. v. Classic, 313 U.S. 299 (1941), 270
U.S. v. Cruikshank, 2 Otto (92 U.S.) 552 (1876), 91, 230
U.S. v. Holliday, 3 Wall. (70 U.S.) 407 (1865), 143-44

U.S. v. Hudson, 7 Cranch (11 U.S.) 32 (1812), 237
U.S. v. Interstate Circuit, 304 U.S. 55 (1937), 56
U.S. v. Paramount Pictures, 334 U.S. 131 (1948), 56
U.S. v. Peters, 5 Cranch (9 U.S.) 115 (1809), 243
U.S. v. San Jacinto Tin Co., 125 U.S. 273 (1888), 270
U.S. v. United Mine Workers of America, 330 U.S. 258 (1947), 238
U.S. v. Williams, 341 U.S. 70 (1951), 88, 230, 233
Uveges v. Pennsylvania, 335 U.S. 437 (1948), 31
Ex parte Virginia, 100 U.S. 339 (1880), 147
Virginia v. Rives, 100 U.S. 313 (1880), 147
Virginia v. West Virginia, 222 U.S. 17 (1911), 219-20
West Virginia v. Barnette, 319 U.S. 624 (1943), 30, 31, 32
Williams v. Board of Education, 79 Kan. 202, 99 Pac. 216 (1908), 104
Williams v. Zimmerman, 172 Md. 563, 192 Atl. 353 (1937), 104
Willis v. Walker, 136 F. Supp. 177 (1955), 186
Wilson v. City of Paducah, 100 F. Supp. 116 (1951), 183-84
Wolf v. Colorado, 338 U.S. 25 (1949), 117
Worcester v. Georgia, 6 Pet. (31 U.S.) 515 (1832), 18
Wrighten v. Board of Trustees, 72 F. Supp. 948 (1947), 104
Yick Wo v. Hopkins, 118 U.S. 356 (1886), 151
Young v. Ragen, 337 U.S. 235 (1949), 252
Youngstown Sheet and Tube Co. v. Sawyer, 343 U.S. 579 (1952), 3, 39

* Noted and discussed at numerous points throughout the volume.

INDEX

Adams, John, 15
Alien and Sedition Laws, 242
Allen, Robert S., 19
Almond, J. Lindsay, Jr., 4
An American Dilemma, 8, 154
Attwood, William, 211, 216

Bickel, Alexander, 66-67
Bingham, John, 59-60
Black, Hugo L., 21, *23-24*, 105,
    148-52, 230, 234, 265, 271
"Black Monday," 4, 6, 141
Blackstone, William, 16
Borinski, Ernst, 160
Bradley, Joseph P., 93
Brady, Tom P., 7, 141
Brandeis, Louis D., 42, 128-29
"Brandeis brief," 128-29, 134
Brennan, William J., 36
Brewer, David J., 18
Brown, Henry Billings, 96, 111
Brownell, Herbert, 270
Bryce, James, 40
Buchanan, James, 244
Burton, Harold H., 21, 34, 230, 233
Butler, Pierce, 108
Byrnes, James F., 7, 9, 13, 31, 66-67,
    78, 100, 112, 198

Cahn, Edmond, 30, 135

Calhoun, John C., 243
Campbell, John A., 89-90
Cardozo, Benjamin N., 17, 57
Carter, Robert L., 4
Chase, Salmon P., 244-45
Chinese, discrimination against,
    151
Citizens' Councils, 187, 218, 269
Citizen's Guide to De-Segregation,
    13
Civil Rights Acts, 87-88, 92-93, 161,
    229-37, 270
Clark, Kenneth B., 135
Clark, Tom C., 21, 35, 230, 233
Class suits, 158-59, *181-85*, 191,
    224-29
Clay, Ky., desegregation in, 212-13,
    217-18
Clinton, Tenn., desegregation in,
    186, 212-13, 217-18, 238-39
"Communism," 8-9
Constitution, interpretation of
    advisory opinions, 43
    avoidance of constitutional ques-
       tions, 42-43, 111
    constitutional standards, 127-28,
       133, 145
    historical analysis, 59-67
    intention of framers and legisla-
       tors, 56-57

Constitution (Cont.)
  interpretation of words, 54-55,
    115-17
  maxims of construction, 57, 72
  plain meaning, 56, 230
  see also Judicial function and
    process; Supreme Court of the
    United States
Contempt powers, 237-39
Cook, Eugene, 31, 71, 73
Cooley, Thomas, 68-69
"Court-packing," 19

Davis, John W., 3, 105, 162, 171,
  177
Davis, Wylie, 104
Desegregation
  arguments in support of: "badge
    of inferiority," 96, 120; for-
    eign policy, 11-12; inherent in-
    equalities, 49, 130, 136; irrele-
    vance of race, 34; sociological,
    105, 130-37; for arguments
    against desegregation, *see* Seg-
    regation
  Attorney General, action by,
    269-70
  by locality, general, 210-14; by
    state: Alabama, 205-9; Arkan-
    sas, 186-87, 221; Delaware, 7,
    160, 174-76, 215; District of
    Columbia, 7, 13, 160, 173-74,
    211, 214; Florida, 193-97;
    Georgia, 203-4; Kansas, 7,
    160, 176; Kentucky, 186, 199,
    203, 212, 217-18; Louisiana,
    188; Maryland, 187, 200-2, 215;
    Michigan, 204-5; Missouri,
    204-5, 215; North Carolina,
    227; Ohio, 222; South Caro-
    lina, 177-79, 188; Tennessee,
    186, 203, 212-13, 217-18, 238-

    39; Texas, 188-93, 212-13, 217-
    18, 222; Virginia, 176-77, 188;
    West Virginia, 186, 222
  contempt sanctions, 237-39
  criminal law sanctions, 229-37
  developments: bathing beaches,
    200-2; golf courses, 203-4;
    higher education, 193-97, 199;
    housing, 204-5, 260; labor un-
    ions, 215; parks, 199, 202-4;
    restaurants, 214; transporta-
    tion, 205-9, 214; voting, 261-62
  legal opposition to, by locality:
    Arkansas, 253; Florida, 253-54;
    Georgia, 258-60, 269; Louisi-
    ana, 246-47; Mississippi, 254-
    55; North Carolina, 250-52;
    South Carolina, 258-60; Vir-
    ginia, 245, 249, 255, 257-58,
    262
  special problems delaying, 212-
    18, 221, 223
  Southern attempts to avoid, 242-
    71
Discrimination, *see* Segregation
  practices
Douglas, William O., 21, 23, 24-25,
  78, 81, 114, 142-43, 230, 233-
  37, 265
Douglass, Frederick, 95

Eastland, James O., 7, 8, 23, 31,
  135, 218
Eisenhower, Dwight D., 13, 21, 37,
  211
Equal protection of the laws, *see*
  Fourteenth Amendment
Ervin, Sam J., Jr., 7, 8, 68, 69, 111

Fifteenth Amendment, 255-56
Fifth Amendment, 50
Fleming, Harold C., 210-11, 216

Foreign policy, 11-12
Fourteenth Amendment
 Black's views, 23-24
 Due Process Clause, 55, 89-90, 117
 Equal Protection Clause, 49, 55, 75, 89, 92, 114-25, 147
 history of, 59-67, 96
 implementation of, 65-66, 71, 161
 "personal and present" rights, 110, 161, 169-70, 204
 Privileges and Immunities Clause, 55, 89-92
 reasonableness, 97-98, 120-25, 141-45, 156
 state action, 93, 95-96, 99-100, 110-11, 155-56, 259-67
 "substantial" equality, 103-4, 106, 109-10, 118, 194
Frank, John, 64
Frankfurter, Felix, 14, 21, 28-33, 117, 230-33, 237
Freedman's Bureau Bill, 87
Freund, Paul A., 11, 22, 111

Gray Commission, 255, 257
Greenberg, Jack, 4, 133-34

Hamilton, Walton, 27
Harlan, John Marshall (1833-1911), 37, 92, 98, 100, 101, 157
Harlan, John Marshall (1899-   ), 37
Hayne, Robert Young, 243
Hoffman, Walter E., 255
Holmes, Oliver Wendell, Jr., 11, 58, 77, 115, 147, 164, 220
Hoover, Herbert, 177
Hughes, Charles Evans, 16, 19, 42, 70, 107

Indians, discrimination against, 142-44
Interposition and nullification, 242-47

Jackson, Andrew, 18, 243
Jackson, Robert H., 4, 14, 21, 22, 33-34, 43, 81, 125, 148, 173, 230
Japanese, discrimination against, 26, 149-52
Jefferson, Thomas, 18, 70, 242
Judicial function and process
 advisory opinions, 43
 cases or controversies, 39, 43, 111
 contempt powers, 237-39
 customs and usages, 97-98, 102, 105, 123-24, 257
 equity powers, 162-63, 224-29
 holding and dictum, 79, 85-86
 interpretation of words, 54-55, 115-17
 judicial law-making, 16-17, 56, 68-75, 98, 127
 judicial notice, 129
 judicial restraint, 39-44, 116
 judicial review, 40-42, 72, 116
 judicial statesmanship, 105, 268
 personalized jurisprudence, 16-17
 stare decisis, 7, 24, 76-81, 102-5, 118, 224-29
 use of non-legal materials, 128-37, 268
 see also Constitution, interpretation of; Supreme Court of the United States

Kasper, John, 217, 238
Kentucky and Virginia Resolutions, 242
Kernochan, John M., 40
Ku Klux Act, 87-88

LaPorte, Cloyd, 76
"Law of the case," 185
Laws permitting or requiring segregation, 6, 139, 186
Leflar, Robert A., 104
Lincoln, Abraham, 244
Llewellyn, Karl, 77
Louisville, Ky., desegregation in, 199, 217-18

McGill, Ralph, 216
McKay, Robert B., 154, 200
McMullan, Harry, 165
McReynolds, James C., 108
McWhinney, Edward, 29
Madison, James, 242
Manley, Michael James, 155-56
Mansfield, Tex., desegregation in, 212-13, 217-18
Marshall, John, 18, 41-42, 56, 70, 72, 111, 243-45 [169
Marshall, Thurgood, 3, 106, 125,
Matthews, Stanley, 43, 151
Miller, Samuel F., 65, 89-90, 146
Minton, Sherman, 21, 34, 36, 218, 230
Miscegenation, 153, 216
Moore, James Wm., 183
Moore, T. Justin, 4
Munro, Robert F., 64
Murphy, Frank, 152
Myrdal, Gunnar, 8, 154

National Association for the Advancement of Colored People (NAACP)
denunciation of, 7
desegregation arguments, 11, 34, 65
implementation arguments, 165-66, 169-70, 182
legal action against, 247-49

National Association for the Advancement of Colored People (Cont.)
opposition to Judge Parker, 177
Negroes
alleged differences from whites, 8, 141-45
"badge of inferiority," 96, 120
legal position: in 1857, 84-85; in 1880, 93-94; in 1896, 96-100
see also Segregation; Desegregation

Parker, John J., 105, 124, 154, 157, 177-79, 206
Patterson, Edwin W., 17, 20
Pearson, Drew, 19
Peckham, Rufus W., 42
Politics, 13-14
Potter, William I., 31, 71, 73
Pritchett, C. Herman, 27
Precedent, see Stare decisis

Rankin, J. Lee, 4
Redding, Louis L., 4
Reed, Stanley, 21, 36, 230, 233-34
Roberts, Owen J., 57-58
Robinson, Spottswood, III, 4
Rogers, Andrew Jackson, 59
Roosevelt, Franklin D., 19, 21
Rutledge, Wiley B., 148, 152, 233, 235-37

School Segregation Cases
implementation decision of 1955, 28, 52, 150-51, 158-79
lower court action, 45-51
preliminary Supreme Court action, 48-53, 162
Supreme Court decision of 1954, 118-120 etc.
social scientists' testimony, 131-33, 136

Segregation
  arguments in support of: biological, 9, 141-45; customs and usages, 97-98, 102, 105, 123-24, 257; religious, 8; for arguments against segregation, *see* Desegregation
  social and political rights distinguished, 99-100
Segregation laws, 6, 139, 186
Segregation practices
  bathing beaches, 153-55; education, 45-49, 62-65, 100-13, 263-65; housing, 204, 262-63; industry, 155-56; jury service, 146-47; law schools, 106-10, 193-97; transportation, 95-96, 205-9; voting, 147, 255-56
Seitz, Collins J., 48, 49
"Separate but equal," 46, 78, 81, 93, *95-113*, 119, 147, 206, 209
Sociological arguments, 105, 130-37
Southern Manifesto, 246
Stare decisis, 7, 24, *76-81*, 102-5, 118, 224-29
State action, 93, 95-96, 99-100, 110-11, 155-56, *259-67*
Stevens, Thaddeus, 60, 66
Stone, Harlan F., 234
Story, Joseph, 243
Sturgis, Ky., desegregation in, 212-13, 217-18
Sumner, Charles, 97
Supreme Court of the United States
  advisory opinions, 43
  avoidance of constitutional questions, 42-43, 111
  biographical data, *see* under names of individual justices
  criticisms of, 8, 9, 18-19, 68-71, 73, 86-87, 135-37, 245-46

Supreme Court of the United States (Cont.)
  "Court-packing," 19
  function of, 39-44, 116-17
  judicial review, 40-42, 72, 116
  unanimity of decision, 19, 27
  see also Constitution, interpretation of; Judicial function and process
Sutherland, George, 69, 91

Taft, William Howard, 102
Taney, Roger B., 18, 19, 69-70, 84-85
Taylor, Robert L., 186
Thomsen, Roszel C., 154, 200
Timmerman, George Bell, Sr., 205-8
Tocqueville, Alexis de, 40
Truman, Harry S., 21

United States Supreme Court, *see* Supreme Court of the United States

VanDevanter, Willis, 132
Vinson, Fred M., 21, *28-29*, 111-12, 230

Wall, Hugh V., 9, 172
Warren, Charles, 94
Warren, Earl, 4, 14, 20, *25-28*, 79, 149-50, 265
Washington, Booker T., 95
Whittaker, Charles Evans, 37
Williams, John Bell, 6, 7
Wilson, Paul E., 4
"With all deliberate speed," 172, 178, 218-29
Wyzanski, Charles E., 127-28

Young, H. Albert, 4